B

TRAVELERS' TALES

THE
BEST
TRAVEL
WRITING
2009

TRUE STORIES
FROM AROUND THE WORLD

TRAVELERS' TALES

THE BEST
TRAVEL WRITING
2009

TRUE STORIES
FROM AROUND THE WORLD

Edited by
JAMES O'REILLY, LARRY HABEGGER,
AND SEAN O'REILLY

Travelers' Tales
an imprint of Solas House, Inc.
Palo Alto

Art direction: Stefan Gutermuth
Page layout and photo editing: Cynthia Lamb using the fonts
     Granjon and Nicholas Cochin
Interior design: Melanie Haage
Production Director: Christy Quinto

ISBN 1-932361-62-6
ISSN 1548-0224

First Edition
Printed in the United States
10 9 8 7 6 5 4 3 2 1

*Wandering re-establishes the original harmony
which once existed between man
and the universe.*

— ANATOLE FRANCE

Table of Contents

Publisher's Preface

I went to see *Slumdog Millionaire* the other night with a friend that does rural development work in Central America, and we were both reminded of the enormous gap between the poor and Those of Us Who Really Don't Suffer Much But Complain a Lot. It's been over twenty years since I was in Mumbai (then Bombay), but India is engraved in the memory rather easily, and the images of the slums caused me to reflect again on our culture in the West, and our own forms of poverty: poverty of imagination, poverty of friendship, poverty of family, poverty of compassion, poverty of life in the streets. I am not saying we're not actually rich in all these things, I am saying that many of us, myself included, are not functionally appreciative that it is these things that constitute real riches. That is to say, our appreciation is occasional, the way we might admire a sunset or a puppy. It is not a deep and abiding way of life. We spend our time chasing illusions of success, wealth, fame, and ignore the wealth that surrounds us and lies within. A culture defined by Miss Piggy—"more is never enough"—encourages a darkness of spirit that makes us cling to the phony, and want the phony more than anything else.

I know it's a tired sermon, you've heard it before, maybe given it yourself. And I don't want to deny the fact that the great economic meltdown that began in 2008 has caused anguish and suffering, with more coming over the horizon. It is in times like these, however, that we can change our lives for the better. Danger and crisis have a way of making us understand instinctively what matters each moment, and what doesn't.

One of the things that always strikes me when reading travel stories is how often the journey strips away illusions of self; a new place, a new culture, chance encounters with strangers—they so often charge the traveler with wonder and inspiration and the courage to live better. The quotidian, rejected at home as tedious and confining, is seen from afar as replete with possibility. Thus one of the best remedies I propose for "Economic Black Swan Flu" is travel—travel that doesn't have to be exotic or expensive—it can be to places nearby about which you've said "maybe later" to the idea of exploring. But travel nonetheless. "Maybe later" can become "maybe this weekend," and "maybe this weekend" can turn into "today" and an experience with as many aspects as a foreign one. Or, in the vivid light of crisis, it might be that you do indeed decide to change course dramatically, and take that trip to a faraway place that has called you your whole life. Perhaps it is even to Mumbai, or somewhere like it.

So back to *Slumdog*. Without giving away the movie, one of the things I enjoyed most about it was the towering and complex web of stories and memories that is the boy's life. We are all like this boy, and if a bad economy is our cruel interlocutor to his police captor, let it serve us in driving the mental and emotional gangsters from our spiritual house. Let us leave our slums, interrogate our demons, and seek to become whole first, and thereby rich—not the other way around.

—JAMES O'REILLY
PALO ALTO, CALIFORNIA

Introduction

TONY PERROTTET

The jungles of Cameroon...the plains of Mongolia... the wastes of Antarctica...I like to think that Herodotus, who was the Father of Travel Writing as well as of History (he schlepped all over Egypt, Greece, and Asia Minor in search of new material), would have loved this riotously energetic anthology.

In its kaleidoscopic scope, *The Best Travel Writing 2009* is firmly part of the grand tradition established by that restless Greek wanderer some 2,500 years ago: It captures the world today in all its wonder, oddity, and comic contradictions. Within these pages, twenty-nine intrepid authors sally forth to explore zones that are sometimes remote and dangerous and sometimes deceptively familiar. (The wilds of Minnesota, anyone? Backwoods Colorado? In 2009, you don't have to travel far.) For these voraciously inquiring minds, the world turns out to be a fascinating and surprising place, where you might cross paths with African witchdoctors, Nepalese tigers, or Franco-American cowboys. And it's heartening to know that we can still enjoy (as Pico Iyer notes in his witty essay about his own escape from the vales of academe to the life of the travel writer, which could serve as this book's keynote address) "the vagabond's freedom of being unknown and off the grid."

Granted, the modes of transport have changed a little in the last twenty-five centuries, as we have traded the romance of ancient oar-powered ships for 767s. (Triremes may have been slow, but they probably had more legroom). Yet the driving passion for travel—boundless curiosity—is still clearly embedded in our DNA. I can easily imagine Herodotus today in the youth hostels of Cape Town or coffee houses of Yemen, gazing about wild-eyed, furiously scribbling in his moleskin. Travelers are everywhere, but great travel writers from Marco Polo to Mark Twain and Bruce Chatwin all knew that a reader's attention needs to be gripped with vivid anecdotes, humor, narrative—in short, good storytelling. These travel tales do not bludgeon us with facts and figures. They are, above all, marvelous yarns—sometimes funny (Jeff Greenwald taking his Jewish mom to India), sometimes melancholic (Kathleen Spivack remembers touring the sex shops of Amsterdam in the company of a once vibrant friend), but always entertaining. Like their classic predecessors, these writers share a noble mission: They seduce us into learning about the world without even realizing it.

In the process, we often discover as much, or more, about ourselves. The new generation of writer-travelers are not passive observers: A dose of cultural confusion is an accepted, even cherished part of the travel experience—we're all lost in translation some of the time—and it can lead to its own form of enlightenment. In a hilarious piece David Sedaris would enjoy, David Farley finds himself living in the forgotten Italian village of Calcata, researching a relic called the Holy Foreskin and trying to make connections with the local population via the enigmatic local slang ("Are you doing a penis?" he inquires of one grand dame, something of a linguistic faux pas). On the other side of the globe, one of America's most insightful travel writers (and the man who has turned "vagabonding" into an art form), Rolf Potts, accepts an invitation to stay in a tiny Cambodian rural outpost and tests the extremes of cultural isolation. Adrian Cole, an Englishman in Texas, recalls his time as "a wandering ghost on foreign soil." It's a sensation that every modern traveler, at one time or other, has to come to terms with.

Then again, on foreign soil, we can sometimes go too far. In this collection, I was delighted to find that a comic whiff of madness still stalks the genre—shades of Evelyn Waugh and Graham Greene—as both expats and travelers lose their bearings and peek into the abyss. This volume is loaded with fascinating new psychiatric freak-outs for travelers to watch out for: Florence Syndrome (a.k.a. Stendahl Syndrome, where tourists to Europe are overwhelmed by too much art); Jerusalem Syndrome (where visitors to Israel believe they are the Messiah); Golden Calf Syndrome (where Jewish visitors to India "go native"); even Stockholm Syndrome (where kidnapping victims start to sympathize with their captors, an experience that hopefully few travelers will have to contend with). David Torrey Peters identifies yet another dementia in his wonderful story "The Bamenda Syndrome," whereby expats in Africa start trying to solve the continent's problems single-handedly. Torrey Peters's lucid meanderings amongst Cameroon's witch-doctors, while his own grip on reality rapidly deteriorates, won him the Grand Prize for travel writing in the most recent Solas Awards.

These stories don't shy away from the dark side. In a riveting piece, Millicent Susens recounts a chance meeting with a teenage waitress in rural Colorado that would alter her life in a way she never expected. One writer tours the American hotel rooms where rock stars died, while another inspects the corpse of Aleksandr Solzhenitzyn.

But there are far more cheery rites of passage in these pages, each one filled with lust for life (and lust for lust, of course), not to mention booze and music and good food and general joie de vivre. In a deliciously intimate report from south of the border, Stephanie Elizondo Griest joins a Mexican quinceañera, a girl's fifteenth birthday party, where the father returns from Brooklyn to lovingly squander three years' wages on a single night of festivities. Some authors are consumed by flirting. Hearts are broken. Men dream of love and drink way too much in bars, waking up with lurching hangovers and pounding regret. (Casanova Syndrome?) Women "of a certain age" slip off to Italy and are surrounded by suitors, much as they were in centuries past, when proper northern ladies would arrive in Venice to meet with handsome young gondoliers—enjoying the potential, if not the actual offer. "We are alive!" Susan Van Allen sums up the ancient Italian spirit, which has lured visitors for centuries. "And what a fun game we play!"

No two stories are alike in this collection, so sit back and enjoy the ride. I challenge any reader with blood in his or her veins not to get itchy feet. Who knows? Maybe you too will feel the compulsion to record your discoveries and share them in print—which, given the financial logic of publishing these days, is the purest madness of all. Luckily, that has never stopped travel writers.

Let's call it Herodotus Syndrome.

~❧ ~❧ ~❧

Tony Perrottet is an Australian-born travel writer and historian who lives in the East Village of Manhattan. He is a regular contributor to Condé Nast Traveler, The New York Times, Smithsonian Magazine, National Geographic Adventure, Slate *and the* London Sunday Times. *He is the author of four books that blend travel and history:* Off the Deep End: Travels in Forgotten Frontiers; Pagan Holiday: On the Trail of Ancient Roman Tourists; The Naked Olympics; *and (most recently)* Napoleon's Privates: 2500 Years of History Unzipped. *His website is www.tonyperrottet.com.*

Escape from Darien

Something here still casts a dark net.

ANOTHER BIG PACIFIC SWELL CAME UP FAST AND silent, moonlight flashing on its face. Hurrying east, it lifted and then dropped our sixty-foot raft with the smooth motions of an elevator. I caught my stomach and adjusted a steering plank. The glowing compass revolved slowly as the raft pointed back on course. I marveled at how quickly it responded, and in perfect measure.

But I didn't marvel for long. My mind was following the eastward-driving swell, thinking on where it would end up. I knew exactly where it would end up, but I didn't want to believe it. I knew that eight miles east the swell would rise and then curl and crash as luminescent foam on a dark, stony beach that cowered beneath thick jungle vegetation. I sensed the Darien out there, to my right, like the open jaws of a medieval Hell-Mouth.

Darien. I said it softly aloud. How many conquista—
dores' tales ended there? How many human disasters
had that monstrous jungle hosted, like a grinning spec-
ter? How many old explorers' tales of the Darien had I
read throughout my life, and had the jungle—like an
enormous net—finally drawn me in?

I took a breath and told myself that none of that mattered. All that mattered now was the wind. If it gave
up completely our raft would follow that swell and run
aground on that beach. There would be nobody to help
us. Our sailing raft, a replica of a native vessel encountered by Spaniards in 1526, was built of logs, rope, and
canvas. We had no engine. Our radio took an hour to
set up, and contact was intermittent. We were halfway
up a 200-mile stretch of primordial jungle that for five
centuries had shrugged off every bloody club and every
subtle wedge of civilization.

Manila rope creaked and clicked as the raft wallowed
ahead. I looked up at the mainsail, a three-story high
triangle of dirty canvas glowing yellow from a kerosene
lamp. The sail fluttered, barely tugging us along. If the
wind died we'd have just a few hours before the swells
drove us aground. I imagined six men scrambling in the
dark to get clear of a heaving raft that weighed almost
as much as a Sherman tank. The breakers would destroy
the little bamboo deckhouse, containing our supplies
and the radio. And then what?

As another swell swiftly elevated the raft I turned and
looked back at the deckhouse. There was no light and I
turned back to stare at the compass.

Hours later the stars winked out as the Earth rolled
sunward. Dowar Medina, a fit Ecuadorian fisherman,
slipped on a t-shirt as he came out of the deckhouse. He

inhaled deeply, smelling the jungle, and glanced at the scraps of vegetation floating in the water. He knew we were too close to shore, but he stood calmly and put a hand on my shoulder.

"*Todos* O.K.?" he asked. "No," I said, pointing at the barely-inflated mainsail. "We're too close to land and the wind is dying," Dowar nodded absently and stepped back inside.

He returned with John Haslett, the mastermind of the expedition. John and Dowar had sailed this route three years before, on a raft that was eventually devoured by shipworms. They'd landed in Panama after thirty-five days at sea. Now it was reassuring to see them coldly assessing the conditions together. John stood with his arms folded and his legs spread wide against the swells. He sucked his teeth and said, "This is no good," punching out the words as cold as tickertape. "We've got to get offshore. If the wind gives up," he said, jabbing his thumb eastward, "we're done."

By noon all six of us were on deck, facing east. The wind had given up and the swells had driven us in. We were only three miles offshore. The entire eastern horizon was a billowing chaos of vegetation that roiled skyward, tier upon tier, like oil smoke. Here and there the greens were smudged gray by pockets of clinging mist.

Through my binoculars individual trees sharpened before swinging wildly away as the raft rolled. I looked up at the sails. They hung like great curtains. We were going in. Our charts weren't good enough to tell us where to drop our anchor. The desperate idea of letting it drag as we approached shore—in the hope of snagging rocks, seagrass, anything—rattled around my mind.

I imagined the pieces of a horrible puzzle sliding into position; the raft would run aground, spinning and heaving against a nameless, cobbled beach; we would escape with minimal gear and perhaps a quick SOS; we would be stranded in southern Darien, where F.A.R.C. guerrillas held dominion; nobody could risk a rescue attempt; we'd try to hack our way out, alone. Maybe some of us would make it.

It was an old story. Darien had a bad reputation. Since the conquistadores arrived in the early 1500s, expeditions had been swallowed up time and again. I imagined a legion of ghosts out there, rags of mist in the treetops.

Perhaps some of those mists were all that remained of a handful of Columbus's men; in 1502, on the Caribbean side of the jungle, they'd paddled up a river for wood and fresh water. They returned as arrow-pierced corpses floating downstream. Later, Balboa lost men by the score, forcing himself across the Isthmus of Panama for the first European glimpse of the Pacific. A little later, seven hundred Spaniards died in a year out there, enfeebled by disease as their colony failed. It was the same gruesome dysentery fate that withered and finally buckled a thousand Scots in their disastrous 1599 colonization effort. Even into the 1800s, Darien's appetite was sharp. In 1854 it took less than two months to reduce a disciplined American expedition crew to maggot-infested, crazed, and near-cannibalistic survivors. And the jungle produced weird tales, like prospector Thaddeus O'Shea's ravings about having shot a ten-foot ape. The jungle remained so impenetrable that a 1970's plan seriously considered "nuclear excavation." The "final solution" to this entangling forest, it was said, was to blast it with civilization's most devastating weapons. The idea

sounded less like an engineering plan than deep human
frustration with Nature in the same days that men
walked on the moon.

Not much has changed. In the late 1990s, the able
adventurer Alvah Simon took on Darien against all advice. Clawing his way up a mere hill through grasping
vegetation, he babbled into his video camera: "This has
become something more than crazy, something that not
anyone could call safe, or even prudent." He retreated
not long after. More recently the Briton Karl Bushby
successfully threaded the jungle from south to north,
avoiding Colombian guerillas by disguising himself as a
transient and then clinging to a log that floated him, like
Gollum, down the sluggish rivers.

Part of the Darien is a Panamanian National Park
now, but it's often closed, and it's never advertised as
a destination. Panama doesn't have an army, and they
don't confront the F.A.R.C. guerillas that wander freely
across the border. A party or two make it through the
Darien each year, and some researchers return year after
year, without incident. But still others go in, and never
come out.

As I recalled all this history, my mind crafted an
image of Darien as a diabolical mirror-house; a place of
quarter-truths where you might look at your watch and
see time running backwards; a place where water might
flow uphill and only the Cuna Indians and the F.A.R.C.
could expect to survive; the former because they'd been
there for thousands of years, the latter because they were
insane. We couldn't survive: I was sure of it.

John broke us from the spell. "O.K.," he said calmly.
We all turned to listen to him. "We're closing in on the
two-mile mark. If we land here, whoever survives is

going to have to go overland on that coast, fifty miles south to the nearest settlement."

Fifty miles overland, wrestling through mangrove swamps! The buccaneer Henry Morgan tried the same thing in 1670, and within a week his crew was eating leather. I gulped as I thought of my friend, Evan Davies, who'd spent months in the Congo and years later was still taking dog heartworm pills to combat parasites. I looked at John's left leg. It was already swollen from a massive infection that had started from a little scratch. I'd always been drawn to snowy mountains, expansive glaciers or open savannah, and now I felt sick.

Nobody liked the overland trek idea, least of all John. In 1995 he narrowly avoided landing on an island that turned out to be an unstaffed prison colony, an event that understandably soured him on uncontrolled landings in strange places.

"So," John said, coolly peeling a half-rotten pineapple, "We're going to turn south and try to sail down and make a controlled landing in that last settlement." We all knew that the settlement, a simple black dot on our chart, might be abandoned, or a drug-runner's lair, or a pirate's cove, or a F.A.R.C. base. "But," John said, tossing a rind into the water with a quiet plop, "anything is better than landing here."

We set to work. Only the meagerest puffs of wind came from the southwest, but we worked the steering planks and the sails to hook a gust that wheeled us around, putting the bow south against the northward-flowing Humboldt current. We moved the sails to the landward side of the raft and worked their lines with the greatest finesse, coaxing them like horse reins. By night-fall we were still just under two miles from shore. Even my landlubber's nose detected the wet, crawling soil, and I could hear the occasional crash of a breaker. By midnight we'd slowed our eastward drift, but we hadn't moved a mile south. Pointed south against the swift current, and shoved from the west by wind and swell, we were on the wrong side of just holding our position. We were edging in. Soon we were only a mile offshore.

In the morning we didn't need binoculars to make out the huge, twisted limbs of ancient trees, netted with enormous vines. Someone spotted a white, box-like shape on the beach. It was a small house, almost overgrown. There was no sign of life, but we doubled our watch for pirates.

Early in the voyage, Ecuadorean fishermen had warned us to stay at least thirty miles offshore, particularly off Colombia, where pirates approached their victims in boats painted like those of the Colombian Coast Guard. We checked out our only armament, a rusty double-barreled shotgun purchased in a back alley in Ecuador. Even if it worked, what good would it be against half a dozen automatic rifles? We all knew we couldn't survive an attack. *My God*, I thought, *if I ever come back here, I'm going to be armed to the teeth*.

After midnight I was on watch again. Now I could hear the soft crash of every wave on the shore. The sail hung limp. The rest of the crew slept, or pretended to sleep, saving their strength for the disaster. Scott, my watch partner, produced a bottle of red wine. At least we would go down in style.

Just as he poured a wind crept up and the mainsail fully inflated for the first time in forty-eight hours. The wine bottle clattered away underfoot as we jumped up and yelled for the crew and set to work. By dawn we were seven miles offshore. The relief was enormous. But we still had to land safely in a friendly place.

At noon we were just five miles out from the bay and the little settlement dot on our chart. We'd successfully navigated the lumbering raft against the current, and with poor winds, to precisely where we needed to be. At two miles out we sailed through a narrow passage between enormous rocks. Soon the little harbor appeared, an ear carved neatly out of the coastline. Several vessels were anchored in the flat water and we were all out on deck for the moment of truth. Come what may, we were headed in, totally visible now, and we would meet the owners of those vessels in less than an hour. Peering through binoculars, John told us he saw a sophisticated vessel, possibly a warship. If it was F.A.R.C., we were finished. We'd be captured for ransom and probably killed even if the money was paid; that had happened to the brother of our Colombian crewmates.

Through binoculars I could see that the ship bore the insignia of the Colombian Coast Guard. I saw figures standing at the ship's railing, watching us as we came in. I couldn't tell if they wore uniforms.

When we were closer in it was clear that the vessel was armed with light cannon and heavy machine guns. We were all very quiet as we let off the sail a little and slowed our approach. A launch was lowered from the ship and motored out towards us. Again we saw the Colombian Coast Guard insignia. This was it. We could only wait; we were at their mercy.

Reprieve! It was the real Colombian armada, anchored here while on patrol for pirates. The executive officer inspected our passports and invited us to dine with the captain that night. Laughing with disbelief at our luck, we anchored right next to the 100-foot *Simon del Benalcazar*, the greatest concentration of firepower on the entire Colombian coast. Even the F.A.R.C. would steer clear of her.

Early the next evening we paddled our inflatable dinghy towards the Darien and waded to shore, setting our feet on land for the first time in seventeen days. The jungle was silent. We explored the weedy ruins of an abandoned settlement, a cluster of leaning houses.

I was overawed by our connection with a bloody history. Over four hundred years ago Francisco Pizarro had landed exactly here, and fought a battle on this very beach. As we looked into the muddy house frames, where filthy mattresses lay abandoned in bare rooms and blackening magazines rotted like leaves, I imagined Pizarro grunting as he poked through Indian huts, looking for food or gold. In the end, despite capturing the wealth of the Aztecs and the Inca, Spain was no better off, and declined as a European power. *All that effort*, I thought, *for what?*

In the end, all that remained here was the Darien; leering, stoic, unassailable as ever. Its greenery would crawl up and engulf whatever was built here. Only a rain of hydrogen bombs could annihilate this forest. And when that happened, nobody would be left to care.

❧ ❧ ❧

Cameron McPherson Smith is an archaeologist at Portland State University and a freelance writer. The 1998 Manteño Voyage—an attempt to retrace a well-established maritime trade route between

Ecuador and West Mexico on a replica of a native balsa sailing raft—was John Haslett's second balsa raft expedition. Smith and Haslett are currently planning another attempt, documented at www.balsaraft.com. You can read Haslett's account of his expeditions in Voyage of the Manteño.

Officially a Woman

She opens the door on an unforgettable
rite of passage.

VICTOR'S DAUGHTER JUMI IS ABOUT TO TURN FIFTEEN, which for a Mexican means one thing: a *quincea-ñera*, or Serious Party. The kind worth crossing the border for, even if you'll have to hire a coyote to sneak back into the United States when it's over. Last week, Victor took a leave of absence from his deli in Brooklyn and flew home for the festivities. Since I'm already in Mexico, I've sworn to bear witness.

I hop a bus through the central state of Morelos and hail a cab to Victor's. He is chatting with a *primo* at the foot of a hill. Out of apron and off bicycle with no hefty cartons upon his shoulders, he looks rested and happy. We warmly embrace, then walk up the hill and through a metal gate. A dozen people flock upon us with kisses.

Victor leads me past some tree-chained dogs to a three-walled home serving as the *quinceañera* storage facility. Cases of beer and tequila are stacked five feet high and twelve feet wide alongside several hundred three-liter bottles of Coca Cola.

"How many people are coming tomorrow?" I gasp.

"*Quien sabe*," says his wife Judith. Who knows.

"Three or four hundred," Victor tries to be helpful. "Maybe even five hundred. Six hundred. We'll see."

I ask for Jumi but she's at a dance lesson. Do I want to go watch? I do, envisioning her waltzing with a gallant young man across a hardwood floor beneath the hawk eyes of an old lady in a hair bun. We walk to Salon Esmeralda, an open-air banquet hall with a cement floor and a sound stage at one end. A young woman runs toward me. It takes a moment to realize she is Jumi. Gone is the girl in the puppy-dog shirt I met a year ago. Grown and curved in all directions, she is wholly *chola* now, draped in a baggy t-shirt of Jesus Christ bloodied by thorns, camouflage pants, hi-top sneakers, and silver hoop earrings. We hug and laugh until someone claps us to attention. A pony-tailed man in a leopard-patterned shirt strides across the floor. The dance instructor. "Places, places everyone," he exclaims, flailing his arms about. You could balance shot glasses on his cheekbones.

Jumi's dance partners are six of her (male) *primos*. One wears a Metallica t-shirt and dog collar studded with silver spikes; the others are clad in hip-hop gear, their boxer shorts peeking above their jeans. Collectively they are the caballeros—or gentlemen—of the festivities. They gather into formation as the dance instructor blasts Cher's "Believe" through the speakers and lowers himself into a thigh-defying squat. "Feel it, move it, BE IT!" he commands between sucks on a cigarette.

Judith and Victor beam as their daughter gyrates on the dance floor. Victor tries to snuggle as they exchange whispers but Judith nudges him away, giggling. After so many lonely nights, their reunion must be salty sweet.

The *quinceañera* court practices another full hour before the dance instructor releases them. Jumi links her arm through mine and we charge a block ahead of the others to gossip. The boy she likes is coming tomorrow. "There's a girl who wants to fight me for him but I don't think any boy is worth fighting for, they should fight for you, don't you think?"

I secretly admire a system where you either kick someone's ass for love or get your own kicked, and that's the end of it. I assure Jumi that by tomorrow night, every *chavo* in town will be throwing punches for her. She squeals at the thought.

After dinner, it simultaneously occurs to everyone that we'll be feeding and liquoring up to six hundred people tomorrow. We whirl into activity. Jumi and I tackle the geraniums amassed in Abuela's backyard, covering each plastic pot with aluminum foil. The *tías* (aunties) crochet serapes for the tequila bottles while Judith stalks around with a hot glue gun and Victor and the caballeros lift heavy objects. First there are twenty of us and then there are thirty, all bustling about. The night grows warm but the wind keeps us cool. I have just wrapped my thirty-eighth pot when a *tía* brings me a plate of sliced mango. "Remember how we picked them from my tree last year?" she smiles.

As we share the tangy fruit, I ask after her family. She points to the Metallica caballero and claims him as a son. Since there are no men her age here save Victor, I ask if her husband is in the United States. Her forehead creases. "He left us years ago. I am still suffering but *ni modo*. What else can I do, wake up every morning and think about how my son's father is a dog? You have to move on, *m'hija*."

A woman appears at the gate with a makeup kit. The nail stylist. All the little girls and I gather around the kitchen table to watch Jumi's hands transform into those of a woman. She opts for the Dragon Lady look, with nails half the length of her fingers. The stylist adorns them with silver tinsel, rhinestones, and tiny stars. Around midnight, Jumi mentions that she will take her high school entrance exams at 7 A.M. Her score will not only determine which (if any) school she can attend but affect the type of profession she can pursue. Yet her new nails are so unwieldy, she can barely grasp a pencil. No one seems to fret about this except me. What is an exam compared to womanhood?

I retire to Jumi's bedroom—which we're sharing—around 1 A.M. The entire extended family waves good-night from their workstations. When I return seven hours later, they are still there, wearing the same clothes and finishing up their projects. Dozens more boxes have arrived. One is filled with 500 shot glasses engraved with Jumi's name and "*Mis Quince Años*" (My Fifteen Years); another has 500 highball glasses. There are hundreds of monogrammed salsa pots, salt and pepper shakers, napkin holders, and tortilla covers, plus place settings featuring Jumi's name embedded in lace and netting. The beer and tequila, meanwhile, multiplied overnight and birthed two buckets of limes.

Commotion erupts at the front gate. The pickup truck is here. Strangers appear out of nowhere to load it. I join

them on the ride to Salon Esmeralda, balancing precariously on the bed rail. At the banquet hall, a lone worker
single-handedly sets up seating for five hundred. I don't
see how everything will be ready on time, but everybody
seems *tranquilo*. I return to the house just as Jumi does
from her three-hour exam, mentally spent. We retreat
to her bedroom, where I pour her into a corset and she
steps into puddles of petticoats.

"JUMI!" Judith shouts.

We race downstairs. The hair stylist has arrived. Jumi
sits beneath the avocado tree as she constructs wonder-
curls in a halo around her head with bobbie pins and
AquaNet. Then the caballeros dart in, decked out in
uniforms modeled off the Spanish Conquest: long white
double-breasted coats trimmed with gold braid, white
gloves, swords, and soldier hats. "Jumi! We're going to
be late." I grab her train and we rush out the gate. The
whole barrio has gathered outside. They clap as we dash
past. The caballeros cram into one car; Victor, Judith,
Jumi, and I into the other. Our driver is a peroxide
blonde who says she once lived in Milwaukee.

The church is forty-five minutes away; Mass starts in
thirty. The blonde lady slams it. The giant pink bow on
our car hood grants us the right-of-way: everyone honks
in *felicidades* as we swerve past. At the church, the caballeros form an archway with their swords. Father and
daughter duck beneath it as the mariachis play a joyous
tune and everyone in the pews rises to their feet. Jumi
kneels alone at the altar, clutching her fake calla lilies,
until someone whispers to Victor and Judith that the
seats beside her are theirs. They scramble forward.

The priest concludes Mass by asking Jumi for the
name of her best friend.

"*Mi mamá y mi papá*," she replies.

"That's right, Jumi," he coos. "Your parents will always be there for you."

At that, he asks the three to stand and face the audience. Victor smiles not just with his lips but his eyes, his chest, his whole being. After a few photos, we roar back to Salon Esmeralda where several hundred people await in a salon magically transformed into a *quinceañera* banquet hall, complete with streamers and balloons. So many party favors and aluminum-covered flowerpots cover the tables, the guests must crane their necks to see each other.

"Where are the security guards?" Judith hisses.

I stare at her blankly.

"There might be fights," she explains.

The tequila is another concern: they don't want to stack it on the bar "because people will steal it and drink it and then we'll really have problems." The blonde offers her car. We stuff the cases inside.

"And the presents?" Victor whispers.

A caballero is stationed beside them.

May the fiesta begin! The first of two bands saunters onto the stage in *norteño* chic (cowboy hats, cowboy boots, and rump-sculpting jeans) and fires up some *cumbias*. After slamming a few beers, couples of all ages and sizes take to the floor as the single, divorced, and widowed people look on. The only soloist dances with an open container of salsa balanced atop her head. We all watch, mesmerized, as she defies gravity and sense. "*Qué loca*," the *tías* whisper.

An hour before midnight, the house lights blacken and opera music blasts forth. The caballeros appear in a spotlight carrying an enormous blinking star. Jumi sits

Indian-style inside it. They lower her onto the dance
floor, now ablaze with the light of twelve candelabras.
Jumi tries to step out of the star gracefully but her pet
ticoats intervene. The caballeros break her fall and
somehow scoop her out. She strides across the floor
with her head held high. We clap. Celine Dion belts out
"Power of Love" as the court begins their recital, which
primarily consists of the caballeros bowing on one knee
whenever Jumi glides past.

Then the *padrinos* line up. One by one, they proffer
gifts to Jumi upon a red velvet pillow: a tiara (which
shows she is a princess before God), a bracelet (repre-
senting the unending circle of life), earrings (to hear the
word of God), a Bible (to read it), a scepter (to symbolize
the responsibility she has acquired as a new adult), and a
four-inch pair of stiletto heels. She slips on the heels and
tiara and looks around for her father so they can share a
dance. He is nowhere to be seen. We chant his name to
no avail. Finally, the house lights flicker on. Victor and
Judith are spotted way in the back, guarding the bar.
The dance instructor swiftly retrieves them.

When Victor takes his daughter into his arms, something stirs within me. Maybe it's the knowledge of what
he sacrificed for tonight. Or the aesthetic of a father
dancing with his little girl-turned-woman. Or the tequila I just shot. Whatever. Tears leak as I rise to my
feet in applause. Others join me for a standing ovation.
The moment is tender but brief: according to tradition,
Jumi must now waltz with every adult on the premises.
This takes over an hour, after which she breaks for the
bathroom for a costume change. She and the caballeros
return in hi-top sneakers and sideways baseball caps to
perform the Kumbia King's techno-mariachi-hip-hop

hit "Pachuco." The crowd goes wild as they shake their asses and pretend to shoot one another. For the encore (Cher's "Believe") Jumi pours back into her corset and a ruffled skirt that commences four inches beneath her pubic bone and ripples down the back. Strobe lights and disco smoke shroud the choreography, but no matter—here come the fireworks! The words *"Mis Quince Años"* shower the eight-tiered birthday cake with debris as the guests dart away, coughing.

And with that, my cost analysis of this event smashes through the roof. A journalist will later tell me that Mexican families traditionally spend the equivalent of three years of salary on their daughters' *quinceañeras*. In Victor terms, that is roughly 12,000 bicycle deliveries of 20,000 bagel-and-egg sandwiches prepared over a hot griddle 2,300 miles from home. And the man is still hustling, bringing his guests plates of food and bottles of beer as Judith trails behind. Never do I see them dancing or laughing or even sitting, opting instead to pass out party favors their guests are too blitzed to notice. I soon cease drinking altogether. It is like guzzling his sweat.

Victor could have spent this hard-earned money on any number of things. A college fund for Jumi. A small business. A car. Investments that could have shaped their future. He elected instead to give his daughter the spotlight, to elevate her status in the community. (No doubt, this also proved his worth as a father. He may have abandoned Jumi for seven years, but look at her now, a veritable princess!) Which would she have preferred, though: this one night—or all those missing years with him?

In *Labyrinth of Solitude*, Nobel laureate Octavio Paz writes, "How could a poor Mexican live without the two or three annual fiestas that make up for his poverty and misery? Fiestas are our only luxury…. [It] is not merely a return to an original state of formless and normless liberty: the Mexican is not seeking to return, but to escape from himself, to exceed himself." Mexicans believe in the here and the now; they strive for the delectable moments of being. And tonight has been chock-full of them. Certainly, Victor's money could have been more wisely spent. But not more memorably. No girl ever forgets the night she became a woman.

By 3:30 A.M., most of the guests have straggled home. Salon Esmeralda is a train wreck, and *la familia* gets to clean it. This is no small order. We have been partying for eleven hours straight. Our heads are throbbing, our ears are ringing. The temperature has dropped thirty degrees. But we are Mexican. We *aguantar*, endure. Like that seven-year-old walking by. Her eyes are glazed as doughnuts, but she has an empty beer bottle in one hand and a drained shot glass in the other. If she can hack this, I can too. I grab a stack of Styrofoam plates and march toward the dumpster.

Half an hour later, I join Abuela at a table. We are going to be here until dawn. Maybe even tomorrow afternoon. I plop my head atop a stack of napkins that say JUMI. Leaving now would be unforgivable. It would break family code. If I'm too exhausted to clean, I should at least patiently snooze while the others do it.

By 4:30 A.M., I reach acceptance. I am not a Mexican who can *aguantar*. I am an American who wants to go home. Full of shame, I ask Victor for the house keys. He hands them over, nimble as a zombie. I search around for Jumi. She is sprawled across three chairs, wearing eight inches of skirt and heels. I help her up and we teeter into the street for a taxi. A passing drunkard does a double-take at Jumi. Though only half-conscious, she pulls up her rebozo.

"My *quinceañera*...is it over?" she mumbles.

"It's over," I reply. "Congratulations, Jumi. You're officially a woman."

୬୧ ୬୧ ୬୧

Stephanie Elizondo Griest is the author of 100 Places Every Woman Should Go, Around the Bloc: My Life in Moscow, Beijing, and Havana, *and* Mexican Enough: My Life Between the Borderlines *from which this piece was excerpted. Visit her web site at www.aroundthebloc.com.*

~≈ ~≈ ~≈

No Sin in Ecuador

Not all curves are what you might think.

TANIA WALKED UP THE STEEP DIRT ROAD, PAST PLAYING children and barking dogs, toward the workshop. I felt light-headed and convinced myself it was the elevation. Below us sat downtown Cuenca, Ecuador, and above lay the ghosts of teenage insecurity and lust. Tania opened the workshop door. A smarter man would have turned and ran. But I floated inside, pulled by a temptation older and stronger than I would ever be.

Boys of a certain age (fourteen) and complexion (pimply) are generally not babe magnets. Girls look at them like stains soiling their prom dresses. So these boys form relationships with guitars. The Les Paul electric is the girl in the short, black skirt with that "when I'm eighteen, I'm so outta here" scowl. The Martin acoustic is the girl with glasses and braids who never knew anyone noticed her.

A boy of a more advanced age (thirty-two) and complexion (less pimply), has discarded most of his teenage insecurities, is married, and has a credit limit his ancestors could only dream of. No longer confined to a single guitar, over the years he's picked up several, which mostly stay in the closet. Les Pauls sit comfortably next to Martins and no one ever gets jealous.

Sandwiched in between his quarter-life crisis and upcoming mid-life crisis, the boy has begun his thirty-second year crisis. The solution is to take a few months off work to volunteer and study Spanish in Cuenca, Ecuador. He goes with his wife's blessing and one condition.

"Since we'll be living off only one salary, please try not to buy any guitars," the wife asks.

"Don't worry. I don't need another one," he tells her.

"But you need the six you already have, dear?" she asks.

"Um. Yes," he replies.

Then there is silence because he always forgets to back up his statements with actual evidence or facts.

"Because..." he says.

"Because?" she asks.

"Because every guitar has a unique tone and is best suited to a certain style of music," he finally says. "To play it right you need the right guitar."

He scans her face for telltale signs of skepticism, then adds, "And my friend Ethan has at least seven, if not eight."

"Yes and your friend Ethan is a professional musician," she says. "You play with yourself in your room."

The boy believes he has outgrown temptation. Once in Ecuador he will not be seduced by a finely lacquered hourglass curve resting on his lap until his Spanish teacher, Tania, mentions her father makes guitars. Then temptation strokes him under the chin and whispers, "C'mere, big boy. I've got something to show you."

On the front wall of the workshop hung a couple dozen guitar molds—flat pieces of cardboard used to trace the S-curve of the soundboard. In the corner sat an electric saw, dusty and unplugged. Mr. Uyaguari works by hand, at the same long, narrow workbench he's used for forty years.

He squinted over a thin piece of pine, working on the inlay around the sound hole. Mass-produced classical guitars usually have a decal. But Mr. Uyaguari made the multi-colored pattern by hand, carefully cutting off tiny pieces of dyed wood and placing them in a carved groove, then sanding them even. Completing the inlay on a single guitar would take at least three or four days.

"Everyone wants a $40 guitar from Taiwan," he said. "But they're not built well and they don't sound very good. They don't last." He has repaired many.

"A lot of people ask why they should pay $500 for these guitars when they can get a Yamaha for $40," Tania added. "And it's a Yamaha, a brand name. Uyaguari is not."

Mr. Uyaguari handed me a guitar neck.

"That wood is over two hundred years old, *capulí* salvaged from an abandoned house," he said. "It's had plenty of time to dry."

Cheap guitars are made from young wood. As the wood dries it warps, distorting the guitar.

I asked if there were any finished guitars I could see.

"He usually doesn't have completed guitars around the house," Tania said. "Every once in a while he'll build one for himself, but eventually someone asks about it and then buys it."

"Whenever the family gets together and someone suggests we play some music, Dad—the great guitar maker—just shakes his head because there isn't a single guitar in the house. And so someone has to run home to get one."

But temptation hadn't pulled me into his workshop just to turn me away. Today Mr. Uyaguari had a few.

We walked into the living room. Tania set three guitar cases on the couch. She opened the first case and pulled out a classical nylon-string guitar. This one was hers.

"You know how to play?" I ask. "You never mentioned..."

She shook her head and quickly handed it to me.

"Someday," she said.

I strummed a few chords, played a minor scale, but got self-conscious and put the guitar back in the case. I pulled out the second, also played it briefly, and put it back in the case.

The third was smaller than the rest, like a guitar carelessly shrunk in the wash.

"It's a *requinto*," Mr. Uyaguari said.

A *requinto*? I'd promised not to buy a guitar, but never said anything about *requintos*. I sensed a loophole.

Requintos are pitched higher than normal guitars and play the melody in many styles of Latin music. But really it's just a small guitar, tuned to A instead of E. Claiming this as a loophole would be like cheating, getting caught, and then complaining "that our vows never said anything about sleeping with *Canadians*."

I started playing the *requinto*. Despite its size, each note had a presence that demanded it be heard, that laughed at the mere suggestion it could use an "amplifier" or "effects pedal." I sounded confident and there was no hiding. If you heard a mistake, well it was because I meant to play that. Strumming "Puff the Magic Dragon" was out of the question. This was an instrument to turn boys into men.

"It was a commission," Mr. Uyaguari said. "A difficult commission. First this guy wanted to add an electric pickup so I cut a hole in back for the plug. Then he decided he didn't want the pickup, so I had to fill it up again. In the end he didn't buy it because he didn't like the shape of the markers on the fret board. They're diamond-shaped and he preferred round."

Mr. Uyaguari had carefully selected the wood for the *requinto*: ebony for the fretboard, pine for the soundboard, and Indian rosewood for the back and sides. The sound came from the right combination of woods.

I turned it over in my hands and then gently put it back in the case. The first date always ends too soon.

"I, um, will need to talk to my wife."

The thirty-two-year-old boy isn't sure exactly how to tell his wife he's changed his mind. The call will probably go something like this:

"Hi dear, it's nice to hear your voice."

"Hi, sweetie," she says. "What did you do this week? How are classes with Tania going?"

"It's been fun," the boy replies. "Did you know that here they have thirteen words for being drunk but only one for being sober? And yesterday we visited Tania's father to see his workshop."

"That sounds fun. What does he do?"

"He makes guitars."

"But you're not planning on buying any more, right?"

Silence. The phone line crackles.

"Did I tell you you look very nice today?" he asks.

"Did you buy one?"

"Of course not. That's not in my travel budget. And I said I wouldn't."

"And are you thinking of buying one?"

Silence.

"And will this one go in the closet with the others you never play?"

The boy reminds himself that having lots of guitars doesn't make him more of a man. (John Wayne didn't have any, he tells himself.) But it's hard to shake the insecure fourteen-year-old, tempted and alone in Ecuador.

A month later, Tania and I returned to Mr. Uyaguari's workshop. The newest batch of guitars was just about complete. Freshly lacquered, they hung drying on a clothesline in the backyard.

"Don't they get dusty drying outside like this?" I asked.

"Yes, we have to sand them down a bit," Tania said. "And sometimes flies stick to them."

"Oh, but flies are O.K.," I said. "They help the sound."

Tania gave me a puzzled look.

"Yes," Mr. Uyaguari said. "Especially when they get inside. They give the notes a nice 'zzzzz.'"

Mr. Uyaguari asked why I was spending months away from my wife, studying Spanish and volunteering. Tania explained that many foreigners came to study while their partners stayed at home. For us it wasn't so strange.

He was skeptical. A while back a lonely, married cousin had shacked up with a co-worker.

"The problem is mixed workplaces," Mr. Uyaguari said. "That's were the trouble starts. When people get tempted at work."

"And what workplaces aren't mixed?" Tania asked. "Your one-man guitar shop?"

Mr. Uyaguari didn't respond. "What does your wife do?"

"She's a university professor. That's definitely a mixed work environment."

"She could be cheating on you right now," he joked.

"Well, in that case I won't need permission to buy the *requinto*," I said. "And I'll have to buy a few more guitars to console myself."

Mr. Uyaguari smiled. "Well, then lets hope she's enjoying herself."

Sanka was Argentinian, handsome, and completely unaware he'd been named after decaffeinated coffee. He was also the only person in the salsa club tall enough to see over the dense crowd. He chatted with Gaby, Amaia, and Miriam—my fellow volunteer co-workers. Gaby spoke the musical Spanish of Guanajuato, Mexico. Miriam's Spanish was slightly inflected with the language of her native Austria. Amaia spoke the staccato Spanish of a Basque.

Sanka turned toward me. "Dude, this music is pretty cool," he said in perfect California surfer English, picked up from his American missionary parents. "But it would be even cooler if they played some Doors."

I nodded.

"The girls just told me you're married. Are you wearing your ring?"

I showed him my left hand.

"Ah, man. This is Ecuador," he said. "You gotta take it off. Enjoy yourself. Just look at all the hot women in here. There's no sin in Ecuador."

Sanka's ambition was to sail a boat from Argentina to New Zealand, cutting across Antarctica. I mentioned that Antarctica was a continent and doing this would be like trying to sail from Las Vegas to Denver. But he seemed undeterred. When you are tall and gorgeous you can walk on water and sail on land.

Sanka had been here four months, entertaining at children's parties. A tall, blond Swede walked past and he caught her attention for a moment. She'd been teaching in Cuenca for eleven months and was ready to go home soon.

"I've been here too long," he said after she wandered off. "The women in Ecuador aren't like Argentine women. They're too conservative, too uptight. This country is too Catholic, man."

A moment later Sanka asked, "Do you want another beer? Let me go buy you a beer."

I nodded.

Salsa music was invented by people who are not Swedes. There is no place for accordions, oompa-oompa rhythms, or floor-length skirts. But the thirty-second-year-old boy, after several drinks and no dinner, forgets he is descended from Swedes. He hears the music and he finds a beat—any beat—and he's off. When the dance floor is stuffed with people he can't make a wrong move. Everyone is moving together.

For a moment the insecure fourteen-year-old boy is long gone and maybe never even existed. But really he stowed away in the luggage, crossing time zones and continents, waiting for his moment. And he wonders if everyone here knows something he doesn't. Maybe there is no sin in Ecuador.

At 2:30 A.M., La Mesa was closing, and we decided to go to a bar. Most people had the good sense to hail cabs, but Gaby, me, and two Spaniards named José decided to walk. We locked arms. Individually, we were little more than human Jell-O. Together we were invincible. Marching through the deserted cobblestone streets, José Two loudly quizzed me on my knowledge of Spanish profanity.

"¡Culo!" José Two shouted. "¿Sabes que quiere decir 'culo'? ¡Culo! ¡Culo!" The word giggled from facade to facade.

"Ass!" I shouted back.

If the salsa club had been young and sweaty, the bar was middle-aged and needed moisturizing. Lonely men sat scanning the room for one last prospect before calling it a night.

The Josés stayed for a couple drinks, but absence of culo had deflated their enthusiasm and they soon said their good nights. I sat at the table next to Amaia, embracing a large glass of water. Miriam and Sanka kissed in a corner. Gaby danced with a young Ecuadorian while his twin brother stared at them from an adjacent table. He looked absolutely miserable. Amaia told me the twin had a crush on Gaby. I couldn't tell them apart.

A series of middle-aged men approached Amaia, asking for a dance. Their clothes were off by twenty years and forty pounds. If they had hair, gel plastered it into helmets protecting them from shame. I missed my wife.

I wandered home and went to bed. Two hours later I oozed out of the covers and swayed toward the bathroom to get ready for work.

"I am a stupid, stupid man," I told the door jamb blocking my face.

On my final visit to the workshop, Mr. Uyaguari had just finished repairing a smashed guitar.

"It wasn't braced properly," he told the young owner and his father. "But now it's better than new." He picked up the original, now shattered top piece and handed it to the son.

"You can keep it if you want."

The son shook his head. "No, I don't want to remember that evening."

I told everyone about the destruction of my first guitar. Moving it to another room in our apartment, I dropped the case on the hardwood floor. This made a loud bang that startled my wife, who then yelped. Her noise surprised me and I jumped, unfortunately with my hand still on the case. The guitar flew out of the case and the neck snapped on the floor. This guitar had survived high school and to destroy it with a flick of the wrist was an insult. It deserved better.

Mr. Uyaguari looked pained. "You probably could have repaired it..."

I shook my head.

Sometimes the break creates too many splinters. And even if you can put it back together again, you'll always remember where it broke, never completely trusting that it won't break again.

The son asked to see the *requinto* and Mr Uyaguari handed it to him. "It has a nice tone, it's different," he said, playing an upbeat melody. "Maybe I'll get one of these someday."

His father gave him a look that said, "first stop breaking your own guitars, and maybe we'll consider it."

After the father and son leave, the thirty-two-year-old-boy picks up his *requinto*. He starts playing, and the fourteen-year-old-boy is impressed with how good he sounds, much more confident than he actually is. They are giddy. This is so much more than lust. They swear it will be the last time.

≈ ≈ ≈

Justin Peters grew up in Santa Fe, New Mexico and now lives in Seattle, Washington with Becca the Wife and Selkie the Dog. He uses his English degree and extensive knowledge of arcane music trivia to build web sites that require neither. His personal web site can be found at vatoweb.com. He is no longer thirty-two.

~ ~ ~

The Bamenda Syndrome

Insanity is very much a point of view.

IN MID-JUNE OF 2003, RAYMOND MBE AWOKE ON THE floor of his dirt hut. A white moth had landed on his upper lip. In a half-sleep, he crushed it and the wings left traces of powder across his lips and under his nose. The powder smelled of burnt rubber and when he licked his lips, he tasted copper. Outside the hut, his eyes constricted in the sunlight. A steady dull thud, like a faraway drum, filtered through the trees. "I hate that noise," Raymond told me later. "The sound of pounding herbs with a big pestle. Every time I hear it, I know that a short time later they will stuff those herbs up my nose."

Two hours later, Raymond's nose burned as the green dust coated the inside of his nostrils. A muscular man in a white t-shirt cut off at the sleeves held Raymond's arms twisted behind his back. Across the table from

Raymond, a loose-jowled old man in a worn-out fedora had measured out three piles of crushed herbs.

"Inhale the rest of it," said the old man.

"Please," Raymond pleaded, "I have cooperated today. You don't have to force me."

Deftly, the man in the sleeveless t-shirt twisted Raymond's elbows upward, leveraging Raymond's face level with the table top. Raymond considered blowing away the herbs. He found satisfaction in defying them, but already his arms burned with pain. He snorted up the remaining piles of green dust. Herbs mixed with loose snot ran from his nostrils. The piles gone, Raymond's arms were given a final yank and released.

"Oaf," Raymond muttered and wiped his face with his shirt. No one paid attention; already the old man had motioned to an androgynous creature in rags to approach him. Four other patients stood in line waiting for their turn.

In the bush that ringed the compound Raymond pretended to relieve himself. Glancing around him to make sure no one watched, he fell into a crouch and crept into the foliage. The scabs on his ankles split anew at the sudden effort. Glancing at the pus seeping across his bare feet, he remembered that he had once had a pair of basketball shoes. They had been white, with blue laces.

One hundred yards or so into the bush, he emerged onto a small path that ran in a tunnel through the foliage. Raymond stood up and began walking, brushing aside the large overhanging leaves as he went. In places, the sun shone through the leaves shaping a delicate lacework on the path. The tunnel dilated out onto the bright road. It had been three months since Raymond had seen the road. Under the mid-morning sun, heat shimmered off the pavement and mirages pooled in the distance. The road appeared empty.

"So, I did it. I placed a foot on the road. Very close to where I had last seen my mother. Then I walked across."

"Oh it was terrible," said the tailor who works alongside the road, "We heard him screaming and laughing down on the road. He was like an animal or something possessed. I was scared."

In June, I traveled to a village named Bawum, outside the city of Bamenda in the Anglophone Northwest Province of Cameroon, to interview a priest named Father Berndind. Bawum consisted of a single road, high in the cool grasslands, lined for a mile or so with cinderblock dwellings and the occasional open-front store. Behind the houses ran a network of dirt footpaths connecting poorer thatch-work houses built of sun-dried brick or *poto-poto*.

Berndind had launched a campaign to eradicate the practice of witchcraft from his parish. Plenty of priests wanted to do away with witchcraft; Berndind was unique because he waged his campaign from a seminary that bordered the compound of a witch doctor. His neighbor was Pa Ayamah, a healer renowned for his ability to cure cases of insanity caused by witchcraft.

I went to Bawum with a post-graduate student named Emmanuel, a thoughtful, good-natured guy who grew up in one of the sun-dried brick houses across the road from both Ayamah and the seminary. We agreed that he would introduce me to both Berndind and Ayamah, as a friend rather than a foreign research student, as long as I paid for food and transportation. He had written a Master's thesis on F. Scott Fitzgerald's *The Great Gatsby.* "It's funny," he said. "You come from America to study Cameroonians, and all I want to do is study Americans."

We arrived on a Saturday night. Emmanuel took me to Mass the following morning to meet Berndind. The church was bright and airy, but struck me as weirdly out of place among the green underbrush and dirt paths. It was built in a pre-fab style; the type of church that I remember having seen in lower-middle class areas of Iowa and Nebraska. On closer inspection, I saw that parts of the church had been hand-built to look prefabricated. Inside, I felt underdressed. I was the only man not wearing a sportcoat. In Yaounde, fashion tended towards the sort of suits worn by comic-book super-villains; lots of bright color, wide pinstripes, and shimmery ties. From the somber colors assembled in that church, I gathered that the trend did not extend out into the provinces.

I felt better when a young man who wore a ratty blue t-shirt and taped together flip-flops wandered in. He was short and strangely proportioned, a squat upper body rested on thin legs. He plunked himself down in the pew in front of me. Seated, his feet barely brushed the ground, but his upper body took up almost two spaces. Halfway through the Mass, he craned his head around and stared at me. He pointed at my chest and whispered loudly, "Hey! I like your tie! Very shiny!"

A wave of heads spun around to appraise my clothing choice. "Um. Thank you." A few older men glowered at me and I blushed.

After the Mass, while I waited outside the church to meet with Berndind, I saw the boy walk by and slip into

a thin trail that led into the bush. "What's the story with
that guy?" I asked.

"Oh, that's Raymond," Emmanuel said. "Nobody pays
any attention to him. He's a patient at Pa Ayamah's."

*"I wasn't there," said Emmanuel's sister, "But I heard
about it. They had to take him back bound at the wrists and
ankles."*

"Your teeth have worms in them." George Fanka told
Emmanuel. We had stopped to visit Emmanuel's Aunt
Eliza, before going to Bawum. "That's why they hurt.
They are filled to bursting with worms."

"Worms?" Emmanuel asked.

"I am good with worms," George Fanka assured him.
"I can pull worms out of pile also."

George Fanka did not fit my idea of a native doctor. He was my age and sported a Nike track suit. He
styled his hair like a mid-nineties American rapper
and a cell phone hung from a cord around his neck.
A few years prior, Emmanuel's Aunt Eliza had come
down with a mysterious illness. She spent a good
chunk of her life savings on doctors unable to give her
a diagnosis before she hired George Fanka to come
live with her and treat her. She was a bulky, ashen-
faced woman, whose frequent smiles were followed by
equally frequent winces. Once too ill to stand, under
Fanka's care she had recovered enough to walk into
the town center.

The night I met George and Aunt Eliza, we sat in
her cinderblock living room drinking orange soda. For
more than two hours George talked about his abilities as
a healer. "Well, Sir," he said when conversation turned

to successful treatments, "I come from a long line of doctors. It's in my blood. My uncle is a famous doctor."

"That's why he came here," Emmanuel said, nodding at his aunt. "She needed someone who could live here and George's uncle recommended him."

"Everyone in my family has the ability. There are contests you know. Yes, Contests. Contests." George repeated certain words, as though his audience were intermittently hard of hearing. "All the doctors get together and we compete to see who is the best. I won a contest, you know." He talked quickly and eagerly.

He took a swig of orange soda, smacked his lips, and hurried on. "I won a contest and that's how I lost my toes. Well, only on one foot but that's how I lost them. I'm a diviner; that's what I do best."

"Wait, you lost your toes?"

"On my right foot," George replied. Abruptly, he dropped his soda bottle on the table. Emmanuel lunged forward to keep it from spilling. George didn't notice; he was already bent over in his chair, tugging off his Nikes. He gripped his sock by the toe and pulled it off with a flourish, like a waiter revealing a prized entrée.

He was right. His right foot had no toes. There was a line of angry, puckered scars where his toes had been. They looked disturbingly like anuses. Aunt Eliza said something in a flustered pidgin to George, who was proudly inching his foot towards my face. Emmanuel moved as though he were going to intercept George's foot, but when he saw me lean in for a better look, he leaned back and asked, "Are you scared?"

"No," I said. "Just caught me by surprise."

"Yes, sir!" said George, ignoring the interruption, "My toes were burned off by lightning. After I won the contest, I was too proud—I had been playing with my abilities too much. So someone threw lightning to hit me, but it just got my foot."

George was still holding his foot high in the air, speaking from between his legs. I peered closely at his foot. "Take a good look!" George said gleefully.

A number of people in Cameroon claimed the ability to throw lightning. I had asked about the phenomenon repeatedly, but while everyone said it was possible—and some had even promised to introduce me to people who could do it—tracking down lightning-throwers seemed to be a wild goose chase. An English anthropologist named Nigel Barley had spent a year with the Dowayo tribe in Northern Cameroon asking about lightning rituals, only to find that their method of directing lightning was to place marbles imported from Taiwan in little bowls set on the mountainside. My own investigations into the phenomenon were inconclusive. My best lead, a professor at the University of Yaoundé, had suggested that lightning could be thrown by coaxing a chameleon to walk up a stick.

Nonetheless, there have been some very strange lightning strikes across Africa, many of them having to do with soccer. On October 25, 1998, eleven professional soccer players were struck by lightning in a crucial game in South Africa. Two days later, eleven Congolese soccer players were killed by a second lightning strike. The worst lightning strike ever recorded occurred at a third soccer game in Malawi, when lightning struck a metal fence, killing five people and injuring a hundred more. The official response of African Soccer officials to the lightning strikes speaks to the common interpretation of these events: they banned witch doctors from the African Nations Cup.

I had no idea what toes burned off by lightning might look like, but if I had to imagine, they would have looked something like the scarred puckers lined up on George's foot. I wondered if he had maybe cut his toes off himself, or lost them in an accident, but the wounds looked cauterized, like they had drawn up into themselves.

"Yes, sir," George continued from between his legs. "It might have been another jealous healer, or maybe the spirits thought I was too bold."

I asked George if he could throw lightning. He dropped his leg and cried, "Certainly not! I am a healer and a Christian." He fixed me with an offended expression and wagged his finger back and forth. "That sort of thing is not what I do. What I do is, see, hold on..." He grabbed an empty glass from in front of him. "I make soapy water and I tell it what a person's illness is. Then I look into the water and I can see which kind of herbs I need to find. The next day I go out into the forest and get them."

"I get headaches," I said. "Do you have something for that?"

"And my teeth hurt," Emmanuel said. George looked up my nose and at Emmanuel's teeth. I needed to sneeze more, he told me. Emmanuel, he diagnosed, had teeth full of worms. We made an appointment to return the next day for treatment.

Pa Ayamah's compound looked similar to all the other compounds that dotted the green hills of Bawum: a few huts of sun-dried brick in a clearing surrounded by dense bush. In places, the sun sparkled through the tall trees and sent shadows flitting across soil padded smooth by human feet. Even in rural Cameroon, I had

expected an insane asylum to look somewhat clinical—
whether or not it was run by a witch doctor. I saw none
of the usual tip-offs: no nurses, no white buildings, no
corridors or wards. Only the weathered, hand-painted
sign, "Pa Ayamah—Native Doctor," marked that I had
found the right place.

In front of a smattering of brown huts, dusty men in
chains shuffled about an open yard. Others not chained
had their feet encased into makeshift stocks of rough
wood. Everyone smiled at me, as if I were a regular
stopping in for an evening beer at the neighborhood
bar. A man with his hands tied to his belt tried to wave
in greeting and nearly pulled himself over. He grinned
ingratiatingly, obviously wanting me to share the joke.
I managed a disoriented smile and realized that I had
never before seen anybody tied up. A very old man
with sunken eyes approached me and held out his hand.
Without thinking, I reached to shake it, but recoiled
when I saw that it was purple with infection.

"Antibiotics?" the man said hopefully.

Behind me, Raymond burst out from one of the huts,
barefoot, and pulling on a t-shirt as he ran. "Hey! I saw
you at church!" he cried.

I turned with relief away from the old man. "Oh
yeah," I said, my voice more eager than I intended, "I
remember!"

"You do?" Raymond came to a stop in front of me.

"Yes. I do."

"And I remember you!"

We beamed at each other.

"What's your name?" Raymond asked.

"Dave."

"Antibiotics?" the old man said again, thrusting his purple hand towards me.

"No, no!" Raymond said loudly, leaning in towards the old man. "He's a missionary."

"What? No, I'm not."

"But you're white. And I saw you at church."

"I'm a student. I came to talk to Pa Ayamah."

"Never seen a student here," Raymond commented. "But, oh, come, I'll show you where Ayamah stays." He grabbed me by the arm and pulled me away from the old man, whose parched voice faded as I walked off, "Antibiotics?"

Raymond led me on an impromptu tour of the compound, tugging me along by my sleeve. A good portion of Ayamah's land was devoted to raising corn, planted in rows of raised dirt. Beyond the cornfields were small houses, where women related to the patients lived and prepared food. Raymond confessed that he had no relations among the women, but many of the patients' families couldn't afford both the treatment and food, so a female relative was sent to care for the patient. The few women I saw did not give me the same welcoming smiles as their relatives. I tried to say hello to a pretty girl beating laundry in a soapy bucket. She returned my greeting with a sneer, as she had caught me attempting to watch her bathe.

Beyond the women's huts were the patients' quarters. The huts were small and dirty with a fire pit in front of each one. An aging man with a barrel chest and wooly hair chased chickens with a broom. He was laughing and shrieking. When he cornered a chicken, he spit on it and clapped his hands delightedly. "That's where Pa

Ayamah is," Raymond said. I followed his finger to a long building with a tin roof. "You can just go in."

"Thanks for showing me around," I said, extending my hand. "It was nice of you."

Raymond shrugged and clapped me on the shoulder. He was significantly shorter than I and had to reach up to do so. "Oh, I know how it is. I used to be a student myself."

Clouds hung low in a leaden sky the morning Emmanuel and I presented ourselves at George Fanka's door for treatment. He had exchanged his Nike track suit for a red Adidas shirt and assumed a businesslike air, though his cell-phone medallion still hung from his neck. He led Emmanuel and me to a small wooden shack, consisting of two rooms, padlocked shut. The first had a bed, a small stereo, and was decorated with magazine cut-outs of American pop stars. A large stuffed baboon guarded the second room. "I'll sell you the monkey," George said to me.

"I couldn't get it through customs."

George shrugged and led us inside the second room. Most of the room was taken up by a large table, filled with old water bottles that contained many colored liquids. Red, brown, and green tree barks lay ground up in newspaper. I sat with Emmanuel on a bench and sniffed at the air, which smelled stale, like corridors of a natural history museum. George perused a few bottles and handed me a little bit of brown powder twisted up in cigarette cellophane. "For your head-aches. It is a type of tree bark, O.K.? You snort a bit of that and then you will sneeze for a while and your head will clear."

I nodded. George pulled out a dirty flat head screwdriver. "Lets get rid of those worms," he said to Emmanuel. "They are in your gums." George poured a white suspension over a cotton ball and directed me to hold a piece of paper below Emmanuel's chin; from my position I had a clear view into his open mouth. I hesitated when I saw the screwdriver poised above Emmanuel's teeth, suddenly worried about tetanus. But, I reasoned, when performing oral surgery with a screwdriver, is the status of one's tetanus shot really the primary concern?

"Hold the paper steady," George chided.

Emmanuel's gums looked inflamed, the inside of his mouth very pink. George rubbed the cotton ball across Emmanuel's gums. Little white spots appeared against the pink, then what looked like whiteheads began to form in the gums between the teeth. George reached in Emmanuel's mouth. He pinched one of the whiteheads between the screwdriver and his thumbnail and began to pull. The whitehead stretched and began to pop out in segments. George grunted and forced another finger into Emmanuel's mouth. The last segment of the white-head thing popped out with a little spurt of blood. George held it up for my inspection. It was a small, white, segmented worm, squirming, and covered in blood. It was about a four or five millimeters long, and fat like a maggot.

"They die fast in the open air," he said, and dropped it onto the piece of paper I held. The worm curled up slowly and was still.

"Fuck," I said. I had watched carefully for any sleight of hand, and saw none. The worm had just appeared, a fat zit growing in stop-motion capture. I wanted to be skeptical, but the disconnect between my eyes and brain created a dead spot in my thoughts. I felt seasick. "Fuck," I said again.

"You say that a lot," said George, dropping another worm on the paper. "Uh-oh, I only got half of that one. If they die in there, they rot." Emmanuel winced. His gums bled profusely by the time George got the other half out and still the whiteheads seemed to swell of their own accord. By the time he was done, George had pulled four more worms out of Emmanuel's mouth.

A few days later, I asked Emmanuel if his teeth felt better. "I think so," he said, "but I also went to a dentist who told me the pain was from an infection. He gave me medicine for it. So I don't know if I feel better because of George or the medicine. I'm glad I covered all the options."

A prominent American biologist who visited the University of Yaounde was skeptical of my story. He had not heard of such a worm. When I returned to the United States, I went to my university library and looked up parasitic worms. To the best collective knowledge of Western biologists, there are no segmented parasitic worms that live in human mouths anywhere in West Africa. Apparently, the worms I'd seen did not exist.

Pa Ayamah was a tall man with folds of skin hanging off his face. His eyes looked coated with oil and slipped around, as if the sockets were too big for them. He spoke no English; Emmanuel translated for us. The three of us sat in a line of rickety chairs, pushed against the far wall of a dark dirt-floored room. Ayamah sat very still, but his stillness seemed to come more from a force of energy held back, like a coiled spring waiting to be released, rather than any sense of relaxation or ease.

Ayamah began by announcing that he was of the sixth generation of healers to specialize in the mentally ill. He was the sole heir to two hundred years of practice. Ayamah spoke to Emmanuel, not me, and Emmanuel waited until Ayamah finished before he translated the words.

"He says that the knowledge will die with him," Emmanuel said. "His sons have left him to try to become businessmen in the cities."

Ayamah spoke again, sharply, and stared at the empty space in front of him when Emmanuel translated. "They will end up as market boys. He says that they have forsaken their heritage to be market boys. He finds it shameful." Ayamah wore an old fedora with a snakeskin band. He took it off after he began to speak in earnest. According to him, there were three causes of mental illness. The first was God, by which Emmanuel explained he meant fate and I understood to mean natural causes. The second reason people went crazy was because they neglected their ancestors. Finally, Ayamah said, people might go crazy because one of their enemies placed a curse upon them.

"What happens after people go crazy?" I asked. Ayamah puckered his lips and blew in exasperation. He gave a response that lasted over a minute. Emmanuel cleared his throat and gave a one word translation, "Encopresis."

"That means shit-smearing, right?"

"Yes, and they fight with it. Many things having to do with shit."

"What does he do about it?" I gave up any pretense of
trying to phrase my questions in the second person. Like
Ayamah, I began to speak to Emmanuel directly.

"He has someone clean it up. They can make a real
mess."

"No, I meant for the treatment." Emmanuel relayed
the question. Ayamah said that he didn't spend too
much time trying to determine what type of insanity a
patient suffered from, since he used the same method
to treat all of them: he and his assistants tied them up
and beat them. Eventually they became docile, and he
then stuffed a special blend of herbs up their nose mornings and evenings. "He also maintains a small shrine
to commune with his ancestors in the spirit world,"
Emmanuel explained. "And he might consult the Bible
for wisdom."

"The Christian Bible?"

"Well, they translated it into the Bawum dialect,"
Emmanuel said.

"Yeah, but isn't it sort of a contradiction to commune
with one's ancestors and then consult the Bible? You
know, one God, above all others?"

Emmanuel translated the question and laughed at
Ayamah's response. "He says 'What's the difference?'
Jesus is just a really old ancestor of yours. If he wants
really old knowledge he talks to Jesus. When he wants
to talk to someone more up-to-date he consults his own
ancestors."

Emmanuel waited a moment to see if I had any more
objections and went on. The only modifications Ayamah
made to his treatments were for those who threw their
shit. He chained shit-throwers hand and foot. For everyone else, he simply took a log, drilled a hole in it, and

after sticking the patient's leg through the hole, nailed in place a second length of wood to close off the hole. Ayamah assured me that it was difficult to get very far dragging a log on one foot.

"Doesn't that bother you?" I asked Emmanuel.

Emmanuel scratched at a five o'clock shadow contemplatively. "I guess it might have, but I grew up in this village. You might say that the sight of madmen in logs was part of my childhood."

Ayamah picked his nose and blew snot on the floor.

"What about Raymond?" I asked, "How come he doesn't have a log on his leg?"

Ayamah chuckled slightly when Emmanuel translated the question. His response had a lot of sound effects. At one point Ayamah acted out hitting something with his walking stick and cried, "Bam-Whacka-Bam!"

Emmanuel turned to me when Ayamah was finished. Again the translation was noticeably shorter than the story. "He said Raymond was a hard case. He never threw his shit, but he made trouble in other ways. He thought he wasn't crazy. They had to beat him to make him understand he was unwell. Once he understood, he was docile."

Joseph, the cook agreed with all the others, "I was one of the people who brought him back. Some other men had gathered and asked me to help them. I like him. He likes the food I make. I wasn't happy to see him like that."

Whenever I try to explain the worms I saw in Emmanuel's mouth, I get stuck on that exact fact. *I saw them. I saw them come out of his gums.* After a while, I came to the conclusion that I had three ways to explain what I'd seen: I could decide that I had been deceived, I could decide that my eyes had deceived me, or, finally, I could alter my entire world view to encompass the possibility of non-existent worms residing in people's gums.

Unconsciously, I think I explored the first and third options, but consciously, I chose the second. Though the first option was probably preferable, the second option seemed more plausible. My disorientation in Cameroon felt like more than simply the result of culture shock, I had the nagging suspicion that I was experiencing things I wasn't equipped to understand. Which was more probable, I asked myself, that the world was out of whack, or that I was?

I had my erratic behavior as evidence. I acted aggressively. I fought with strangers. I went to the unrestricted pharmacies and invented pill cocktails. I felt unafraid of garrulous and dangerous men. For someone who prided himself on having lived alone in foreign countries since he was young—who worked to approach other cultures on their own terms—I was suddenly, disturbingly, patriotic. Cameroon may be a rough and difficult place, but millions of people have no problem catching its rhythm and logic. My experiences elsewhere, or maybe my youth, had made me arrogant. Rather than admit to myself that I had arrived unprepared for certain experiences, I narrated my own explanations to myself. But much like a lie built upon a lie, I found myself unable to revise my stories to fit events without admitting that I knew nothing, and so instead my stories, and therefore understanding of the events around me, grew more and more fantastic.

By the time I met George, I was frequently making up the world as I went along. More to the point, I didn't know when I was doing it, and when I wasn't. Given all this, I was willing to believe that I saw worms come out of Emmanuel's teeth, and I was also willing to believe that worms did not come out of his teeth at all.

On my way home from my interview with Pa Ayamah, I came upon Raymond crouched on a log, reading a pamphlet that outlined how to set up a library in accordance with the Dewey Decimal System. "Hey, the missionary!" he called out, grinning. "How's the church work?"

I took a seat next to him. He held the pamphlet up for my inspection. "I'd like to go to a library again. Now I just read about them."

"Did you used to go to libraries?"

Raymond laughed. "I wasn't always like this. I used to study economics at university. I was good at it, too."

Like what? I wanted to ask. In my few encounters with him, he struck me as odd, but living in Ayamah's compound would give anyone a few quirks.

"Why did you quit?" I asked.

Raymond waved his hand airily. His wrists were too thick to make the gesture look natural; it came off as studied or affected. "My uncle. He put a curse on me." Once he started talking, the story rolled out of him. I got the sense that no one had ever asked him before, he kept skipping back and forth through his story, trying to construct it in words.

Raymond was the son of a polygamist father who died when he was six or seven. As tradition dictated, Raymond's father's brother took Raymond and his widowed mother to live with him. Raymond's uncle and his jealous wife beat and underfed him. While we talked,

Raymond pulled back his lips to show me how hunger had ruined his teeth. "Worst of all," Raymond confided to me, "My uncle was an evil man. He was a member of a secret society. The only thing he was good at was witchcraft."

After finishing *lycee,* both Raymond and his uncle's son were awarded opportunities to study at the University of Buea. "My uncle was furious that I should go to the same university as his son. He kept asking me who I thought I was. But he couldn't stop me and my mother secretly gave me some money." During the school year there was not enough money for Raymond and his cousin to come home, so Raymond stayed at the university studying economics, while his cousin came home during breaks.

"What type of economics did you study?" I asked when he paused to breathe.

He furrowed his brow. "How do you mean?" he replied.

"I mean what exactly did you study economics for?"

Raymond inhaled sharply and shifted his seat next to mine so he could grasp my knee. His face was mottled with little scars, but beneath them the skin was unlined. The whites of his eyes were completely clear, which was remarkable given the dust and dirt on the path. "Oh you, know," he said in an off-hand tone. "Lots of different things."

Abruptly, Raymond lifted his head and looked off towards the tops of the trees. "Do you smell something burning?" he asked.

I sniffed the air. "No. I don't smell anything."

Raymond shrugged and continued his story. After months without seeing his family, Raymond's uncle called him home just before exam period. When Raymond left, his uncle gave him ten thousand francs. His uncle had never done anything like that before. Raymond later found significance in the action. "The money was cursed." At this point in his story, Raymond stood and began to wave his hands, acting out his words. His crisp accent contrasted remarkably with his torn blue t-shirt and the caked dirt on his legs and pants.

Raymond returned to school in time to begin cramming for exams. Although he felt he had much work to do, his thoughts kept on focusing on the ten-thousand franc note he had stashed away in his economics textbook. "It was calling to me. Like a beautiful prostitute. Something you know is wrong, but attracts you so much." Twenty or thirty times in a day he would stop what he was doing and check to see if the money was still there.

"It got very bad," Raymond said, his voice almost pleading, "This obsession with the money. I was studying all day for the exams, but I was thinking about the money. The night before the exams, I got sick. It was like a fever, and my chest was tight. I was sweating and moaning and I put the textbook with the money in it in my bed."

"The experience you describe kind of sounds like an anxiety attack," I interjected. "Maybe you were stressed over exams."

Raymond rolled his eyes as though a child had interrupted him. "This," he said slowly, "was not an anxiety attack. I was afraid to trust anyone. It was terrible. I locked myself in my room and held the book with the money in it to my chest. I was like that for twenty-four hours; I missed my exams. Finally it was too much. I took the ten thousand francs and went to the market to buy medicine. But instead of medicine, I asked for poison."

"They sell poison in the markets?" I had never seen any, but then, I hadn't looked.

"For animals. But they wouldn't sell me poison, so I tried to buy Valium to take an overdose, but I was wild and out of control, so they wouldn't sell me any."

"If you could spend the money on Valium, why didn't you just buy a shirt or a radio or something to get rid of it?"

Raymond shook his head impatiently, his wide-set eyes bulging. "Don't you see? They controlled me! I couldn't spend the money on anything but poison! Why of all the ways to kill myself did I try to use the money to buy poison? The money made me do it!"

Raymond noticed he was shouting, lowered his arms slightly, and gave me a weak smile, "Sorry, I forget myself sometimes. Not exactly a smart thing for madman to do."

I shrugged "Go on."

"I went home in a rage and pulled down the light from the ceiling of my room and tore it open." He forgot his fear of yelling and began to act out tearing apart a light with flailing arm gestures. "And I took it so there were two wires, full of electricity, and I grabbed one with each hand so the electricity could flow through me and cure me of the fever." It was quiet on the path; I could hear the whir of grasshoppers and the gurgle of a nearby stream. Against those noises Raymond's long toenails scraped the bare dirt while he stood in front of me. His arms grasped imaginary wires and his body writhed while muted screams escaped through clenched teeth as he pantomimed his suicide attempt. It lasted long enough for me to grow frightened. Just as I was about to say something, his body dropped motionless on the dirt.

"He was shouting about being on the road." The sun-blackened man whose job seemed to be to remain ever-seated on the lawn chair in front of the tailor's shop agreed with everyone else. "So what? I'm down on the road everyday. It's nothing to get so excited about." He took a pull on his cigarette and nodded sagely at his own words.

By American standards, most foreigners I met who were living in Cameroon behaved bizarrely. Every ex-pat I met had his or her quirks; some of the Peace Corps volunteers were downright zany. A volunteer named John, who had lived in the desert for a year and a half without running water, electricity, or a telephone, had, after a few beers at bar in the Hilton hotel, repeatedly called room service demanding to know why they kept calling him.

In Yaounde, I had met a group of wealthy expatriates who had set up something of a European infrastructure and society nestled subtly within the world of Cameroonians. That wealthy, European bubble was not one that was particularly easy to find, and I was happy to have gained their acceptance. They were the twenty-something offspring of diplomats and exporters and they lived a lifestyle that struck me as quite glamorous at the time. Plus, they seemed taken by me; I was new, strange, and for short periods, I had enough money to keep up with them.

It ended when I forgot which person to be with them. One night they took me to a club, some fancy club, where I was ripped off on the entrance fee. Inside, I went to the bar and ordered myself a beer. I asked the barman if he had change for a five thousand. He said he did. He took my money and brought me a tiny beer.

"And my change?" I asked.

There is none.

I decided to be friendly, "Look man, you can keep two thousand of it as a tip if you want, but there is no way a beer is five thousand francs. I pay two hundred at the bar by my house."

"This isn't the bar by your house."

"Just give me the money."

The barman didn't say anything more. He simply nodded to a large Frenchman who had a whore hanging from each arm. He shrugged off one of the whores and grabbed me by the chin. He yelled something in my ear in slurred French. I told him I didn't understand what he said. I understood him the second time, when he told me to fuck off and slapped my cheek Godfather-style.

I got angry then, and forgot where I was. I forgot that I was a twenty-one-year-old middle-class American boy, who was very far from home. I forgot that a flashy nightclub in an expatriate inter-city was not my turf. I forgot that I have not been in a real fight since fourth grade and I forgot that any large Frenchman who has two whores and slaps my cheek like the Godfather is someone not to be fucked with. Instead, I swelled with the sort of self-righteous pride that you find among students at small liberal-arts schools in the United States. Places where things are fair, prices are marked, and some cheesy-looking French Mafioso-wannabe is an abstraction of the movies.

Who the fuck does this mustachioed and obvious low-life exploiter of the African people think he is?

I bitch-slapped him.

The music was loud enough that only a few people heard it. There was a moment where no one moved, not me, not the whores, not the French guy. Then I remembered where I was. With as much dignity as possible I turned my back and walked out of the club. Behind me, the Frenchman was organizing a group of large men. Once outside, I got in the first taxi I saw.

My girlfriend was at the club. She was very confused by my disappearance. I called her on her cell phone and told her what I had done.

She paused a moment, then said, "But a beer here *is* five thousand francs."

Raymond awoke in a hospital, his burned hands fastened to the side of the bed. He had been examined while unconscious. A foreign doctor, an Arab, Raymond thought, had found evidence of possible brain anomalies and ordered a few basic tests to be conducted at the provincial hospital. The doctor concluded, though, that Raymond was most likely suffering from something like anxiety or depression. Raymond felt otherwise. The pieces fit together easily in his mind. His illness was caused by witchcraft on the part of his uncle, most likely with the help of a secret society and most likely with the help of other members of his family. Why else was he suddenly called home? Why else the sudden gift of ten thousand francs, from a man who had never before given him anything? His uncle had given him a gift of bewitched money.

Raymond's conjecture wasn't implausible. Although I found it hard to draw the same initial conclusion as he did, the description of his relationship with his uncle and his uncle's actions follows an almost classic model of bewitchment. Accusations of witchcraft most often occur within families, or at least along some form of kinship lines. Witches and the bewitched nearly always know each other. If Raymond suspected his illness was caused by witchcraft, he would look to the person who hated him most: his uncle. With a little knowledge of witchcraft, the seemingly innocuous gift of money becomes more suspicious as well. While traveling around Cameroon, I found that while I could not leave any of my belongings lying around because they inevitably would be stolen, loose cash left in plain sight was never touched. In the town of Kribi, a group of children went into hysterics when I picked a hundred-franc coin off the beach. The instant I touched the coin, the children screamed "No! Drop it! Drop it! Mami Water, she'll get you! Mami Water! Mami Water!" The youngest of them were nearly in tears. In Kribi, no one touched lost money because of the belief that Mami Water—a mutation of the mermaid myth—used money to entice men into the ocean to drown.

The story varied place to place, but the theme was the same: Don't take money from strangers. Cash was the perfect medium for sorcery.

Although Raymond remained distrustful of his uncle, he nonetheless left the hospital with him. His uncle remained silent, while his mother pressed his hand and told him that they had borrowed a car and arranged to bring him to Yaoundé where he could be given modern medical treatment. Instead, they drove west into the grassland regions along the Ring Road. In the village of Bawum, they parked the car on the path that led to Pa Ayamah's compound.

"My uncle got out of the car and walked away. He came back with two men, who opened my car door and pulled me out. I was so shocked I didn't do anything. I fell out of the car and they began to beat me while my uncle and my mother watched. I cried out for my mother to help me, but she kept repeating, 'These men are going to help you.' Then my uncle stood between us. I cried her name many times as they beat me and I began to bleed." Raymond inhaled audibly and pulled at his ear. "My mother began to ask if it wasn't enough, but my uncle pushed her into the car and they drove away."

Almost an hour had passed since I had sat down next to Raymond on the path. We were both sweating in the sun. He lifted the bottom of his t-shirt to wipe his sweat away, leaving trails of dark blue in the light blue fabric.

"They had me chained to a post the first two months," Raymond said, and picked at a stray thread on his shirt. "At first I tried to reason with them. I yelled for days about the rights of man and how it was not right to treat me as they did."

"Were you speaking in English?" I asked.

"Yes, some pidgin, but mostly English. I don't speak quite the same dialect as they speak here. It's really kind of funny, because I was trying so hard to reason with them, but I was talking about the rights of man, you know, *Liberte, Egalite, and Fraternite*, which must have sounded like complete nonsense. It's no wonder everyone thought I was crazy. A total madman!" Raymond laughed at the memory, but the sound came out dry and mirthless.

By midway through my stay, I had so convinced myself that I was unbalanced, that it took me a while to notice when other people were acting more absurd than I. In a crowded market, I had been pulled out of a taxi by a gendarme with the disgruntled, bovine face of a cop who once had a desk job. He demanded my passport and vaccination records. I produced them and he scowled at the vaccination card. "Your records are not in order," he declared. He blew his whistle and told the taxi driver to move along. The taxi man said he would wait for his fare.

"What is the problem with my records?"

"Are you contradicting me?"

I reviewed what I had just said in my mind, wondering if I had accidentally misused the French words. "No," I said. "I am not contradicting you."

"Good." He squared his shoulders and adjusted his gun belt. Three other gendarmes, brandishing automatic rifles, appeared behind him. They couldn't resist a white kid in a taxi. Tourists hemorrhaged cash at the sight of a couple of Uzis. I sighed and asked what could be done to "remedy" the problem.

"You're missing a vaccination," he said.

"Which one?" I asked.

"You don't have an AIDS vaccine."

"What?"

"You need to have an AIDS vaccine. You don't have an AIDS vaccine."

"There is no AIDS vaccine."

"What?"

"I said, there is no AIDS vaccine."

He blinked and turned to one of the other gendarmes. "This guy, where does he come from? He says there is no AIDS vaccine." He guffawed loudly, the other gendarmes coughed out half-hearted laughs.

I stepped towards him. "Look, I'm telling you there is no AIDS vaccine."

He laughed, "Oh yeah, then how come so many people are sick?"

My words came out soaked in condescension, despite myself. "Well, vaccines cure sicknesses. If there was an AIDS vaccine those people wouldn't be sick. What you have here in Cameroon is an epidemic, something that happens when there is no vaccine."

A small crowd had gathered around as soon as I was pulled out of the taxi. It must have been an interesting scene: an angry white boy who sneered out broken French at four gendarmes who patted their guns like puppies.

The cop tried a new tact. "You think just because there isn't an AIDS vaccine I can't arrest you for not having one?"

I was mad then, and didn't bother to control myself. "What's it going to take for you to leave me alone?"

"You're under arrest."

"For what? Not having an imaginary vaccine?"

The growing crowd cackled with pleasure. A young man cried, "Careful, they almost arrested me for killing my imaginary friend! But I swear, I wasn't anywhere near that imaginary car crash!"

One of the other gendarmes told him to shut up, but couldn't totally repress a smile.

The bovine-faced cop was less amused. He put my passport in his pocket and reached for his handcuffs. "You're under arrest."

I pulled out my cell phone and told him I was dialing the embassy. The cop hesitated. The crowd hooted in surprise. It was a new trick for them; they didn't have an embassy to call.

"You lack respect!" the cop screamed.

"On the contrary, I have only used the *vouz* form, where you call me *tu*."

An Anglophone who corrected his French was the final straw. Exasperated, he threw my papers back in my face and told me I was too clever for my own good. This was apparently an insult powerful enough to redeem him. With renewed swagger he turned to berate the assembled crowd.

The taxi man clapped me on the shoulder as we drove away, "Hey, you argue like a Cameroonian," he said. "I planned to overcharge you, but forget it now."

After months of striving to fit in, I had only to mock a half-witted policeman in order to be accepted.

Raymond squinted at the sun. "I think I will go get a snack."

"What are you having?"

"It's mango season. Mangos."

I walked with Raymond to the center of the compound, where he had left a plastic bag of mangos. The fruit was everywhere; at night the falling fruit thumped in the forest like giant raindrops. We sat against a plank across from a schoolroom chalkboard posted under an overhang.

Rules
Take medicine at 9:00 and 5:00.
Clean personal space.
No fighting.
Bathe twice a week.
Attend nightly prayers.

No crossing the stream.
No crossing the road.

The letters were written in a shaky hand, and it looked like there had once been nine rules, but the last two, too low to be shielded from rain by the overhang, had washed away. "Can I take a picture of that?" I asked, pulling a little point-and-click from my pocket.

Raymond looked eagerly at the camera. "I've never taken a picture before."

I gave the camera to him and showed him how to zoom in and out. "Can you take a picture of those rules?" He stood up and carefully lined up the shot, trying different angles. Behind him, a large man carrying a load of wood walked around the corner. His hair was cut in a flattop, and his t-shirt sleeves had been torn off to reveal arms that looked like they had been drawn by a comic book artist. In a single fluid motion, he dropped the firewood, caught one of the falling sticks and flung it at Raymond. The stick flashed past Raymond's ear as the shutter clicked. With a roar the man was upon us, towering over me and dwarfing Raymond. Raymond smiled benignly and lowered the camera. There was a quick exchange in pidgin and Raymond handed me back the camera. The man fixed me in a hard squint, and I, in an attempt to look away, ended up reading his t-shirt, which advertised a music festival. "That is a madman!" he growled. "You don't give him your things." I didn't say anything. He backed away with a menacing finger pointed at Raymond and I stayed quiet while he gathered his firewood and stalked past us.

Raymond switched back to English and said in a steady voice. "He is one of the men whose task is to beat and control us. He doesn't want me talking to you."

"Why not?"

"Because I am a madman, of course. Just as he said." Raymond picked at the gaps between his teeth during the silence that followed. I couldn't tell if he was serious. He may have been a bit odd, and perhaps he talked in church and wouldn't explain what he knew of economics—but in the time I knew him, he was always lucid. In fact, he was the most friendly, forthcoming, and sensible person I had met in days.

"O.K.," I said finally, "but you don't really seem like a madman. Forgive me for saying so, but mostly you just seem unlucky."

Raymond held out an empty hand and a sour look crossed his face. "As I told you, I am a simple man. It was my uncle's witchcraft that drove me insane. The madness is there, even if it doesn't show. Not to you. Not to me. But it is there."

I put the camera back in my pocket. "People write books about that, you know. The insane are insane because they don't know that they are insane. By that logic, I would say your belief in your own madness proves you are fine."

Raymond sighed and spat on the ground. In the sunlight, his scalp shone through his hair. "That's a fun word game," he said at last. "But some of us in places like this require more than that. We must prove our insanity to ourselves."

"How could you possibly have done that?" I cut in.

Raymond pointed at the chalkboard. "Do you see rule number 7?"

"Yeah. Don't cross the road."

Raymond turned and pointed in the direction of the road. "You might think that Pa Ayamah has that rule to keep us from wandering through town. That's not it. Pa Ayamah says that this area is protected. Out on the road, we are exposed once more to the demons that cause our madness. If we cross the road, we go mad again."

Raymond tapped his head. "A few days before you arrived, I went and tested his rules. I'm a madman all right."

After the AIDS vaccine incident, I wrote an e-mail that described the event to my professors in the United States. It was meant to be humorous, but apparently taunting armed police just doesn't strike the same funny chord in the States. I got a call from my journalism professor shortly afterward. Rather than saying outright that he felt worried, he told me about two psychological syndromes.

The first was the Florence Syndrome. It is a condition that affects young people—usually artists—when they travel to Florence, Italy. Suddenly they find themselves inside a world that they had only seen in books. All their lives, they studied art printed on a page or projected from a slide. But in Florence, there is no book to close, no switch to kill the projector. They overdose on art. Their brains overload and they lose perspective. The art becomes an obsession, an addiction, as crippling as any drug, and the importance of their lives before Florence slowly fades.

The Jerusalem Syndrome is more serious, and religious, rather than artistic, in nature. People from a culture like America's—only two hundred years old—go to Jerusalem and find themselves inside of *history*. Scraps of the Bible, or the Torah, or the Koran, are made tangible before their eyes. They have no chance to close the Bible and decompress, instead the Bible is all around them, they are inside the Bible. A man with the Jerusalem Syndrome finds himself at the wide road of religious history, the course of which traces its path all the way to *him*. And what must it mean that all that is holy and recorded leads to the moment of his arrival in Jerusalem? Simple, he is the Messiah.

While my professor talked, I thought of the spring leaves outside his office in Massachusetts and contrasted it with the bare dirt and open sewers I saw from the balcony. Was he really paying five dollars a minute to tell me these stories?

"Let's talk about this other pattern I've noticed," he continued. "Lots of young people go to Africa. But they all go through programs and organizations. They have a safety net, Peace Corps, NGOs...but when they cut themselves loose, they change. They become disillusioned, they get mad, they take on Africa single-handedly." My professor paused, I heard static. "They pick fights with men carrying guns. Any of this sound familiar?"

"I see what you're getting at," I said into the mouthpiece, "but tell me, does this particular syndrome have a name?"

His laugh sounded dry across the line. "Not that I know of. But in your honor, we'll just call it the Yaoundé Syndrome. Take care."

"A moth that tastes like copper?" The eminent biologist frowned.

"That's what he told me."

"I really don't know about that. But hey, maybe he was he having a seizure when he ate it. Epileptics taste copper and smell burning rubber before seizures. The "Epileptic Aura." The eminent biologist's belly shook with a chuckle.

Raymond stood on the far side of the road and waited to go insane. Nothing happened, and it wasn't long before it was clear that nothing was going to happen. It was all bullshit, the rules weren't worth anything. He was fine.

"Please," Raymond shouted to the empty road, "I have crossed the road and nothing happened. What's more, I will cross it again!" He was almost hysterical with laughter as he sprinted back across the road. Three months of beatings had almost convinced him. He remembered how seriously he had begun to take Ayamah's mumbo jumbo and hooted at the thought.

"I felt like celebrating. It felt wonderful to be so free," he told me later. "It was a wonderful celebration. I knew at that moment that I was cured. Probably there was nothing wrong with me in the first place."

Four times he crossed the road. Each time he proclaimed his accomplishment to the uncaring trees and dusty rocks. Then it was ten times. His voice was hoarse with laughter and he barely had enough breath to keep it coming. Standing in the middle of the road, he raised his hands heavenwards and shouted, "I am free to cross the road. Free to cross the road!"

Just beyond the far side of the road, a stream ran fast and clear over brown pebbles. A young girl had been wading in the water, her red dress turned dark at the hem. Frightened by the shouting, she ran to the nearby cooking shack where her mother was pounding huckleberries. The mother wiped her hands on a rag blackened by kitchen smoke and told her daughter to go inside. Outside the sound of shouting carried across treetops. On top of a bridge made of split logs, a group of villagers all faced the same direction. The mother followed their gaze. A young man skipped and laughed as he crossed and re-crossed the road, proclaiming his accomplishment each time. The women clucked their tongues in dismay, while the men discussed how to subdue him. How sad that so promising a youth could be so hopelessly and so obviously insane.

꙰ ꙰ ꙰

David Torrey Peters is an MFA candidate at the University of Iowa. He has lived in the Dominican Republic and Cameroon, and worked for The Newshour with Jim Lehrer. *His essays have been selected as finalists in contests held by* Narrative Magazine *and* Third Coast Magazine, *and his work is forthcoming in* Fourth Genre: Explorations in Nonfiction. *"The Bamenda Syndrome" won the Grand Prize in the third annual Solas Awards for Best Travel Writing.*

Mother, India

A traveler's mom meets the Mother
of all destinations.

THE DRIVER TOSSED OUR BAGS INTO THE TRUNK OF A
white Ambassador cab, and pressed his palms
together.

"Welcome to India, sir. Is this your wife?"

"No, she's my mother."

My mother smiled. I was less sanguine. It was a
dubious start to an adventure that I already had my
doubts about. Bringing my mom to India had seemed
an inspired idea; I'd wanted to give her something
spectacular for her seventy-fifth birthday. An eight-day
tour of northern India's signature sites—New Delhi, the
palaces of Rajasthan, the Taj Mahal—would provide an
indelible impression of the country's history and culture,
which had so profoundly altered my own world.

My misgivings befit the enterprise. Not only was this my mother's first trip to Asia; she and I had never traveled *anywhere* together before. My inspiration was short on precedent, and long on bravado—a fact that caused considerable panic as our jet approached New Delhi.

Because India, truly, is like nowhere else on Earth. It is not a destination you *visit*, like Paris or Beijing or Barcelona. It's a place you must surrender to, dissolve into. No matter where one touches down, first contact is overwhelming.

During my first visit to the subcontinent, in 1979, I spent my first two days barricaded in a hotel room. On the morning of the third day, I emerged, mole-like, onto the crowded streets. Every sense was immediately overloaded. I felt like a visitor on an alien planet; a place where sounds and sights, tastes and odors, were dialed up to an unbearable volume.

Then—as I strolled along the sidewalk—something inside of me let go. My chest loosened, and my neck relaxed. I began to meet the eyes of the people around me, offering a self-conscious *namaste* in answer to their greetings. The responses were astonishing. Every single person seemed to welcome interaction with me, and to accept me as I was. A huge weight evaporated from my shoulders.

I had broken through. I shed my bulky space suit, and let the atmosphere in. This "alien planet," I realized, had a name: Earth. For the first time, I realized how little I knew about the world's inhabitants. They had a great deal to teach me about this planet—and my own humanity. My spiritual journey in India had begun.

Then and since, India has always been a place of pilgrimage for me; a doorway into mind-blowing personal growth. No matter how short my visit, I always come home a changed man.

But this trip wasn't about me. It was about my mother. A lifelong educator, occasional artist, and very spiritual woman (she had become a *bat mitzvah* at the age of sixty-seven), Mom was overdue for a glimpse into the world so familiar to her eldest son. Granted, a trip to India isn't the most luxurious gift (she might have preferred a Caribbean cruise), but it was the kind of gift we're meant to give: something that we ourselves cherish.

India can challenge even seasoned travelers, and any number of things might go awry. Health is one issue. I'd gotten violently ill during my first trip to India in 1979, and several times since. Mom is in great shape—but even the mighty have been laid low by the parasites of South Asia.

A second concern was diet. My mother keeps kosher, at home and in restaurants. She's never touched bacon, or eaten a prawn. Would she be able to eat, let alone enjoy, Indian food?

Finally, there was the freak-out factor. India is just too much for some visitors. The crowds, the beggars, the sheer intensity of life pushes some people over the edge. When I lived in Nepal, a doctor friend sometimes treated tourists who lost their marbles, and had to be booked on the next flight home. He stamped their medical forms with the anagram PUTIA: "Psychologically Unfit to Travel in Asia." Would my Mom, who had never visited a non-western country, be branded with this tragic moniker? How would she fare in a country where the Star of David is a symbol of tantric union, and the *svastika* a sign of good luck?

Mom hit the ground running. Our first morning in Delhi, we toured the grounds surrounding the twelfth century Qatb Minar: the tallest brick minaret in the world, and the earliest example of how Islamic architecture would transform northern India. I was fascinated by the ancient foundations, and the chunks of classical Indian sculpture arranged in railed-off pits.

"Hey, Mom," I said. "This monkey-god..." But she had vanished. I saw her across the plaza, surrounded by a crowd of schoolchildren in starched white shirts. They clamored around her, shouting answers to her queries and jostling for group photographs.

"I doubt," I said, leading her back toward our cab, "that Amitabh Bachchan himself would have received a warmer welcome."

"Who?"

"He's India's biggest film star—sort of like Harrison Ford, Clark Gable, and Cary Grant rolled into one."

"He must be very handsome."

"I'd say so. He might be the best-looking guy in India. The best looking middle-aged guy, anyway."

The next afternoon we were invited, by our well-connected guide, to visit the Sri Kalkaji Mandir, which may be Delhi's most important temple. It was the beginning of the ten-day Dasara festival, dedicated to the blood-thirsty goddess Durga. Incense filled the air, so thick it muted the beating of drums and strains of a harmonium. The temple was so crowded that we had to be ushered in amid a police escort.

I was astonished to see my mother—who lights the
Sabbath candles every Friday evening—kneeling in
the inner sanctum, receiving a blessing from an opium-
addled sadhu and pressing her head to the huge silver
shrine, upon which stood an ancient image of Durga,
wearing a necklace of human skulls.

Outside in the courtyard, wailing infants—just over
six weeks old—were having their heads shaved with
straight razors. Once shorn, the hair was offered to
Durga, while red *svastikas* were painted on the babies'
bare scalps.

"Oy, vey." My mother, at last, seemed rattled. "Why
are they doing that?"

"In India, the *svastika* is an ancient and much-loved
design. The Nazis stole it, but that doesn't matter here.
To the Hindus and Buddhists, it's still a symbol of good
luck, and a sign of protection by the gods."

"The religion here," she said, shaking her head, "it's
all-encompassing. I was never aware of it."

At sunset, we hired two sinewy rickshaw *wallahs* to
take us through the seething markets of Old Delhi on
their creaking bicycles. It was like being injected into
the guts of a kaleidoscope. We wove through fallopian
lanes blinking with colored lights and draped with
saris and bangles and glass bead necklaces, past show-
cases full of earrings and bright glass gems, between
vats boiling with swirls of frying honey, date-sellers
and pan-spitters and mules, pineapples and *pakoras*
and a dozen varieties of dates, past printers' stalls selling tinseled wedding invitations, illuminated statues of
elephant-headed Ganesh and blue-faced Krishna, beneath clouds of spice and hookah smoke, our rickshaw

drivers' acrobatic legs performing a constant dance of approach/avoidance, back and forth on the pedals, as we threaded through alleys so narrow they'd challenge an anorexic unicyclist.

Emerging out of the bazaars and onto a main street, we dismounted and caught our breath. Even our *wallahs* seemed exhilarated. Above us loomed a huge billboard, upon which a familiar face endorsed a brand of Indian cement.

"Look, Mom!" I pointed. "*That's* Amitabh Bachchan."

My mother glanced upward. "Oh, Honey," she said. "You're better looking than him."

When I think back on the influences that made me a travel writer, I think mainly of movies: epic films like *Lawrence of Arabia* and *2001: A Space Odyssey*, which made me long for the universe that lay beyond the suburban tracts of Plainview, New York. But I suspected a paternal cause, as well.

My dad and I were never very close, and he died of heart failure when I was thirty. Once in a while, though, when I was a teen, we'd drive into Manhattan together. That's when he'd open up. One story that stuck with me was set near El Paso, when my Dad was in the service.

"Your mother was pregnant with you," he said. "And I'd just been discharged. I was driving away from the base, alone, down one of those long, flat highways. I remember coming to a junction, where a dirt road snaked off into the hills. I stopped right there, and stared up that road—thinking of all the places I wanted to see, all the adventures I'd never had. It was a real dilemma. I could take that road and disappear, live the life I'd dreamed of living. Or I could do the right thing—and go back to your mother."

I never resented my father for his ambivalence. It often seemed, in fact, that I was my father's other half: looking back over my shoulder, wondering what the world would be like if I'd stopped moving long enough to have a family. There seemed little doubt that my wanderlust was in my genes.

And it had brought me here, to the city of Agra: first in 1979, as an astonished twenty-five-year-old, and now with my mother.

For almost every first-time visitor, the highlight of a trip to India is Agra's main attraction: the Taj Mahal. Built during the first half on the seventeenth century, it is the most iconic—and ironic—building in the world. Intended as a mausoleum, it is conclusive proof of immortality.

Nothing compares with walking through the domed gateway, and watching in awe as Shah Jahan's marvel in marble explodes into view, filling a place in one's heart that one never even knew existed. The closer one gets to the Taj itself, the more one appreciates the words a forgotten historian wrote of the Mughals: "They built like giants, and finished like goldsmiths."

"It's awesome," said my mother, gaping at the pearlescent dome and slightly tilted minarets like a child. "It's as beautiful as a *natural* wonder. And like a natural wonder, it is exquisite because it's not showy; it is in absolutely perfect taste. Every aspect of its design is perfect—down to a level that approaches magic.

"But for all its opulence, for all the wealth in India," she observed, "the poor can't come and see it."

"That's not so," I replied. "The admission charge for locals is a tiny fraction of what we paid to get in."

"Yes; but how could they even *dress* to come here? Most of the people who visit wear their finest clothes, and their children are well-dressed and clean."

She was right: The Indian women were dressed in their best saris, their outfits flashing against the white marble and blue sky like a fireworks display.

Though it was my third visit, I shared her sense of wonder. The Taj does this for everyone. All who visit are beatified, transformed, united by a common sense of awe and appreciation. It's the opposite of what happens after an earthquake, or tsunami. People are brought together by a shared experience of the transcendent, a statement that blesses all with its indelible proof of the human spirit, its celebration of imagination, its testimony to the power of love.

We strolled together around the grounds, viewing the building from all angles, watching as the late afternoon light faded and the white marble faded into orange, pink, and blue.

"It's like a dream come true," my mother whispered. Then added, "Although I can't honestly say that."

"Why not?"

"Because I never dreamed I would be here."

Food-wise, my worries had been for naught. Sticking to a vegetarian diet—easy to do in India—Mom developed a taste for the local cuisine. Lentil soup, vegetable cutlets, *masala dosas* (enormous, crispy crepes stuffed with potatoes and peas) and fresh lime sodas became our staples, enlivened by the addition of *palak paneer* (soft, cube-shaped cheese with spinach) and *aloo gobi* (sautéed potatoes and cauliflower).

The one thing she could *not* handle was the aggressive selling near the major monuments. Outside the Taj Mahal, and at the gates of Jaipur's Amber Fort, packs of touts descended upon us, pressing in with carved wooden chess sets, silver bracelets and mirrored sandals, onyx eggs and marble trivets. They surrounded my mother on all sides, tugging at her sleeves. "Hello...you buy...fifty rupees.... O.K., twenty rupees...yes, yes... ten rupees...."

My mother spun away, waving her arms as if surrounded by gnats. "I can't stand this!" she'd cry, trying to find an escape route. I took her arm and led her away, toward the safety of the entry gate.

"There's something I don't get," I said. "How could a woman who once directed a New York day care center for welfare mothers, surrounded by screaming kids, be intimidated by a couple of guys selling postcards and necklaces? Why were the kids easier to deal with?"

"I was bigger than they were," she replied.

I knew this issue would not be a factor in Udaipur, one of my favorite places in India. The small city—with its labyrinthine palaces, art galleries, and fierce tradition of independence—is a porthole into Rajasthan's past. Posh restaurants serve Mughlai food, and festooned boats ply the romantic lake. There are mosaics made of millions of mirrors, and murals enlivened with yellow paint made from the dried urine of sacred cows fed a diet of mangos.

One of mom's only complaints (or observations; in India, they often amount to the same thing) was that

there had been little natural charm in the places we visited. "The beauty in India," she observed, "is all in the
culture, the history, the monuments."

We arrived at the Fatepur Prakash Palace hotel, and
found a table at the outdoor Terrace Restaurant. It was a
sultry afternoon, and the view over Lake Pichola—with
the Lake Palace Hotel resting on its surface like a mirage—was like a scene from a James Bond film (i.e.,
Octopussy). A hammered gold sun set behind the Araveli
hills, and swifts dipped crazily in the sky.

"Well, this is lovely," Mom said. We munched on *pakoras*, and sipped Kingfisher beers. A sitar and tabla duet
played an afternoon raga. "It's good to finally see some
natural beauty."

I was loathe to remind her that the lake was artifi-
cial—built by King Pichhu Banjara in 1362—but she
was a step ahead of me. "At least the mountains are
natural," she shrugged.

The next morning we drove out of Udaipur to visit
Nagda Sas Bahu, a nearby temple complex built in the
tenth century. It was an unexpected gem, surrounded
by flowers and trees, the small Hindu shrines covered
inside and out with exquisite marble carvings.

Before leaving, we stopped by a small table where
a local artist was selling small, modernistic statues of
Ganesh: the elephant-headed god of auspicious beginnings and protector of travelers. Mom looked them over,
and purchased one of the deities.

Idol worship is forbidden in Judaism. But Indian gods
and goddesses are so seductive that Jewish travelers in
India often go native, succumbing to the "Golden Calf
Syndrome." I have several Ganeshas at home, which I
touch for success before any journey. But my mother?

"Amazing," I said. "I never thought I'd see you, of all people, buying a graven image."

She shrugged. "It doesn't mean the same thing to me that it means to you. To me, it's just a souvenir: a fanciful, mythological creature, and not a manifestation of God."

After a week in India, my mother had seen enough monuments and temples. She no longer cared where Aurangzeb's second cousin was buried, or how Mughal observatories predicted the solstice. The questions she was asking had changed. She wanted to know where people shopped for clothes, and to see where the middle-class families lived. Most of all, she was interested in visiting the places she knew best: schools.

On our final day in Udaipur, I cancelled a visit to an art gallery and directed our driver to the Rajasthan Mahila Galeda Senior Secondary and Primary School. This was the first institution in Rajasthan to offer education to young girls, founded by the grandfather of the current Maharana of Jaipur.

Mrs. Usha Kiran, the vice principal, had luxuriant graying hair, and red blessing cords tied around her wrists. "There are 1,500 girls studying in this school," she explained, "which is funded 90 percent by the Indian government."

In America, if two foreigners showed up at an all-girls school asking for a tour of the classrooms, there might be some complications. But a mother and son are above suspicion, and Mrs. Kiran instantly arranged an informal tour of the campus.

The grounds were spacious; big white buildings surrounded by arched porticoes, separated by gardens and playgrounds. Four female teachers joined us; they proved adept at answering my mother's questions about curriculum, testing, and further education. We ducked into six classrooms, finding walls covered with the same basic posters, maps, and animal drawings one might find in a school in Whittier. The girls were immersed in their studies (or, in one case, their nap), but always managed to roust up a big "Good Morning," or sing us an approximate version of their ABC's.

Mom was in her element. This experience clearly meant more to her than the sight of any marble monument. She had been floored by the Rajasthani palaces and the markets of Old Delhi. But here was a place where, rather than be astonished by the exotic, she could appreciate the similarities between her life and the lives of the Indian people. It was a hinge that swung everything into place, and taught my mother what I had learned, with difficulty, nearly thirty years ago: The people here are not aliens; they're earthlings.

When the tour was over, I returned to Mrs. Kiran's office. "Thank you so much," I said. "This meant the world to my Mom. I know it seems strange to see a grown son traveling with his...."

Mrs. Kiran held up her hand to silence me. "There is no need to explain," she said. "Mother is Mother. There is no supplement."

Our last evening in New Delhi, as I rode with my mother to the airport, I asked what she'd liked most, and least, about India.

Topping the list was the Taj, and the school in Udaipur. For the low points, I expected her to mention the aggressive touts, the traffic, the ceaseless crush of people in the bazaars of Jaipur and Delhi. But her answer surprised me.

"I didn't like taking my shoes off," she said, "and walking barefoot on those dirty temple floors."

But the thing with India—as centuries of invaders have discovered—is that it transforms everyone it touches.

Two months after the trip, I asked my mother how the trip had changed her. Her reactions echoed my own—and by that point, even her discomfort had become a virtue.

"It's not for everyone," she admitted. "The heat, noise, and dust are oppressive. You have to be ready, physically and emotionally, because it assaults every sense. Sight, sound, taste—even the sense of touch—because you have to take off your shoes, and be in contact with the ground. It's a *sensual* experience, to a degree I haven't found anywhere else.

"It was almost like being in another world," she reflected. "But I loved it. I felt very comfortable. And I realized that no matter where I go, what clothing people wear, or what traditions they practice, we're all human beings. We all want the same things: to enjoy our lives, live in peace, and be allowed to practice what we believe in. That opened up a whole new vista for me. There's no doubt that India changed me, for good."

The other person changed by the trip, of course, was me.

India, I'd seen before. My mother in a Hindu temple, receiving a blessing from a holy man in a loincloth, not so much. By coaxing Mom out of her comfort zone, I was pulled out of mine. But the world that changed for me was not in Asia, but inside my own skin.

Looking back on the experience—on Mom's openness, and her ability to take the world in stride—I had a startling realization. Since adolescence, I'd believed the wanderlust in my veins had been put there by my coltish, distracted father. My restlessness, maybe. But the ability to steep myself in other cultures, and thrive in alien environments, may have come from that other set of chromosomes.

Mother India, that rascal, tricked me again. She sneaked in another lesson, and blew my mind once more.

~᷂ ~᷂ ~᷂

Jeff Greenwald is the author of five books, including Shopping for Buddhas, The Size of the World, *and* Scratching the Surface. *His travel writing is widely anthologized, appearing in* The Kindness of Strangers, In Search of Adventure, *and many Travelers' Tales books. Greenwald divides his time between Oakland and Kathmandu, publishing stories and essays in a variety of print and online publications. He is also Executive Director of* Ethical Traveler *(www.ethicaltraveler.com), a global community of traveler/activists.*

~·≈ ~·≈ ~·≈

Crazy Diamond

The best reasons for leaving home
are revealed.

I COULDN'T REALLY EVER TELL YOU WHY I LEFT HOME. I'D
come up with some superficial reasons, of course, but
just so that we could avoid an awkward and unhelpful
silence. The deeper truth probably lies somewhere in the
inherited murkiness of the human psyche, a monkey's
inclination to wander, always, one has to assume, looking for larger bananas, taller trees, and perhaps a place of
fewer predators.

Soon after I had arrived in Texas I read the book Bruce
Chatwin wrote shortly before succumbing to AIDS: *What
Am I Doing Here?* It did not necessarily answer that particular question for me, nor did it really help me in figur-
ing out the reasons for my perambulations. But it did

at least allow me to ask that question of myself, which
before I had perceived but never really articulated: What
the hell *am* I doing here? The particular question obviously had existential undertones which were exaggerated by the author's untimely death, and seemed to refer
both to a geographical place and to the human condition
itself—the ultimate existential query. Chatwin's question, presented as the title to a collection of serious travel
essays, cast a cloud of shadowy doubt over the whole
enterprise of being a stranger, what it means to be away
from our family, and to some extent from ourselves, and
I found that useful.

Reading about those who had made similar journeys,
sometimes in the distant past, clarified one thing: most
people voyage with a sense of promise, with a belief or
an inkling that there is gold under a distant rainbow, and
the inclination oftentimes is sustaining, because people
seem to put up with a lot of pain and suffering which,
you imagine, could be avoided by staying home. But I
was no Cabeza da Vaca, let's be clear on that. I mean
that I did not consider myself intrepid because of this
particular sojourn, although I often identified with this
luckless sixteenth-century Spanish explorer, and sometimes, navigating my way across the Texas hinterland, I
would catch glimpses of human figures on the horizon,
reduced by the distance to shimmering stick-men, and
I would be struck by their fragility in the maw of the
elements. These figures always reminded me of da Vaca
and his hopeless companions, lost on a wild and distant
continent, and although I too felt somewhat lost, I was
grateful that I had a varied diet, a roof over my head,
and a bank account guaranteeing escape should it become necessary. What in the end did I have in common

with him? I could not even speak Spanish. But I did come from the landmass of Europe (or somewhere just off the coast) and I did see America as a New World.

I had been sent to the southwest by a publishing company; my mission was to sell high-quality university textbooks to professors. In the enormity of Texas I came across universities much like a parched desert nomad might happen upon Saharan wadis, covering huge distances over the semi-arid terrain in my Texan camel, a pearl-white Ford Taurus. I grew to love that car even if at first I had looked at it with something bordering on disdain. After the fist couple of thousand miles I realized that when I beheld it, first thing in the morning, sitting sedately outside my motel room, I was overwhelmed by a sense of comfort, even love—the kind of feeling one might experience when looking at a benign dictator who shows you leniency after a crime, or a dentist who after drilling your teeth speaks soothingly and gives you refreshing liquid with which to gargle. This vehicle was my sanctuary, my fifteen square feet of sovereign space, and its graceful steel curves and its competent wheels guaranteed me a certain insulation from the threateningly foreign environment.

The land over which I guided the car was the same hard land over which Cabeza da Vaca had stumbled five hundred years ago. The ultimate objective of his expedition had been Florida and the riches that everyone believed lay there. After shipwrecks and desertions, most noticeably of the captain and expedition's leader, da Vaca and a handful of companions were left helpless and adrift in an unfathomably vast and unexplored territory without a map, without language, and without even the vaguest hope of rescue. An isolation not unlike someone stranded on the moon with no spaceship—a terrible existential imprisonment.

After the rest of his party had disappeared or been killed by local tribes, Cabeza da Vaca was left with three others: Andres Dorantes, Alonso del Castillo Maldonado, and a slave from Morocco called Estevanico. They spent months on end eating nothing but oysters (at this time they were not a delicacy and there was no horseradish or cocktail sauce), shucking them with rocks until their hands bled. And months again eating roots, and sometimes if they were lucky, extremities of dog. These were the good times. They survived off the morsels of flesh scraped from skins; they stayed with nomads who suckled their children until the age of twelve because food was so scarce that otherwise their offspring would stand no chance of surviving. America, as it came to be known, was then a vast amorphous wonderland full of boundless wildness, beauty and barbarism, a fluid world strewn with gaping portals into the afterlife. Those were the days when you really could not count on the recognition that another human being must owe to you—to you as a human being, that is—the recognition that prevents him from otherwise doing you harm, like the Spaniards were doing to the Mesoamericans: tearing them limb from limb, boiling them alive, feeding them to the dogs, hanging children from the legs of their dangling mothers. Most strange fruit. Still, the small group of lost Europeans wandered across the desert landscape of the Southwest, sometimes in what would become Mexico, sometimes in the future United States, both sides of the future border equally harsh and unforgiving. Having been separated from

his companions, da Vaca, alone in the desert wilderness, would think he had actually died, so profound
was his sense of isolation.

Some of the colleges I visited were harboring professors from far-flung places and my arrival occasioned
long talks about New England, Old England, and on
one occasion a writing instructor in southern New
Mexico asked me longingly where I bought my trousers.
"Not in this state," he guessed wistfully. A professor of
forensic anthropology in Waco showed me her personal
photos of the carnage at the Branch Davidian compound, which she had been in charge of analyzing after
the FBI siege.

"See," she said smilingly, "some shit happens down
here, too!"

My relative isolation made my identification with da
Vaca grow, slowly. I was soon bored selling books to
pompous professors; whenever I could I crept off campus early and found desolate rivers in which to bathe,
or I walked in arid, dusty hills. Often I found myself
far from the nearest habitation and able to contemplate
these distant historical eras, without the meddlesome interruption of the present, able to tap in to the raw reality
of the lost medieval Spaniards. But more often than not
I found that isolation was hard to come by in Texas these
days, and just as da Vaca had his fair share of interac-
tions with locals, I had mine, too.

On a July afternoon, when, thankfully, the endless
American collegiate summer was in full session, I was
sitting by a river. It was hot—the kind of heat that
drugs you and slows down your metabolism. I had
been perched on a rock for a few minutes when a truck
drew up behind me. A pair of dogs jumped out of the

back then plunged into the water next to me, having inspected me first by pushing their noses into my face. A boy of about ten or eleven soon followed them.

"Is it cold?" he asked me with an English accent. We had a brief conversation in which he didn't seem to notice my accent—maybe he hadn't been here long enough to find another English accent strange. Soon an elderly couple came struggling down the bank hauling a large steel canoe, forcing me to move from my rock to avoid being driven into the river at the prow of their vessel. The man, who must have been in his sixties, wore a moustache which drooped on either side of his mouth in Sancho Panza style. His eyes were also characterized by a droopy effect which made him appear either sleepy or in an advanced state of meditation.

"Sorry ta interrupt your readin'," he said in a sincerely apologetic way. The canoe found the water and bobbed obligingly on its surface. Meanwhile the boy had fitted a mask to his head and began examining the underwater life. The dogs were jumping in and out of the river a little too close to me, occasionally sliding onto my towel with their large mud-filled feet. The woman, overweight, with a ruddy complexion and an ill-fitting bathing suit, stood over me.

"What ya readin'?" she asked in a chummy tone, taking my book by its cover and turning it towards her. I felt myself stiffen instinctively. I told her it was a book about early American history, smiling weakly.

"Which chapter are ya gonna be tested on?" I told her I wasn't actually reading it for a test, that I was too old for school, unfortunately. She handed it back to me, apparently disappointed. As if history, for its own sake, was an eccentric's game. She was silent for a couple of beats.

"England or Australia?" she said, fixing me with a piercing stare, beaming now, as if delighted to find another way to extend our conversation.

"England," I admitted, impressed that she had tumbled my game with so few words being exchanged and feeling all the more of an outsider for it.

"We're from England, too, ain't that right, Jason?" Jason reared his head out of the water and gave an incomprehensible grunt from inside his mask.

"Yeah, that's right," she continued, drinking from a plastic cup which appeared to be brim full of bourbon.

"We're just slumming it here in Texas!" She gave a gravelly laugh.

"Well we're not English, exactly. But Jason's dad is. Oh yes, his dad is over there in Dagenham. Do you know Miller Street, that's where they live, down there by the river. You know what's it called, Jack?" She appealed to her husband who was busily attempting to mount the canoe.

"What, honey?" he said.

She threw her cigarette butt into the river. "You know, Jack, that pub right there on Miller Street, the Dead Duck, Royal Duck, whatchamacallit?" Jack was in the canoe and with his huge belly pointing to the bows he was engaged in extracting the paddles from under the seat.

"The Duck and Rabbit," he said, causing her to explode with another hoot of laughter. "The Fuck-like-Rabbits, whoops! Excuse my French! That's right ain't it Jack?" Jack gave me a long-suffering smile from his position of readiness in the canoe.

"C'mon honey, lets get this ship movin' and leave this poor guy to his recreation," he said, encouraging her to lift herself from the rock.

"You're right. I'm sorry; we've just ripped up your nice peaceful afternoon here, lets go to sea—we're here to have a good time, right Jason?" Jason was face down in the river, too absorbed to be listening. She staggered to her feet and walked gingerly into the water where the canoe awaited her. I was curious—apprehensive even—about how she was, in fact, going to get into the canoe, bearing in mind the characteristic instability of canoes. First of all she lifted her right leg onto the gunwale of the boat like a ballerina stretching on a bar (I was surprised to see that she could perform this maneuver at all without serious damage to ligaments). Then, when it was clear that no other part of her anatomy would cooperate from this position, she decided to start from scratch and with some effort removed her leg from the boat, letting it plop back into the water.

"Here," Jack offered her his hand, and she suddenly lunged head-first into the canoe causing it to tip drastically towards her. As it did this Jack presciently steadied it by instinctively falling in the other direction, one hand still in hers. Now she was half in and half out, and she wriggled the rest of the way, like a matronly mermaid, to end up lying face-down on the bottom of the vessel. Soon she was seated on the bench and was cradling her cup of whiskey which Jack had been looking after and miraculously had not spilled.

"Hey Jason," she yelled at the boy who was still engrossed under the surface. "You wanna come over to the other side with us? C'mon, we're goin' explorin'!" They were about to set off when one of the dogs reappeared on the bank, whining.

"Oh my baby! I can't go without my baby!" The dog launched itself at the canoe from the riverbank, and Jack dragged it, bedraggled, into the rapidly-filling canoe. Once Jason was aboard they set off against the current waving to me and promising to return shortly.

With this advance warning I slipped off my rock and swam upriver against the current and found that I was just about moving forward, at a snail's pace. My identity. Why was it so difficult to get beyond it, beyond the basic fact of difference? With barely any language being exchanged, too! It was as if there was an aura around me screaming of foreignness. This had been da Vaca's curse. The medicine man who had captured him had recognized the vulnerability of his alien identity, which set him apart from others and made him a perfect candidate for lifelong servitude (he escaped, of course, after several years). And slavery was no passing concern for da Vaca—it was endemic in the Southwest back then, human beings traded as eagerly beads, or skins, or edible meat. And it was not only the Indians who were doing it. The first white men da Vaca saw after all his years of wandering, the first glimpse he had of his very salvation were mounted, *Spanish*, slave traders patrolling the plains for stray Indians. If he was enslaved, it was to his identity, and what seemed almost more painful than anything to him was the knowledge that he was one of them.

The river was shallow, its flow interrupted by long weeds which reached up from the sandy bottom to float on the surface of the water. I tried to avoid these patches of weed. I never like to touch anything when I'm in the water. However I suddenly found myself caught up in a throng of this vegetation, kicking and thrashing as against an animate enemy. Just as I thought I was free of the river flora, I felt something move in the pocket of my shorts. My shorts have large, billowing pockets, which are actually very inappropriate for swimming, as they balloon outwards when they fill with water and act as water brakes. But something was in my right pocket, and it appeared to be alive. I was filled with a terrible panic. Short of putting my hand into the pocket and pulling out the offending creature, I didn't know what to do. I grabbed the pocket and its contents and gave it a quick, vicious squeeze—a cowardly, mean reaction to the fear instilled by the thought of a smaller being. Whatever was there was hard and shell-like: crustacean, I realized. This only increased my terror, to know that a crustacean was in my pocket—a crustacean! In all its primeval, unfathomability, face to face with my most vulnerable and intimate areas.

I sensed stillness now in my pocket, and thought that maybe I had actually killed whatever had been inside—the instinctual fear of further contact with the unknown was coursing through my veins, and enabled me to overcome my scruples about killing. But I needed to take further evasive action, and the only measure left to me was to take the shorts off and shake the creature loose. I did this in one swift movement without even un-tying the shorts. Treading water as I drifted downstream through yet more weed, I shook the shorts in the air in front of me, and as I did so I almost collided with a family of Mexicans swimming my way. They altered course to give me a wide birth, alarmed by my antics, shepherding their children out of my reach. From the corner of my eye I noticed something float away from the shorts, downstream, of a reddish-green color.

I soon reached a grassy area of riverbank where I made landfall and attempted to regain my composure. I noticed a scattering of crawfish remains, as if people had enjoyed an al fresco seafood meal. Clearly these creatures were common in this river. I rooted in the weed on the riverbank with a long stick and sure enough I soon encountered the bulbous eyes and spine chilling pincers of a live crawfish. Admittedly, the creature was not large. In fact it was about the size of a small hamster. But a hamster is a rodent and, noxious as some rodents are, they do not belong in the same league as crustaceans. Personal preferences apart, crustaceans are scientifically, *typologically*, different, and different not just in an equal kind of a way, but indisputably *worse*. I offered the beast the end of my stick and it backed into the weed with a passivity which surprised me, but its movement made me shiver; its little legs folding midway to embed their spearlike feet into the sand for purchase.

The part of the river where I had alighted was populated by small groups of people who had parked their cars under drooping trees and were sitting on rocks drinking from beer cans and some of them were throwing fishing lines into the slow-moving current. Soon a jeep pulled up on the grass behind me, and two young boys and a man of about fifty stepped out. The boys raced for the water and hurled themselves in, whooping. The man walked over to me. He had a gray beard of medium length, and a face weathered by the sun. He walked with a slight roll, like a sailor, and notwithstanding a fairly muscular, squat build, he had a pronounced belly.

"Me and my boys like to swim here, with the rope and all," he said. "It be alright if we share the space?" His voice was broad Texas, and deep. He reminded me of Stacy Keach—a mixture of the rough and ready and the civilized. I told him that there was plenty of space, to feel free. The boys ran back onto the bank and started playing with the rope. The younger one, around ten, said: "We were here before, you know."

The father now had his shorts on and was gingerly entering the river. He immersed himself up to his waist and stood there, facing the sun and moving his hands around in front of him, in arcs in the water. He turned around to face me.

"Where're you from, man?" His tone was almost challenging.

"I'm English," I said after a pause. He scooped the water in his hands and let it run down his chest.

"Oh yeah? Scots-Irish-Comanche, myself." He held his head high, and spoke with an air of pride. I wanted to tell him that if he wanted to play the origins game then I would have to start over; we can all identify with the underdog if we dig in our heritage a little. In reality he was American in the same way that I was English. Sure, I might have some Polish-Jewish-Celtic blood, but I don't bother to pull all of the possible strands out every time I state my nationality. I hold a British passport, I speak English. But it seemed that he wanted to connect with those who had suffered at the hands of the American colonials and those who resisted the English colonial administration. It was a pity and an irony that the Scotch and the Irish were no great improvement over the English, as far as the Comanches were concerned, making their lives nasty, brutish and short and almost wiping them out with their guns and their European diseases. But I got the message.

"So what's your name, Limey?" He said, after a pause. It was a strange tone—challenging yet friendly. It was as if he had set up his perimeter, established a boundary, and now was exploring it a little.

"My name's Richard," he said, and then looked up at the sky, "Richard the Lionheart." There was only the slightest hint of a grin on his face. *Coeur de Leon,* I thought to myself, now there's a true infidel-killing Brit, if ever there was one. He immersed himself in the water and executed a few short strokes, and then came back to the beach and walked out of the river. The boys by this time were busy swinging off the rope.

"Dad, are you gonna swing or what!" The younger one pestered him until he stood on the bank and pulled the rope back, gripping tightly with his hands, and with a delicacy which belied his size but bespoke his age, he swung out over the water, released the rope and plopped the death-defying two feet into water up to his knees. His son was ecstatic and grabbed the rope, handing it back to him: "Again! Do it again!" Richard winced, "Ah, no Sammy, your old man's too fragile for that, why don't you give it a shot." He stood on the bank next to where I was sitting and dried himself vaguely with a towel. He was a handsome man and had a knowing gentleness about him. He was old, I observed, to have such young kids and I wondered if he was divorced and this day, Saturday, was his "time."

He threw down the towel and turned to me: "I'm gonna smoke some of Mexico's finest. Care to join me?" He produced a reefer and ignited it with a Zippo lighter, inhaling sharply before handing me the joint. We passed a few moments enjoying a quiet smoke while the two boys swam, and soon Richard started reminiscing about his time on a warship, and how he met some British sailors in Jamaica who knew how to drink. Then he

talked about working as a roadie for Eric Clapton
who, as he pointed out, was one of my compatriots.
We passed the joint back and forth. On the bridge a
truck had pulled up. Some men got out and started
preparing to fish. They left the doors of the truck
open and its stereo filled the area around the bridge
with the dolorous sounds of classic rock, heavy on
the bass, which came snaking over the surface of the
water to where we sat in the hot sun. I was beginning
to get the feeling of being pulled into something, inevitably. He had traveled with rock bands, and drunk
with sailors and now here he was swimming with his
kids on a hot Saturday afternoon in Texas. He looked
out over the river, at the houses up on the opposite
bank, perched with the best view in the Texas hill
country. Then he was into a story about West Texas
some forty years ago, about where he grew up, and
the army base which was the original reason for the
town's existence, established mostly for black soldiers
to man after the Civil War. They were posted out on
the frontier as cannon fodder, while the "crack" white
troops were inland being saved the hardships of the
desert. The black soldiers became fed up with the
local intolerance of their presence and ransacked the
town, pillaging and looting and destroying property.
The base had since closed, but the town found that it
didn't need the base as a raison d'être anymore with
the arrival of oil. I felt the sense of the conversation
drifting away from me. It was all I could do to ask
the occasional question, hoping that I was vaguely
connecting with his train of thought. We were both
sitting on the grass now, Richard with his legs in the
water and me leaning back on my elbows. My head

was feeling increasingly as if it were boxed in with a three-dimensional crystalline structure which shimmied every time I moved it. Sensation had all but fled most of my body; Richard's eyes had taken on a vaporous quality.

"But things have all changed now," said Richard. "I've changed, I dare say; not the crazy-headed son-of-a-bitch I used to be. Sometimes I can't believe the things I did when I was young." And for some reason as he spoke I wondered whether Cabeza da Vaca had remembered who he had been in his life as a Spanish nobleman, when slave traders had galloped up to him in his starving, filthy, crazed state. And did he ever really become that person again, once the dirt was washed off, the hair was cut, and he was back in Castile? Did he remember those times when, walking naked, his identity had come to seem like an enigma?

Sammy came sploshing onto the bank, holding a crawfish claw.

"Look dad, I got a crawdaddy." Richard took the claw and examined it with interest. "That's great, son. Yep. Ain't much left of that poor sucker." He snapped it at Sammy, who squealed with glee and ran back into the water. I got up and entered the water slowly, feeling its cooling affect rising over my legs, and I began to swim steadily upriver against the persistent current. With the sun ahead of me I had to squint into its rays, and its reflections off the water looked like a field of wheat in the evening light, or a night of bright stars in a clear sky, and I kept on swimming, holding level with the bank, keeping the current at bay. The glass cube which encapsulated my head was floating on the surface of the water, and shards of light refracted around it. On my right I perceived Richard on the bank holding up his fist, and yelling, "He's gonna make it to the bridge, goddammit! He's gonna make it to the bridge, and climb up there like a pirate!" and I noticed after some time had passed that the vibrations coming over the water from the large black truck were in fact the familiar refrains of Pink Floyd—a sound intimately connected to my adolescence in England. The music seemed to encapsulate something essential about me, was even largely responsible for who I was now, for better or for worse, and in that warm canyon, surrounded by Comanches and Mexicans and the ex-roadies, I hovered above the waving river weed captivated by noises produced twenty years before in a studio in London now being echoed around these Texan hills and washed down the river to Austin, and felt buoyed not so much by the water as by the sound, and the light and the heat: *Nobody knows where you are. How near or how far. Shine on you crazy diamond.*

I am sitting on an underground train leaving Wimbledon Station. Rain is gently falling, and the streets of row houses gray under the cloud. I am wearing a pair of blue-and-white striped drainpipe trousers that I shoplifted three weeks ago, and a pair of black leather winkle-pickers. I have not showered for a number of days and I can feel the grime from the train already lifting itself off the seats and the floor and adhering to my skin, making me feel like the filthy character in *Charlie Brown* whose name I forget. I open a new packet of cigarettes, enjoying the newness of the shiny silver foil, unmarked, before dropping it on the floor along with the plastic wrapper. I pull one out and light it, dully remembering how I never enjoy cigarettes on the Underground, where I always feel soiled. I blow

the smoke against the window and through it I see wet
school playing fields.

   The train clatters through deserted sidings and empty
urban spaces, scattered with used oilcans, rags, and
pieces of brick. In one old overgrown parking lot stands
what seems to be an ancient water tower, rusting,
twisted metal lying whale-like, belly-up in the middle of
an open field, half tarmac half-feeble blades of grass. We
move on at our steady forty miles per hour. The track
is elevated now, affording a view of a housing estate
below. In front of this is a bowling green surrounded
by small sycamore trees, the houses are gray in the rain,
semi-detached, Victorian. An industrial chimney belch-
ing smoke blocks the view; it has a waistline, like a
huge headless woman rooted into the ground standing
resolute in front of the houses. Past this there is a pub,
standing in an island between two roads looking as if
once it were attached to something, now standing like a
rock when the tide has washed away the sand. A small
white dog sits outside the door and its mouth opens and
shuts silently as it barks at the train. Suddenly we are
in a station, pulling to a standstill; a number of human
beings stand in the rain, randomly arranged on the concrete, some with umbrellas. They shuffle forward as the
train stops. I look on as a young skinhead boy skulks
away from the train, his Doc Martens splashing in the
puddles. On the wall next to him someone has scrawled
I suck cock. The man opposite me is wearing red socks;
we both stare at each other's shoes. His are huge shape-
less blobs with rounded, bulbous toes. I do not think
they signify any particular political persuasion. He is
probably a conservative with a small c, an upholder of
the status quo; he spends a lot of time in pubs and has

an allotment somewhere near here where he goes to escape his ugly wife and tend to his potatoes. He gets out
yesterday's *Sun*, and opens it to page three. I read on the
front cover *Stick It Up Yer Junta! Argies Go Home.* This
is the eighties and Britain is in the Falklands.

Later I am in Surrey, with Duncan and James. We
drink from cans of beer and talk, and James in his
pompous, arrogant way, makes fun of people and speaks
far too loud. He always embarrasses me, as he is too
obviously a public-school boy. His fine blond hair, his
confident look and his booming, hollow voice, which he
uses with theatricality that only a public school boy can
exhibit. We are in a carriage with a few other individu-
als in it. We are drunk, James is telling a story, with his
cowboy boots up on the seat opposite him. He is holding his cigarette in a way that makes him look gay. An
elderly woman sitting behind James has, I notice, been
bristling at his words. James has no sense of social difference; everybody, as far as he is concerned is like him,
or if they aren't then they aren't even worth thinking
about. The woman clutches her handbag, and I can
see the stern outline of her face, her mouth tight and
twisted, ears pinned back and listening, not embarrassed
and humble, but aggressive. Luckily the woman chooses
the next stop to disembark.

We are on our way to stay in the shell of his parents'
old holiday house in Dorset. The house is an empty,
filthy place with an overgrown garden. Five of us are to
camp in it, with copious quantities of alcohol. As soon
as we arrive at the village we go to the supermarket
and buy alcohol, bottles and bottles, and condiments to
soak it up, chips, gherkins, pickles, and then we make
our way on foot to James' house and set up camp in the

damp, empty living room with sleeping bags. On the
first night we are all out in the garden drinking; James,
wearing a collarless white shirt, "y-front" underpants,
and cowboy boots is standing with one foot up on an old
urn, a tumbler full of liquor in one hand and cigarette
in another, mimicking Hamlet, while the rest of us are
sprawled around, stupefied, on the long grass. One of his
old neighbors walked into the garden, and with a look
of horror encounters James, half naked and very drunk,
saying: "Seems, Madam? Nay I know not seems, it *is*."
The rest of us are howling at him. Facing us with his
back to the driveway he has not noticed her, but we all
go silent, as this short middle-aged woman shrieks above
James' voice.

"What on earth is going on here?"

James pirouettes on the heel of his boot, spilling liquor
from the glass extended in the air, gracefully, and sees
the woman. His shirt is long and gives the impression
that he is not wearing anything underneath it. Instantly
recognizing her he says, "Ah, Mrs. Mullins, how good to
see you, I'm James Pembroke, we used to live here, don't
you remember?" She looks suspicious, so he goes on.

"Perhaps you don't recognize me dressed like this. I
assure you I don't always go around in my underpants,
but it is unseasonably warm this evening, don't you
think?" Her silence continues; so does James.

"Would you like some wine?"

She looks increasingly confused. "So you're the
Pembroke lad are you? Good Lord, I never thought
you would turn out like this! Well it's all that education I expect."

James nods dolefully. "Yes, that's it I s'pose, rum
sodomy and the lash, what else is there?" He lets out

a high-pitched laugh. She looks around at us variously arranged in the decaying flowerbeds. Duncan, sitting in a pair of filthy shorts, his chunky, thick legs, covered with hair, draped over the remains of a sun chair. He is grotesquely nestling a large beer can in his groin. Of all of us he seems the most at ease in the situation, sitting back, taking it all in with an expressionless face, like some country idiot watching the world go by. It amazes me that he can sit through this bizarre encounter without exhibiting even the first indications of anxiety. Does he really not care? Duncan does not let on, but maintains a strict obliviousness to his environment. Mrs. Mullins, having confronted the beast, is reassured at least that we are not totally unknown devils. She makes her demands for tranquility and James hammers out a bargain with her before she leaves us.

The time between that drunken teenage summer and now seemed like a fold in the fabric of the universe, a black hole of some kind. The place that had formed me so much diluted by the knowledge of so many other, distant places. The people I knew, gone from my life now, left only as fading recollections, and the person I had been was gone too, changed cell by cell, transformed by incomprehensible time into flotsam on a Texas river. By what process this had happened I do not know, the same process that made of da Vaca a wondering ghost on foreign soil.

After what seemed like hours I stopped swimming and let myself be washed back towards the bend in the river where Richard sat. I noticed that the music from the truck had turned into chat on some Austin radio

station. On arrival at the riverbank Richard's kids were
still jumping in and out of the water. I walked up the
bank and sat down next to him. He was finishing a joint,
looking for all the world like one of Cabeza da Vaca's
medicine-man acquaintances. One of his sons came running over holding what seemed to be the claw of a small
lobster, "Dad, I found another one!" Richard took it
from the boy and turned it around in his hands. "Well,
I'd say that's one dead crawdaddy." His son leapt back
into the water and Richard took the pincer between his
fingers and inserted the roach of his joint between the
claws, using them as a vice to grip the burning joint as he
sucked on it one last time. The whole scene—the father
on the bank, the remnant of local fauna, the indigenous
drug, the children in the water, splashing, and the hot,
hot sun, looked so authentic, as if this was what was
done in this place, here was the daily spectacle of life in
this particular corner of the world, and the participants,
the *players,* were so naturally a part of the environment,
belonged in some organic and indisputable way that I
began to think of Chatwin's question again, began to
think of it in terms of the hapless da Vaca first. But then
I realized that here was the difference between him and
me: He had no choice but to plunge in and take part
in whatever form of life was around him. As for me, I
wondered whether the answer wasn't after all obvious: I
was a voyeur. I was skirting the perimeter of experience
where I could observe the comings and goings of others
from a safe distance, and avoid being drawn into close
conflict with them; I was walking on the water, afraid
to put my foot down in case it should get wet, in case it
should sink, and take the rest of me, thrashing and kicking, to the bottom to sleep with the crustaceans, as da

Vaca had done, afraid perhaps to see what *I* was when all else was stripped away. But there were similarities, too. For both of us the promise at the end of the voyage had been a mirage—for him far more so than for me. For it only becomes clear who you really are when you leave and find yourself amongst strangers, and by then it's too late to go back—you can never go back.

Richard grinned, holding the crawdaddy's pincer towards me with the joint still in it: *Texaaas*, he hissed, exhaling slowly.

◦≫ ◦≫ ◦≫

Adrian Cole moved to the United States from the U.K. for graduate work in Middle Eastern Studies. After working for several years in Middle East-related fields, and living, variously, in Washington, Texas, and France, he recently moved to Maine where he lives with his wife and three children. His writing can be found at www.adrianvcole.com.

Raw Meat, Barry White, and the Brothers

This is why he keeps going back to Italy.

Ⅰ SEE HER SPIDER TATTOO BEFORE I SEE HER FACE. IT'S ON the back of her right hand, a fat-bodied camouflage-green spider crawling along a web that covers knuckle, wrist, all five fingers. For a second, I think she's going to throw it at me.

"*Ciao, ciao. Salute,*" she says from far back in the throat, in a rasp usually reserved for the dying.

I run my eyes from her hand to her face and am arrested by her worn beauty. She must be forty or so, long black paintbrush hair going gray at the tips. She has the face of an old house—the only one in the neighborhood that survived that fire all those years ago. Her skin is more olive pit than olive, but leathery, somehow soft and impenetrable at the same time. There are those rare times when you can tell the texture of something just by looking at it. It works with a few species of cacti and it works with this woman's face. She is dressed all in black and her body seems assembled from the discarded broomsticks in some wicked witch's dumpster. When she wraps her fingers around a red velvet menu, I can almost hear her bones click. She is the most beautiful corpse I've ever seen.

"*Ciao*," I say, "*Non ho una prenotazione. Ho bisogno di una tavola per uno.*"

"You do not need reservation for this night," she rasps and my heart jumps hopscotch in my chest.

"You speak English," I say, stating the obvious aloud.

"A little," she says. "Your Italian sound very American."

My laugh is so dry it becomes a cough, and I sneeze again.

She leads me out the back end of a tunnel of trees, the persimmons spreading themselves into an open outdoor courtyard with clay-potted plants spilling white flowers. Low, bass-driven music pumps like diesel from the speakers, rattles the tables' glassware. She seats me at the table closest to the restaurant's entrance. I peer inside to the yellow walls lined with wine bottles, and sit in the wooden chair. As she sets the menu on the table, a frenzied voice bellows from inside, "Loredana!"

I look to the right of the entrance and see two small open windows near the roof of the restaurant. They are lit cave-white, and from them, I hear the banging of skillets, the chop of knife through vegetable, the simmering of stock, the opening and closing of an oven door, and the wild mating call, "Loredana!"

"*Uno momento*, Ercole!" she shouts to the windows.

In the kitchen lights, I can see the shadow of someone shaking their head and probably throwing their hands in the air.

"The chef," Loredana says to me, "is a little crazy."

I laugh and, despite the crazy chef's insistence, we talk a bit. I tell her about Il Gioco dell'Oca, the place where I've pitched my tent, and Sandrone, the vintner in whose fields I've toiled, and she tells me that she knows Raffaella and Luciano.

Taking the unread menu from my hands, she says, "I bring you something nice."

She walks into the light of I Cannubi's interior and I expect her to fade like a ghost. An inside realm of yellow-tinted walls and chandeliers, of pseudo-Mayan design. Only two other courtyard tables are occupied: an old man in square glasses and brown brimmed hat hunches over a demitasse cup of espresso; on the other side of him, a young couple takes turns feeding each other spoonfuls of orange custard. I watch them and wonder what it would feel like to be fed in a courtyard like this. My eavesdropping is scored by I Cannubi's strange dance music, a shrill woman's voice struggling to be heard over the swollen bass, shrieking, in accented-English refrain, *I'm horny, I'm horny...* Where am I?

A muffled argument sneaks through the kitchen windows. The sky goes dark. By the time the music switches to Barry White, Loredana has brought me a 1990 Marchesi di Barolo.

"This is very good, uh, year. Very full of, uh, the mouth. You understand?"

"*Si*. I think so," I say.

She pours my glass half-full. I bring it to my nose and am taken to a scene of which I've never been a part—not in this life, anyway. I imagine myself as a child thrown into a burlap sack that once held potatoes or onions or both. The smell assaults my nose, chases any further sneeze back into the recesses of my brain. I sip and the sack opens. I look to the sky and expect it to rain needles of rosemary. This wine is, indeed, full of the mouth.

"It is good," Loredana rasps, wiping her forehead with the spider side of her hand.

I swallow. The stars come out.

"Yes," I say. "*Sì*," I say again.

"Good. I tell Ercole. It is his selection, the wine. I tell him about you."

"The chef," I say.

"Yes," she says. "He is crazy, but he know the wines."

As she turns for the inside, I am struck with the desire to have her back at the table. It's not loneliness, per se, but I feel as if her presence supports my own, like a fourth table leg.

"Loredana," I call after her.

She twists around like a ribbon. "Yes?"

"Will you have a glass of wine with me?"

She smiles, reaches to some hidden shelf at the inside right of the entrance. I expect her to retrieve a brass jar containing her own soul, or her ashes. I expect to have a campfire story to tell. It's not a testament to her own death that she retrieves and holds out toward me, but a tight and shiny red can of Coke. Her smile drops closer to her mouth.

"You drink Cannubi Barolo," she says, "I drink Coca-Cola."

With that, she disappears into the restaurant and I sip the wine without her, awaiting the first course. Barry White's voice pulls at the back of my neck like a shot of rum, and I hear the two voices dueling in the kitchen. Loredana and Ercole jab at one another with an array of *Si's* and *No's*. I sip the wine. The old man in the brimmed hat stands to leave, then loses his balance and falls into his chair again. He succeeds in his second attempt and tips his hat to me as he passes. His eyes are as wide and as blue as a baby's. Leaves rustling, persimmons dancing like light on water, the kitchen quiets just enough for me to hear Barry White croon, "Oohhhhh, yeaahh..."

For a while I sit and smell the herbs in the air, finger a white petal curling from a clay pot. I am about to doze off, about to drool when Loredana's footsteps patter across I Cannubi's wooden floor. Stepping from in to out, she holds one plate in her hand, but the contents, like the grapes in Lodovico Borgogno's picture of his father, are obscured in the light. Hope running from my eyes, I look to her as a woman about to toss me an edible liferaft. Strangely, the colors of the plate define themselves only in the dark of the outdoors. In the plate's center: jewels of rose stacked and folded over one another as if a napkin trick. At the plate's edge, scrambling for space: an inverted cone of gelled cream. At first, it looks like a dessert.

"*Carne cruda*," Loredana announces from the great beyond, "with *parmigiano*, uh, *panna cotta*, and the oil of *tartufi bianchi*."

As she sets the plate down with a dull bass thump, Barry White putters his lips, and I am attacked with the desire to lean in and kiss her spider. But instead, I bow my head and sniff Ercole's invention. The raw beef comes at me first with the caress of blood, then the soil-rich syrup of the white truffle oil, and cutting it all, the honeyed parmesan flan.

"Oh, Loredana," I say, hand on my heart, "this looks amazing."

"Yes," she says, "the chef is very good. Ercole, he is invited to, uh, uh, food exhibit in Hong Kong in March. They know of him there. Very famous in Asia."

I shake my head, barely find my fork with my fingers. "Amazing," I say.

Here, in this speck of a town, in this tiny, contained utopia, in this restaurant at the base of the Cannubi hill, in the middle—dare I say—of nowhere, lies a chef who is big in Asia. How, from Barolo, Italy, does the word get out?

"Have dinner now," Loredana says, fingernails tracing through her hair. "Then Ercole want to meet you. He and Sandrone have, uh...great respect."

Thinking of Sandrone, of his glasses, his hands, his suspenders, I pick up my fork. The weight of the world is in my fingers like a pencil. I reach for the plate, Barry White vocally beds yet another perfect woman, and Loredana, huntress-cum-waitress, stalks back into the restaurant.

My fork falls into the parmesan flan like a penny into a pool, settles to the bottom and, miraculously, re-emerges coated in cream. Rolling the forkful of flan over the beef, and swathing the bite in a paint-streak of white truffle oil, I hear the young couple at the other end of the courtyard moaning over a plate of sugar cubes soaked in a green liqueur. I bite as they bite, our flavors commingling, coupling. In this bite of *carne cruda* with parmesan flan—this pinnacle of earth and animal—I am one step closer to my fellow human and the notion of being alive. *Oh, baby.*

On my last bite of my first course, the couple kisses with sugared and exhausted mouths. Come midnight, they will surely float off to the heavens. Ercole and Loredana are finally silent in the kitchen, the only argument being between what I imagine to be the caramelizing leeks and the shellfish stock. I wonder what Ercole looks like. I wonder where this couple is going back to, the woman in her long black skirt and white blouse ruffled at the wrists, the man in his red sportcoat with cowhide elbow patches. Are these their special-occasion clothes? Will I ever see them again? Were we all only meant to share one wordless evening of tastes?

I stare at my empty plate, baring itself wide open to the sky, its ribcage exposed, and I wonder...

Alone in I Cannubi's courtyard, as I await Ercole's arrival at my table, the air temperature drops so quickly, it's as if the floor has collapsed beneath it. I wonder: how crazy can this crazy chef really be? Crazy enough to create for me, for no good reason, a spontaneous menu above and beyond what was printed between the set red velvet covers—*carne cruda* and parmesan flan, fresh *lasagnette* with porcini slivers, pork fillets in peach-moscato gastrique, veal fillets in rosemary sauce, persimmon *panna cotta* (the fruits plucked straight from this courtyard), chocolate soufflé, almond, peach, and chocolate tarts with hazelnut cream...

I don't know what to say. I don't know what to do except lean back in my chair, stare the stars into hiding, and lick the slick graininess from my teeth. I consider for a second never brushing them again, never eating again, letting myself go the way of Loredana. This courtyard begins to become as cold as my tent, until a small pocket of air behind me, as if heated with a small, but intense campfire, wraps the back of my neck.

I straighten without thought, my hands grip the table, and I turn to see the source of heat as a pea-sized glow of perforated orange light, winking in a desperate tango. It is the cherry of Ercole's cigarette, dangling ashen from his lips. His hands are on his hips, hands far too large for his arms, flaring from his wrists like the persimmons from their branches. He is barrel-chested and young—early thirties, maybe—and he has the face of that one small-town boy who has never left home, but somehow knows everything about the world. He is plainly intense, eyes squinted, nose perplexed from countless childhood fights; he lifts his giant hands to the capped blades of Loredana's shoulders, mysteriously materializing directly in front of him. I am both comfortable and uneasy, as if sleeping in my own bed, but with a brand new blanket.

"This," Loredana says, "is Ercole. The chef. He speak no English."

His hand flits forward, swallows my own hand as if the head of a lamb.

"*Come va?*" he says.

His voice is like gunfire, each word a tin can, bullet-plucked from a picket fence top. He could say the word *surreptitious* and it would be an exercise in cacophony.

"*Bene* Ercole," I say, "*Mille grazie per la cena.*"

"*Ay, ay, é niente,*" he fires, wiping sweat from his forehead, "America, *si?*" he continues, his curly grenade of a hairdo threatening to explode from his scalp.

He turns his face to the light of the restaurant and I notice a large scar on his cheek. I think of Ivo and his Rottweilers.

"*Si,*" I say.

"Ah, ah," he shouts, drowning out the techno music blaring from the speakers, and kissing the air six quick times, "*Bellisima!*"

Shivering, I search the air around Ercole for lightning bolts, the source of his heat, and see that Loredana has disappeared into the nebula again. Ercole opens and closes his right hand.

With three quick hand movements, each movement corresponding to a syllable of his speech, he says, "Bill Clinton."

His I's are extended as double, no, triple-E's, his O is longer than his fingers, and the name comes out as *Beeell Cleeentone.*

"*Si,*" I say.

"Ah!" Ercole cackles like a warlock finally successful in spawning the Armageddon.

A waterfall of Italian streams from his throat, and he ends it not with a period, but with the phrase, "Billy, Billy! Billy, Billy Clinton!"

As his laughter deteriorates into a cough, he takes one final and enormous drag from his cigarette and flicks the filter like a fastball fifty feet across the courtyard. He exhales a bodyful of smoke and in it, appearing as the magician's beautiful assistant, is Loredana, holding three half-full snifters on a brown bar tray. Ercole turns to her and shoots her in Italian. She shoots back, her rasp somehow matching his fire, and then turns to me.

"He want me to move more fast than I do."

I shrug. I smile. Again: comfortable and uneasy.

"Ercole make this himself. A, uh, not wine, but, uh, thicker with dessert...uh..."

"A liqueur," I say.

"*Si, si,*" Loredana rasps, and I feel like I've answered the bonus question and am now eligible for the really big money. "Of hazelnut."

I look at the brown liquid, a log cabin in a glass.

"Does he make everything himself?" I ask.

"Yes," she says, "he teach himself everything. To cook everything. He is the only person in the kitchen."

She looks at Ercole with big eyes. I look at him, too. His arms are folded, his gaze fixed on me. Loredana sets the three snifters on the table and the two of them pull up chairs. The sight of Ercole sitting shocks me. It is as incongruous as a roadrunner taking a nap.

Ercole snatches a snifter in his fingers and raises it nearly to the persimmons.

"Billy, Billy!" he shouts, and we clink glasses.

The sip is like rolling the finest tobacco in the Dead Sea Scrolls and smoking it. This inky hazelnut liqueur—the mad genius invention of this mad genius chef—is intoxicating and informative all at once. It teaches my taste buds new things: to open like flowers, then lie down and accept their fate. Loredana swallows first.

"He is, uh, an obsession with Bill Clinton. He love how he, uh, do everything."

Ercole begins wrapping on Loredana's shoulder and I expect her to break. He is asking her what she said. She tells him and he laughs, shooting a string of *Si's*—"*Si, si, si, si,*"—from his throat like a clogged faucet trying to expel its water.

I sip again, and then again, and soon, in the combination of Ercole's vocal rapids, Loredana's mist hovering over it all, and the sweet hazelnut running through me, I feel I am immersed in the most tepid and happy of the oceans. I feel pre-born.

I try, to the best of my Italian ability, to tell Ercole my story—how I got here, the tent, the grapes, Raffaella, Sandrone...

Ercole throws his head back with the mention of each name. With Raffaella, he runs his thumb over his scarred cheek to indicate her beauty; with Sandrone, he palms the air as if searching for a hidden doorknob and mutters, "Sandrone...*uva, uva, uva. Che é uva in inglese?*"

"*Uva,*" I say, "*in inglese? Uva é* grape."

"Grape?!" Ercole exclaims as if it's the most preposterous word he's heard.

"*Si,*" I say.

"Grape?" Ercole questions, then pauses, thinks the word over and says, "Oh, *come* grappa!" He pauses again, thinks about grappa, then says, "*Desidera* grappa?"

"Oh, no," Loredana sighs, her spider-hand over her eyes. "He want to give you the grappa now. This is how his mind work."

"*Si, si,*" Ercole says and springs from his chair.

Loredana and I watch the stars. He returns a minute later with tiny crystal grappa glasses and a tall bottle. As I learned the hard way in Sandrone's cantina, grappa is made from the grape mash: skins, branches, seeds; that leftover steaming junk that attacked me from his holding tank, sending the man himself into cheroot-rattling hysterics. Like certain cultures who use all parts of an animal after the hunt—the fat for lamp-oil, the skins for clothes—the Italians use all parts of the grape. I have never sipped so much in my life and I sip again; this sip of Nebbiolo grappa is the smoothest of its kind, running into my belly like silk soaked in kerosene. If the earth were a grape, this would be the taste of its core.

The three of us talk long into the night, drink deep into the bottle of grappa. We talk of Chicago, of Hong Kong, of cooking and eating and drinking; we talk of the upcoming Salone del Gusto. They tell me to return to I Cannubi tomorrow night to apprentice for an hour or two in Ercole's kitchen. I can't believe it, or I'm too drunk to believe it, and when he pours me yet another glass of grappa, Loredana now sleeping or pretending to sleep on the table, I have to wait until he averts his eyes, and dump my entire glassful into one of the neighboring clay pots. I can't take anymore. I am filled from belly to brain. I'm not even close to cold. Somehow, I don't believe my grappa discard could have flown under Ercole's radar, but he doesn't let on; he just continues to stroke Loredana's hair, fanned over the entire tablecloth, muttering, "*Mia moglie, mia moglie...*" My wife, my wife...

Later, another day, the air is so crisp you can break it like a cracker. And as the crumbs fall to the truffle soup, they hit bottom and become mountains. The Alps break from the Piedmont haze and I open my arms to them. Adriana's day-old apple cake still sits crosswise on my teeth like a cement that refuses to dry. The vineyards are everywhere, pitching me over slopes less drastic, but more numerous than those on the way to La Morra, Italy. The occasional residence asserts itself, pushing its washed-out white stone, cracked orange roof, rusted black gate from between the rows, then, just as quickly, disappears like a lioness. I feel I am somehow being stalked by structure and, as always, barely escaping with my life.

Persimmon trees tower above the rows, but hang still today, keeping their secrets. Somewhere around a curve, behind a slew of vineyards, Sandrone is commanding his grape-picking crew, Ivo and company are loading the crates onto flatbeds, Ercole, local chef extraordinaire, is washing leeks for a stock, Raffaella, my host at the Il Gioco dell'Oca agriturismo, is smoothing sheets for the day's guests, raw *grissini* is getting its cornmeal dust, wine is being sold, the Borgognos are harboring their quiet, cross-eyed animosity, and Adriana, Raffaella's mother, is doing my laundry. But here, now, curving left around a profiled slope, the hamlet of Monforte pokes its rose-colored head from a distant hillside like a turtle testing for rain. Finding none, finding only clarity and windlessness, it remains, pushing shop front after shop front, terrace after terrace up from the dirt and into the air.

It is a vertical town, even more so than La Morra, stacked, switchbacked, and as the trail descends at my feet, Monforte disappears once again behind a swell of green earth. I stop. No sound. No wind. I drop my hands to my sides. The air, like an Egyptian plover, cleans my mouth of breakfast. But there is no wind.

If there is no wind, why do I hear the grapevines slushing on the down-slope? To the right, the crops gather together as clouds. The vineyard is imploding in front of me, closing its leaves into a fist, a concentrated heart of green. I expect Nebbiolo grape juice to run like blood over my shoes. I expect it to open itself into a first beat. And when it does, leaves deafening as wings, the vineyard spreads its aorta wide open and belches, at my feet, not blood, not love, but two hunch-backed old men.

They are more wrinkled than wrinkled. They are over-wrinkled, über-wrinkled, sun-dried as tomato. The liquid was cooked from their skin long ago. Will the circus of Italy never end? What next? Will I look to the sky and see a helmeted brown bear riding a unicycle along a tightrope?

The men's noses come at me first, riding parallel in the air as two brown bodies on a slab. They shake the vineyard leaves from their white hair, loose rooster necks shuddering. Their eyes find me, laser blue, and two steady smiles spread like jam across their faces.

"Ciao," the man on the left sings in a surprising and pinched soprano.

His voice reaches like an unoiled hinge: rusted, stiff, but still functioning.

"Ciao, ciao," I say.

He squints at me, studying the accent that laces my *"Ciao's."*

"Americano?" he asks.

"Si," I say, smiling, nodding.

"Mi chiamo Guiseppe," he continues, fanning the hinge open, closed, open, closed, *"Questo é mio fratello,* Renato."

Guiseppe holds a hand at his thick throat and covers his mouth, indicating that Renato can not speak.

Both men push their hands to me and I shake them— each one heavier than it looks, grittier than granite. Renato takes a step back toward the vineyard that, not two minutes ago, birthed him onto this trail. His hands reach for his hips, find them, and, staring at the snarl of grapes, the wrinkles run from his face. He is so placid,

I'm not sure if he can't talk, or if he just doesn't need to. The pride in his newly smoothed face, the pride of a father whose child has just successfully pedaled a bicycle for the first time, tells me that this vineyard belongs to him, or to both of them. But I have to ask.

"*Queste uve...*" I say, struggling with my Italian this morning, "*le tue?*"

"*Oh, si, si,*" Guiseppe sings so much like Farinelli, I expect his gray hair to tie itself into two waist-length castrato braids.

Renato looks from the grapes to me. His wrinkles are back. He kisses his fingertips and holds his hands to the sky. The gesture is saturated in so much drama and summoning power that I expect the weather to change at once.

"*Desidera* Barolo?" Guiseppe enunciates slowly, chasing the clouds away.

I should be surprised, but I'm not. Am I becoming desensitized to charity and luck? I should be chastised for this, but instead, a sigh springs from my stomach to my throat. It is the sigh of the poolside lawn chair, of sipping lemonade through a straw.

I shrug. I look toward Monforte. It remains in hiding behind the hillside. I wonder if it is still there. Barolo, Monforte, Barolo, Monforte? Barolo.

"*Si,*" I say.

Their cantina is tiny. If Sandrone's cantina is the penthouse, theirs is the broom closet. It is more ancient than their faces; it must be the entity that spawned these two gentlemen—the Alessandria brothers, as indicated by a wooden hand-carved sign over the cantina's doorway: *Fratelli Alessandria*. Indeed, the entire cantina seems constructed of wood and sawdust, a relic, a holdover, an unsafe rollercoaster from three generations past. The cantina is rickety and dim. A single brown light bulb shines as if from the bottom of a coffeepot. The whole place, including the brothers themselves, seems in the process of fermenting.

Medieval wheelbarrows line the walls and I expect to see them full of bodies, crushed by catapult and plague, ruined by arrows and hot tar. But instead, they offer, in both smell and sight, the organ meat tangle of flattened grapes, skins, branches. The brothers parade along the wheelbarrows as if soldiers guarding a drawbridge, and Renato holds his hand to the wall behind me. I turn and am stunned to see steel. In the muddy, reflected light, three tanks stand equipped not with scaffolding as in Sandrone's cantina, but with makeshift ladders, crooked rungs, wooden to be sure.

Guiseppe begins to pull thin scarf-strings of Italian from his throat, telling me about their business, how wine-making has been in their family for centuries. Renato punctuates Guiseppe not with voice, but with gesture, oftentimes karate-chopping upward to either dispute or emphasize his brother's statements. Only one is speaking, but these brothers interrupt each other like Abbott and Costello. They are *choreographed*.

Renato reaches for the ladder in the middle as if for an axe. I strain to hear any trace of a dungeon torture scream from inside the tank. But only: the gong of his ancient knees against the steel and the silk sloshing of three wine glasses being filled. Renato hands first to Guiseppe, then to me. In this light, the wine is black. Guiseppe offers his glass to the ceiling shadows. I hold mine to my nose and: hay, sawdust, slaughter; then: truffle, blackberry, pine; fruitcake baked in a coffin. Even here: even in the dungeons of Italy, elegance is fostered by four seventy-year-old hands. Guiseppe mutters a toast like a private prayer only Renato can understand.

"Bravo," I say and clink glasses with the brothers.

I sip and am immediately struck on the tongue by a sense of the unfinished. This wine seems to be in the process of coalescing, each element intermingling for the first time. My mouth goes yeasty and robust, sticky almost with fat and marrow, oxtail and liver. Then, on the greasy swallow, the wine inexplicably sparkles like a champagne—an element I haven't yet experienced with a Barolo—leaves the mouth cleaned and ready for another sip.

Another sip leads to another sip and then another, the dark privacy of the cantina now bright enough, the outdoors fading into a morning dream, disappearing like Monforte behind a hillside.

I sip the last of my third glass and Renato, obviously trained to balk at empty crystal, grabs it from my hand and fills it a fourth time. The more he drinks, the more comfortable he seems on the ladders. He hands me my glass and climbs down like a cat along a window-ledge. He's becoming younger with each sip. I wonder if, after ten glasses, he will get his voice back. We toast again to Guiseppe's mystery prayer. We talk of Il Gioco dell'Oca and Sandrone. In mid-sip, Guiseppe, dribbling wine from the corners of his mouth, invites me to stay at their house. He scowls at the idea of sleeping in a tent.

"*No, no,*" I laugh, "*Va bene, va bene.*"

Soon, this glass is vanquished like the others. The thought of the outdoors and Monforte returns. I buy a bottle of Barolo from the Alessandria's; Renato drops it into a paper bag, and they walk me to the front of the cantina. Guiseppe lays a hand on my left shoulder, Renato on the right. They are pressing a story into me that won't find its words until later. They say *ciao* with their eyes.

The outside cool plays in my hair, rests on my head like a helmet. I turn back to the cantina and see the brothers' faces poking like trolls from the doorway, which itself seems disguised in the pattern of a giant tree trunk. When the door closes, the world becomes relatively real again, the fable receding into the vineyards behind me. The air smells only of early afternoon and, rolling my shoulders toward my ears, I am struck with the desire for words in any form.

Taking small steps toward Monforte, I pull the bottle of Barolo from the paper bag in the hope of simply reading the words *Fratelli Alessandria*. I am greeted instead with the final hammering of the brothers' rustic operation. An unusual joy expands from my chest to my ribs. Monforte lifts itself once again from behind the hillside and reflects the sun from its windowpanes to the bottle in my hands which reclines in a lawn chair of its own: dusty, purple, entirely unlabeled.

❧ ❧ ❧

Matthew Gavin Frank's work has appeared in numerous publications, including The Best Travel Writing 2008, Gastronomica *magazine,* Best Food Writing 2006, Literary Review, *and* The New Republic. *He lives in the Chicago area. This story is an excerpt from his book* Barolo, *which will be published by the University of Nebraska Press in spring 2010.*

～ ～ ～

A Chance Life

A connection forged in the imagination
takes a strange turn.

D ESPITE ITS UNSAVORY NAME, THE CUTTHROAT CAFÉ
looked like the place to be. Its tiny parking lot
full of cars, diners visible through the large window—the
modest structure occupied its bit of Bailey, Colorado as
if it had always been there. Nothing about it signaled
that this ordinary place, like the rest of Bailey, would
soon become extraordinary—struck by a kind of collective death. For now, a pleasing innocence enveloped the
Cutthroat Café.

We opened the door and waited on the landing, startled by the number of people crammed inside.

"Anywhere," said a blond woman with a quick smile
as she hurried by.

Down a few steps in the official dining area, we slid into wooden chairs at the one unoccupied table, awkwardly close to a party of six teenage girls. At just after three o'clock on a late September Tuesday, it made sense that most of the thirty or so customers in the room would be escapees from the magnificent high school we knew to be a little farther down the road.

A poised, dark-haired young woman in her late teens took our order. We then amused ourselves scrutinizing a miracle of woodcarving on the windowsill behind me. A log twenty inches in length, perhaps four inches high, featured at one end a tiny fisherman—his rod missing—in mid-cast on the edge of a river; slivers of minutely rendered pine trees; and, at the far end, a matchbox-sized log cabin with billowing wooden smoke pouring from its chimney. Centered within this Lilliputian mountain idyll the words "Cutthroat Café" had been carved in a craftsman's tour de force. Our waitress later told us the fisherman's rod had been stolen so many times they'd stopped asking the artist to replace it.

A young man with a green-tinged Mohawk, an incongruous apron tied around his black pants, entered the upper landing from the kitchen. I wondered how this quotidian country town accepted a teenager trying hard to be a renegade. Just how narrow might this picturesque valley be, only ninety minutes southwest of Denver but seemingly a vast distance away from an urban *frisson* and its possibilities? Here the visible attractions included hamburgers, hot dogs, a few other cafés and businesses, and, next door, the Bailey General Store—one of those phenomena of space utilization stocked to anticipate anything on a hypothetical shopper's list.

Our waitress came from the kitchen balancing two plates along one forearm, one plate in the other hand, followed by a younger girl similarly burdened, her dark blond hair pulled back except for a flourish of a wave along the side of her high forehead. They distributed the plates of sandwiches and fries among the girls at the table next to us. Our waitress left immediately, but her partner stayed, gently hovering.

"Is everything O.K.?" she asked. I admired her small, well-proportioned body and her barely contained animation. She stood surveying her table of peers, her apron tied low around her jeans. "Does anybody need anything else?" An eagerness to please colored her young voice.

I used to teach American literature to high school juniors and I guessed her to be that age. The girls at the table—two of them in black-and-gray school warm-up suits—might have been her classmates or members of that sacred state of seniordom.

"We need salad dressing," one of the girls said, although none of them had ordered a salad.

"What kind?" the waitress asked. They discussed the choices.

"I'll bring big bowls," she said, holding up her hands to indicate something substantial.

She soon returned and placed two cereal-sized bowls on the table. Her customers began dipping their sandwiches, one bite at a time.

What must this be like? I wondered. Waiting on—essentially working for—one's peers, and at this age, when finding out who you are and where you fit into this life, this *day*, can be so viscerally charged by an admired classmate who ignores you, or a mean-spirited one who doesn't.

I found myself feeling protective of this girl, although she clearly had all sorts of positives on her side. Her strong features somehow composed a face delicate and compelling. Her body language and the expression in her large eyes, clear and blue, reminded me of some of the girls I knew now as a substitute teacher at an all-girl high school. There is a way of living that suggests experience without its reality. A certain amount of footage viewed and you are far more worldly than your surroundings or passport might suggest. Some of my students seem consummately innocent; some have traveled way too far down the road already; and some—perhaps this girl—occupy a middle, amorphous territory. Sex and brutality and death on a screen large or small can implant a hypothetical passage of time, a vicarious journey that returns the viewer as not quite the same teenage girl, even though she hasn't left her old and tattered beanbag chair.

I guessed that this girl didn't wear the title of most popular or most beautiful or the smartest in her school. Despite perhaps being a contender in all these categories, her demeanor, her mantle of uncertainty, suggested that she spent more time trying, seeking, practicing, than she did reveling in triumphs.

She disappeared, then reemerged from the kitchen and headed straight for our table. With a small smile and glancing eye contact she placed two large, iced lemonades before us.

"Thank you," I said, reaching for the frosted glass. She smiled again without looking at me and turned back to the girls next to us.

"You guys doing O.K.?" she asked again. A few girls responded indifferently, the others not at all.

I felt a little miffed on her behalf. "Be nice to her," I wanted to say, my own high school days as a relative outsider still too accessible. I couldn't call this girl an outsider. She didn't *feel* like one. But I thought I felt the presence of a need.

Eventually the girls finished eating and paid at the counter. After some discussion, one of them came back to the table and dropped a bill folded into a tight square. I don't recall seeing the waitress come to pick up her tip or clear the table. I just remember the green bill, folded into eighths, as perhaps a minor insult. Would it seem to her like enough or too much? Would it somehow demean her—this offering?

After lunch we resumed our long drive south to Crestone where my parents-in-law retired in 1972. We had driven Route 285 dozens of time. Not often enough to say that we knew it, but often enough to be disappointed earlier today, after picking up a rental car at the Denver airport, to discover our usual lunch stop just north of Bailey had closed. And often enough to be dazzled several years ago when the handsome new high school and middle school had come into view as we rounded a curve of the valley to the south.

Today the schools—still gleaming and pristine—soon appeared on our right. They faced a narrow fork of the shallow, exuberant South Platte River and a hillside behind it banked by aspen trees at their golden height and dark green, invincible pines.

"Their students must come from all over the county," I said to my husband. "That town couldn't possibly build a complex like this." The athletic fields across the road along the river stood well maintained and empty. A few cars flanked an administration building just north of the two schools. In the clear mountain silence, all of it reflected the order and promise that schools are meant to convey. In another moment we had curved out of the valley and resumed listening to a book on CD evoking a world—art and politics in nineteenth-century France—antithetical to this one.

The next day disappeared while we repaired the bridge over the arroyo and excised the weeds my mother-in-law loathes in her garden, planted at 8,300 feet up the side of one of the Sangre de Cristos' tallest peaks. No time for the news or going into town to pick up the mail. The following morning my husband returned from the post office with an armful of catalogues, envelopes, and a newspaper.

"Look at this," he said, his face ashen. He handed me the *Valley Courier*.

I stared at a black, bold headline. "Gunman, girl dead after hostage situation in Bailey." A photograph of a counselor, according to the caption, comforting a hysterical girl in a pink sweater, her face contorted as she sobbed, accompanied the story. In subsequent articles similar images became ubiquitous—photographs of teenagers, girls mostly, distraught and emotionally shattered by the kind of pain seldom wholly forgotten.

The orderly black print belied its content. A drifter armed with at least one handgun and claiming to have enough explosives in his backpack to blow up the school had entered a second-floor Honors English classroom late yesterday morning. He fired one shot to prove his mastery of the moment, ordered the teacher and male students out, and lined up the girls along the blackboard—to make his terrible choices from among the helpless contestants. He then released all but six blond girls. A scenario impossible to reconcile with that idyllic school, real and exemplary, in a pristine Rocky Mountain river valley. A scenario that served as an ugly template for a similar event at an Amish school in Pennsylvania just five days later.

The ensuing four-hour crisis in Bailey included all the too familiar reference points: SWAT teams surrounding the school; desperate cell phone calls; students streaming out a back door to that uniquely American symbol of safety—the big yellow school bus; multiple squad cars and trained negotiators; frightened parents convening from all directions, then sent to another school to wait.

The details remained sketchy but emphatic enough. The gunman sexually assaulted some of the girls and released four of his hostages, one at a time, as negotiations transpired. To the sheriff and others speaking with him by cell phone, he expressed no specific goal.

Several hours into her captivity, one of the remaining hostages wrote a text message to those outside: "Why won't you come get me?"

By 3:30 P.M. negotiations had stopped. The gunman, no longer willing to talk, remained in the classroom with two last hostages. "Something," he had told the sheriff in their final communication, would happen at four o'clock.

The sheriff then made a decision he later said—expressing the warped clarity violence begets—he would second-guess for the rest of his life, while also maintaining that he had had no choice.

With explosives the SWAT team blew a hole in the classroom wall. One of the two girls ran toward the opening and her would-be rescuers, blocking the sharpshooter's line of fire and giving the gunman just enough time to shoot her in the back of the head. He then turned his weapon upon himself. Whether his bullet or one of the many fired into him killed him is of no consequence. The girl, Emily Keyes, died soon after being airlifted to a Denver hospital.

"Keyes," the article continued, "was a member of the volleyball and debate teams and was getting involved with cheerleading.... Keyes also worked as a waitress at the Cutthroat Café...."

Innocence is not something lost only once. There is hope, and then despair, and then, somehow, hope again. J.F.K.'s assassination broke our hearts, but then Bobby emerged as the future. The Vietnam War pressed us down into the mud and Watergate kept us there, until, it seemed, Nixon's maniacal wave before his last helicopter ride from the White House lawn signaled that America—its laws and its public—would not long tolerate bad men in high places.

As a teacher I believe in the sanctity of the school—students entering classrooms each morning to learn, evolve, thrive—despite the times one may wonder, at the end of the day, what exactly has been accomplished. High school students are heavily invested in immediacy. What is around them, who is next to them, why they are compelled to do this deed rather than that one. These Bailey High students were between five and nine years old in 1999, when what is known as "Columbine" occurred less than an hour away. Frightening as it would have been to their young sensibilities, the intervening seven years would have effaced recognition of that violence—what they might have known of it—from life in Bailey. A sense of well being, of the comfort of an ordinary day, would have been allowed to reestablish itself like the vibrant blue lupine growing out of the hard gray rock of the mountains.

It was the mowing down of this innocence that pervaded this tragedy and made it matter—just as much as the loss of one young girl.

Reading about sixteen-year-old Emily Keyes, I felt chilled and anxious. The Cutthroat Café had eight or nine tables. How many part-time workers would they have?

The enthusiasm if not the dynamism of a cheerleader fit the picture in my mind. But volleyball? I couldn't quite see the slight girl who had so engaged me forty hours earlier powering a ball over the net. Nor could I picture her on the debating team, standing before an auditorium of listeners and confidently, meticulously dismantling her opponent's position on capital punishment.

But that night on the televised news my speculations abruptly ended. A photograph of the girl accompanied the story, her chin tilted downward slightly, giving us not an exuberant here-I-am-world smile, but a face filled with light, with an I-love-life-and-aren't-we—you and I—lucky kind of smile.

I left the room to cry while my husband explained our distress to his mother. "A murder!" she said later, when discussing the event with visitors. Expressing the kind of egocentrism common to those lucky enough to live ninety-three years, she added, "Who could imagine that they'd be involved in a murder on their way *here*?"

As her guests sipped drinks with us on the porch, our clothes softly reflecting the brilliant pinks and oranges of the sunset, I considered that word "involved." How *were* we involved? Emily was a face, a lithe body, an imagined connection based on nothing tangible or resolute, a blip of a presence near us while we traveled a thousand miles from one place to another on this screen of random existence. She had touched my lemonade glass. That's as close as we had come to each other.

A sense of shock and sorrow pervaded the next few days as further details emerged. The gunman's brother received a letter in the mail the day after the shooting absolving all five siblings of any responsibility for what was about to occur (the letter suggested suicide but nothing else), thanking him and the others for their attempts to help him temper his demons, and attributing full blame to their father, a man the letter depicted as volatile and terrifying.

The obviousness of this equation—violence begetting violence—insulted the scope of the pain engulfing the people of Bailey. They included a sixteen-year-old boy— Emily's twin brother and only sibling—left to wonder how to survive without his figurative other half. Parents with a sense of loss too deep to measure. Five girls—the other hostages—who shared some part of Emily's nightmare and will, to varying degrees, re-dream it probably forever. An entire school occupied by students who no longer believed in their own safety, and a staff of teachers, counselors, and administrators left to set aside their private distress in order to begin recreating a place of peace. And the sheriff, the man in charge, whose son once shared a little grade school romance with Emily and whose decision it was to "go in"—in the parlance of these contemporary maelstroms.

Driving back to Denver three days later—the day following Emily's memorial service—I felt a sense of dread as we approached Bailey. Rounding the curve just south of the school, the beautiful, empty building with just one or two cars visible in its lot shone in the bright sun. Across the road a portable electronic sign flashed "No parking, no stopping along the road." A few satellite news trucks remained parked near the athletic fields. Farther on, in the meager town, pink ribbons fluttered on highway dividers, light poles, fences. Business signs offered consolation and solicited prayers for Emily and for the people of this stricken community.

I wanted to stop at the Cutthroat Café just long enough to contribute to the memorial fund mentioned in the newspapers. Entering the tiny building, I felt as if I had been there many times before, as if the fundamental honesty of the place would always stay with me, even if I never returned.

A large photograph taken inside the café of two laughing teenage girls, one of them Emily, stood propped against the wall at the end of a counter. Cards and other offerings surrounded the photograph. I spoke brief, clumsy phrases of sympathy to the woman who had greeted us five days earlier as another young waitress, who looked disconcertingly like Emily, listened. Instead of treating me as the stranger and intruder that I surely was, they seemed to appreciate my concern. I stuffed some bills—a completely impotent gesture—into the five-gallon glass jar on the counter already filled with money and left.

At the airport, awaiting our return flight to San Francisco, we bought the Sunday *Denver Post*. The front page featured a large color photograph of Emily's family at the memorial service—her brother, Casey, seated between the parents, his pale face tilted downward, eyes closed, an icon of sorrow. The mother, seen from the side, looks delicately strong and bewildered. Her hair is pulled back with a clip revealing long earrings made of very thin silver passing through the lobe, dangling several inches both front and back with a tiny ball at each end. They are elegant yet whimsical, not funereal. I'm convinced that Emily gave them to her—perhaps with a recent birthday card, quoted in an article citing the girl's thoughtful ways, in which Emily wrote now ironic promises.

Emily's father is wearing wrap-around reflective sunglasses and his face could be made of stone. In another photograph he and the sheriff embrace at the service, the two men holding on to each other in shared anguish. But here the father is ramrod straight, his lips a thin, bitter line. I sense that he would have insisted upon seeing Emily's body, her once lovely face transformed in death.

In our literature we find archetypes of young American girls who die: Henry James's Daisy Miller and Milly Theale; Stephen Crane's Maggie, so-called girl of the streets; Edith Wharton's Lily Bart. The playwright Thornton Wilder, in *Our Town*, named his version of this character Emily. Sixteen-year-old Emily Webb of Grover's Corners, a New Hampshire town not unlike the way Bailey might have seemed a hundred years ago.

In *Our Town*, Mr. Webb—Emily's father and editor of the local newspaper—responds to a question about how much culture there might be in Grover's Corners. "We've got a lot of pleasures of a kind here: we like the sun comin' up over the mountain in the morning, and we all notice a good deal about the birds…. And we watch the change of the seasons; yes, everybody knows about them." Later another character, the Stage Manager, adds that "There's an early afternoon calm in our town: a buzzin' and a hummin' from the school buildings...."

After her marriage following high school and eventual death in childbirth, Emily Webb joins the others in the cemetery on the hill and shares their ability to gaze down upon life in Grover's Corners as it proceeds without them. Among those who greet her arrival is Simon Callow, formerly the church organist and chronic inebriate, and a suicide—Wilder's unembellished symbol for what simmers beneath the veneer of towns like Grover's Corners.

In response to Emily's imploring, the Stage Manager grants her the privilege of returning to Grover's Corners to relive one ordinary day. She chooses her twelfth birthday and while immersed in this visitation, reliving the day with her family and friends, she "can't look at everything hard enough." But soon Emily decides to return to the dead, overcome by a sense of the things she failed to notice and appreciate when they were hers.

On that reclaimed and benign twelfth birthday morning, this spectral Emily—who knows that before long her brother will die on a camping trip and her own death, while some years off, awaits them—urges her family to engage with one another before it is too late. But they can't hear her words. "Oh, Mama," she pleads, "just look at me one minute as though you really saw me.... Just for a moment now we're all together. Mama, just for a moment we're happy. *Let's look at one another.*"

Would Emily Keyes suffer similar regrets if given the same chance to reenter her life? She seemed to signal something else—a realized love for life—in that birthday card for her mother; in the relationships she established with her classmates, co-workers, and many Bailey residents; in her selfless text message to her father moments before her death in response to his asking if she was all right ("I love U guys"); in her archetypal full-of-the-moment face. Integrated with the disappointments she no doubt experienced, I suspect that she did notice the dawn behind those dark mountains. Certainly she heard the birds and the laughter or concerns of those she loved. And on some level she felt at the end of the day the evening sun slipping away to the west.

A Park County broadsheet I picked up in Bailey en route home included over two thousand delinquent tax listings—a name, address, and sum of money in arrears. A sale would occur in two weeks: "Remember—you are NOT buying the land or mobile home. You are buying a lien against the property...."

Did Emily see beneath the surface of this Colorado idyll, see around the curves of Route 285 and into the darkness awaiting here and there—behind the kind of scenes of ordinary life that one of Wilder's characters describes as "wonderful"—in preference to which Simon Callow chooses a noose, in reference to which the dead Simon Callow scoffs?

It remains just an existential question.

How does this girl matter? Why *that* school chosen for a private Armageddon? Why *that* café, her hand on that lemonade, when we had never stopped in Bailey before? Why do I think I know her and the quality of her love?

If I had known Emily Keyes, I would now have a shaped sorrow. As it is, my sense of loss—my own inescapable egocentrism—spreads in an amorphous

constancy over that lovely valley and school; over
Emily's family and friends missing her still—as always—missing her in real time; and over the image of a
young, vibrant, unforgotten face.

~≈ ~≈ ~≈

*Millicent Susens is a playwright, essayist, and writing coach living
in San Francisco. A former high school English teacher, she writes,
edits the work of others, and substitute teaches at an all girls' high
school. Previous essays have appeared in* The Best Women's
Travel Writing 2008 *and in regional publications.*

≈ ≈ ≈

Choices Rejected

Love takes an unexpected path.

MID-JULY IN LOS ANGELES, MY NEWBORN GRAND-child needs no more than her diaper. Less than a mile from the Pacific coastline, offshore breezes from Venice Beach wring out warm and dry as they flow up the slight incline and cross Lincoln Avenue. These hot winds embrace us; Nora cradles in the crook of my left arm, a pink flannel receiving blanket between her skin and mine.

Unlike the creaky old Craftsman rocker I used when Nora's mother was my first baby, this silent glider won't even whisper as Nora and I drift silently forward and back, forward and back. Will her eyes stay blue? Will her skin stay this parchment white, so like her name-sake, my mother?

Gently rocking newborn Nora, daughter of my daughter. Rocking, rocking, back and forth. Will Nora have a daughter? A granddaughter? She is born at the beginning of this new century; I lived nearly sixty years in the last. Who will she be in her future, when I am gone?

Hear baby moans. Baby sighs. Deep, slow breathing. Sudden startle!

I rest my palm on her chest. "Shhh, Nora. Shhh." She calms with a loud exhale. I feel her warmth against my palm; my body heat warms her unnecessarily, but I will not put her down. I learned with my own girls, rocking a sleeping baby completes my world. Nothing satisfies me more, there's nothing easier to do, and there's nothing better for babies. I rock, slowly forward and back, and my life and world comes into my mind, anyway it likes.

"Gramma loves you. Just rocking, rocking. Um hum, um hum. Now you hush, hush. Shhhhh."

Rocking, swaying, dreaming memories. Choices accepted. Choices rejected. Drift, daydream, imagine a future, remember a past.

Mysteries open to me. Faded memories back bright and strong. End of August, 1966 rainy season. My little two-room house in Addis Ababa, near Arat Kilo. I'm completing two years of Peace Corps teaching in Ethiopia.

"Everyone says you won't be happy if you go back. And they're right," Guy says as we sit together on the couch having our morning coffee and an Arab roll.

Our friends also want me to stay. They say I'm more Ethiopian than they are because I've lived for two years among the common people in the provinces while they've lived only in cosmopolitan Addis Ababa—in addition, that is, to their time abroad for higher education, at the behest of Emperor Haile Selassie. They are good, dear friends to me, the first in my life to give me a nickname. I arrived named Carol and now I am Kay.

"But I have to go home and finish school," I explain once again, holding my cold fingers between my knees for warmth, my shoulders hunched up close to my ears. Will anyone at home believe that Africa is actually chilly at times? Without a fireplace, there is no way to heat this house, and it's downright cold on a cement floor at 8,000 feet during the rainy season. I'm wearing my blue mohair cardigan against the damp chill. Morning's first rain has yet to begin, but thick, dark clouds already have blacked out the sun and blocked its welcome warmth.

"My dear Kay, you have become Ethiopian. You will not be happy back home."

"Perhaps."

"I'm sorry, I should let you go," he says. "But I don't want you to." He looks away.

"You don't need to be sorry. I'm sorry to leave." We have known each other for two years, and now only days remain for us; I deeply regret leaving.

"Will you come back? I know you can't say right now. But do you think about coming back? Will you try?" He looks at me, waiting for my answer.

"Of course I think about it. All the time."

"I'm sorry for so many things. That I can't ask you to stay. That I can't offer you a future. Not until my family problems are settled. Soon, I hope. Soon."

"I know that. It's O.K."

"But there's something else." He pauses, waiting. "There's something I don't understand." His left forearm rests comfortably across his thigh, and I'm admiring the beauty of the back of his left hand, the way his smooth brown skin contrasts with the stark white cuff of his fresh business shirt. He raises his right hand, cups my chin and gently lifts my face to his. It's only when we're this close that I smell the spicy, evocative fragrance of his aftershave.

"Yes?" I ask. I'm still in love with the sight of his brown eyes, especially those alluring quarter moons above the lower lids, yet today they make me almost sick with loss. His fingers are cold on my chin, just as cold as mine.

"I've always hoped that you would leave me with our baby."

"What?" I pull away.

"I don't understand why we haven't started a baby. I always think it will happen, but it never does."

"Of course not. I don't want a baby."

"You don't want a baby?"

"Well, someday. But not now."

"I don't understand."

"You don't? Oh, wait a minute." Of course. He returned from college in the U.S. before birth control pills were in common use. Our times together were intermittent—school holidays, Easter week, the rainy season—but each time he thought I possibly might have become pregnant? "Do you mean you don't understand why I haven't gotten pregnant?"

He nods. How odd, we never discussed this. No, not so odd—it was my business, not his. How could he possibly have thought—oh well, some things that happen here are unknowable. And here's another one.

"Guy, I'm on the pill."

"The what?"

My usual frank tone is replaced with a new gentleness. "I take the pill, the birth control pill. I'm not ready to have children, and—"

"I didn't know," he says, interrupting me, his kind, calm voice that is richer, deeper. He takes off his glasses and wipes at his eyes with a neatly ironed and folded white handkerchief and again I see the beautiful contrast, his reddish-brown color against crisp white.

"Guy, I'm so sorry. I just assumed you knew—knew I did not want to be pregnant."

"No. You should have told me. I would have asked you to stop."

"What? Why?"

"For a baby. We could do that now, yes? Would it hurt you to stay that much longer? You could leave me with a baby. Please, my darling Kay. It's all I ask of you."

I don't know what to say.

"We would have a beautiful child," he continues, speaking slowly in a logical, even tone of voice. "And then I would always have something of you. It's all I want. Please."

"But what about me?"

"You may do as you wish."

"But I wouldn't be able to leave a baby here."

"Good. Fine. Then stay."

"But I have to finish my degree."

"Then do that. And come back. Or not. It would be up to you."

"This is impossible, Guy."

"Why is it impossible? I have two aunties who would love and care for our child."

Ah yes, I know of these women, and they know of me, but for some reason, Guy's mysterious "family problems" prevent our acquaintance. Yet the only problem I know about is his family's agreement, made when he was a child, that he someday ought to marry one of Emperor Haile Selassie's daughters. That's unlikely to happen, however, since neither of them want to do this. So what would everyone say if he suddenly produced our offspring into the mysterious "family problems?" I can't imagine, though I know such a thing would not be forbidden here, not the way it would be in my culture.

"I guess it's impossible for me to do that," I say. "Just impossible for me."

For all the talk of my friends in Addis Ababa—Guy's friends, actually—that I have become an Ethiopian, I know in this moment I've hit my limit. Yes, this culture would embrace our beautiful biracial child, but for the first time my culture succeeds in pulling me back to itself.

"Guy, please listen. I don't want to have a child until I want one, and I won't want one until I'm married. And I can't even think about being married until I go home and finish college."

"Then you'll come back in a year or two? I'll fix all my family problems in the meantime. Yes, then we'll be married, and we'll have our baby."

"You're being very persuasive, you know. Why now? Why didn't we talk about this before now?"

"Because I kept waiting for us to start making our baby."

We fall silent. I'm trembling; is it the chill? I imagine a letter: Dear family, Sorry, but I won't be coming home right away because I decided to marry that nice Ethiopian man I told you about. Oh, and I'm pregnant. So I guess you were right, Mother. I never will complete college.

No! Unthinkable.

I'm aware of Guy again, and he's sitting up straight and tall. His brown, thin-soled Italian leather shoes, highly polished, are placed firmly on the floor. With long, elegant fingers folded together, his clasped hands rest between his knees. Eyes closed, as if asleep, his glasses folded on the arm of the couch, I watch him for a long time, trying to figure out what he's doing, why he seems so intent and still, wondering how he can be so still when I'm shivering.

The electric bulb overhead blinks off and back on once, just as lightning cracks below the black clouds. A thunderous roar comes with the rain's sudden deluge, and it's the usual deafening sound of falling nails banging onto the tin roof. But nothing disturbs his reverie.

"What are you doing?" I finally ask, in a voice louder than I'd like, trying to speak over the din.

He startles, as if I've awakened him.

"Oh, I'm so sorry," I say, leaning toward him to lay my hand gently atop the middle of his chest, under his tie. I feel his warmth against my frigid palm. Even the small white buttons are warmed up. "I didn't mean to give you such a fright. I just wondered—I didn't know what you were doing."

"I was praying." He looks to me, and I feel sorry. So sorry. For both of us. "That's all," he says. "Just praying."

This is too hard. We want to cry. And I want to imagine a future, one that somehow includes this loving, gentle man whom I love and respect with all my heart.

But these would be our last times together. Now only Guy's letters remain as testament, mere words scribbled in blue pen. I still ache as I read again his fast loopy scrawl, sometimes on a folded blue aerogramme, other times on onion skin stationery mailed in envelopes with the return address of the Ethiopian Tourist Organization printed in both English and the lovely, exotic Amharic script.

> My darling Kay—I have many times asked
> you in a not serious way to marry me, with the
> purpose of you to start asking whether I am
> serious or not, in order to help me explain all
> the problems. You never did, and you never
> took it seriously. I decided that your interests
> were more across the ocean. My dearest of all
> human beings, now at this stage I have to solve
> so many problems that you do not know. God
> knows whether I can solve it within a year. Love
> love love and a million kisses, Guy

Faded memories back too bright. Old mysteries open with something to reveal. How could I have known he wanted to tell me the family problems? That he wanted me to ask? Sensing his reticence and respecting his privacy, I never did. I never took the hint. I'm still no good at hints. So I went home to California. I completed my college degree. Guy and I continued corresponding for two years, until I married the beloved man who is the father of our two daughters. We are married to this day. We are Nora's grandparents. And all these years later, I remember a past as I imagine a future.

Sweetest Kay—You are gone, you have left me,
it is only your memory that is haunting me. I
sometimes wonder whether you have ever been
in Ethiopia. I know two years were long, but
when I try to remember those two long years
they are just like thin air. I miss you my love, I
long to see you. I do not know, perhaps we will
or will not meet again, but on my part, as I have
repeatedly told you, I will try my best to see you
even if you get married and have ten thousand
children. I miss you and will always miss you.
Guy

Now drifting, daydreaming in today's dry, hot summer, I regret that Guy has not found me. But I will always wait. His goodbye letter, written two months after
my marriage, was brutal—for me, for him.

I am left all alone. No one can either see me or
find me. I'm kind of a monk. No more Carol.
All of us missed you very much. You know how
much we loved and respected you. You were
our exception among the *ferengis*. You were the
noblest of all women. We loved you, adored you
and admired you. Now we are separated, yet we
will never stop remembering you. *Arivaderci.*
Buona fortuna to you and your husband. Please
write me again. With very great love and
respect. Guy.

I never wrote him again. And I've never stopped
feeling we still deserve more than that goodbye. So I
honor what's past by remembering, even while today I

also imagine a future. I gently sway, rocking and knowing; newborn Nora is a future. Baby purring. Gramma knowing. Choices rejected, choices accepted. Knowing Nora, knowing love.

～※ ～※ ～※

Carol Beddo served in the Peace Corps, Ethiopia, 1964-66, and traveled throughout Ethiopia and East Africa. A lifelong adventurer, she retired from a challenging career in politics and public policy and at last is writing about her years in Africa, playing her violin, and learning to speak Spanish. She and her husband of forty years are parents of two adult daughters and grandparents of two youngsters.

MICHAEL McCARTHY

❦ ❦ ❦

The Floating Coffin of Tonle Sap Lake

The threat of death focuses the mind.

AT $25 A TICKET, IT'S ONLY THE RICH, OR WESTERNERS touring Angkor Wat, who can afford the fast ferry that runs down Tonle Sap Lake 180 miles from Siem Reap to Phnom Penh. On this particular morning in late fall the 120 seats of the main cabin were full and the roof packed with another two dozen foreigners keen for an adventure. So we were well over capacity but in Cambodia it's not like there is anybody in charge of such things, and the sun was shining in a pastel blue sky, and off we went only an hour late.

About thirty minutes into the trip the horizon disappeared and all we could see were the dazzling blue waters of the huge waterway disappearing into the distance. The rainy season was over and the vast lake was completely full of water, fish, and crocodiles. Those without books or cameras to keep them amused started to nod off, which was when the first trickles made an appearance inside the cabin. The front doors were open—in fact, the doors up front were the only exit to the outside—and the great speed we were making must have allowed water to creep in. We all hauled our bags into our laps, lifted our feet off the floor, and grinned at the sight of a single crew member attempting to dry a 150-foot boat using only a small mop and a couple of old plastic Pepsi bottles.

The nose of the cigar-shaped ferry was tilted up in the air and we were going like hell, and soon the back of the boat was inundated with several inches of water. This became rather irritating and people began to grumble. My friends Roger and Ian shared my row, all of us crammed in like sardines, and we grinned at this small annoyance, just one of those situations that make countries like Cambodia so charming.

I looked around to see what other passengers were doing and noted with some alarm that three women at the very back row were making an effort to open a window. This, I thought, would let yet more water into the boat, but when I saw them pounding on the window and subsequently kicking at it, it dawned on me they were trying to escape. The water by this time was over our ankles amidships, and even deeper at the back.

I noted with greater alarm that passengers all over the boat were quietly opening the overhead storage compartments and bringing down life jackets. Ian thought he might go up front and find out where all this water was coming from. He put on a life jacket, as did Roger, who handed me a vest but it fell into bits in my hands, leaving me with a useless albatross around my neck. Two elderly ladies in the seat in front of us started crying, and then everyone stood up and tried to put on life jackets. As the ferry turned, water sloshed back and forth and the boat made slow sickening slides from side to side. I peered out the window and casually looked for some sign of a treetop to which to swim. There were no treetops. Behind me I heard talk of crocodiles.

At the front of the boat Ian was conferring with a young Aussie named Michael. They had been remonstrating with the driver of the boat, using a Cambodian passenger as translator. Ian came back to report that it might be necessary to stop the boat and find the source of the water because we were listing so heavily. The captain had panicked and was trying to run away from the problem. Ian went back up front and several passengers surreptitiously followed, the increased weight causing the water at the back to run forward, whereupon other passengers suddenly stood up and started to shout. Then the boat stopped and large accumulations of water started to flow back and forth on the cabin floor.

Ian and Michael emerged from the captain's cabin with looks of grave concern. Both of them possessed mariner's certificates. Apparently the driver of the boat was not the captain and would not listen to their advice. They had forced him to stop, using the translator to explain what was transpiring back in the main cabin. Here I learned the crew had secured life jackets for themselves—apparently the only new life vests on board—and retired to the front bow ready to jump overboard at any moment. The captain (finally convinced of the severity of the problem) then jumped overboard himself, attempting to locate the leak.

Water was emerging from underneath the entryway in large amounts and several passengers started to tear away the wooden steps. A very slim passenger went down into the muck of the bilge and found the leak, a hole in the hull the size of a soccer ball, just above the waterline. He reported that all three compartments underneath the ferry were completely saturated with water.

With the captain overboard, Ian and Michael had effectively taken control of the ferry. They politely asked all passengers to remain seated in order to stabilize the boat and drain the water overboard with pumps. This is when we discovered that not only were the life vests effectively useless but there was no rear exit, there were no life rafts, all the windows were welded shut and the bilge pumps did not work. We also discovered that the hatch to the lower compartments had not been opened in many years and was rusted shut. The hatch was subsequently attacked with extreme vigor by several passengers using a hammer and chisel, and finally opened to confirm that the forward hold was completely full of water.

Roger, who had been sitting next to me and calmly reading (albeit while wearing a life vest) announced that according to his Lonely Planet guidebook there were two fast ferries that plied the waters of Tonle Sap, one of which actually ran on a somewhat regular basis; the other was known as "The Floating Coffin" for its sad state of disrepair. Evidently, from time to time, various bits and pieces like the propeller would fall off the Coffin and the crew would be required to hail passing fishing boats or call Phnom Penh for spare parts, although—unlike today—the boat didn't usually sink. Being adrift for days on the vast lake waiting for repairs was a nasty thought, but there was also the more immediate horror that we would sink to the bottom at any moment.

By now Ian and Michael had come to the conclusion that the captain was a complete idiot and an extreme danger to all aboard. They couldn't work out what was worse, the seaworthiness of the boat or his seamanship. Michael solicited several volunteers and formed a water bucket line, and soon six strong men were throwing five-gallon buckets of water overboard from the hatch, using old paint cans we rousted from the motor room. At the rate of one bucket every ten seconds, Ian estimated we were bailing approximately forty-four gallons per minute from the bilges, or several tons of water over the four hours we bailed. We finally got a small portable water pump going, and soon a steady waterfall erupted over the side of the boat.

The captain, who had refused to stop in the first place until faced with a mutiny, now decided it was time to proceed again. An announcement was made that we were heading back to Siem Reap and a huge sigh of relief went through the boat, but Michael soon produced a compass from his bag and deduced that the captain was lying. We were in fact heading south to Phnom Penh, even though the ferry was leaking like a sieve and at least fifty miles from the nearest shore. It appeared as if the captain might be thrown bodily overboard until the Cambodian translator revealed that we were exactly in the middle of the vast lake and it made just as much sense to proceed as to retreat. The captain agreed to make for the nearest point of land, and to drive at a much more relaxed pace so that we didn't take on any more water, and we crept forward.

All the time the bucket crew were bailing water the captain had been banging away with a hammer underneath the stairs, a most disconcerting sound inside a crowded metal boat, vaguely attempting to do something to repair the huge leak. Finally one of the passengers—a Russian mechanic—grabbed the captain by the throat and went down into the bilge himself, armed with a fistful of t-shirts, a rubber sandal and bits of wood pillaged from the stairs. He reported that a great deal of water was coming in, but the flow might possibly be stemmed enough to keep us afloat long enough to reach the shore if we all bailed like mad.

I took up a position in the aisle amidships, smiling at passengers from the rear of the boat as they attempted to go forward but in effect blocking the way. Michael came down the aisle occasionally, offering tidbits of news. Yes, various embassies had been notified by cell phone and perhaps a rescue craft would soon appear. Aside from one elderly couple suffering from extreme stress that was allowed up on deck, all the passengers simply sat and prayed. The hammering and bailing continued for several hours as we proceeded south. By mid-afternoon we entered the waters of the Tonle Sap River and talk turned to who could swim to shore if the boat suddenly went down.

Finally we approached a small town and a police boat came out to meet us. Conjecture was that our frantic cell phone calls to various embassies had produced results, but of what nature we could not be sure. Certainly we were going to be welcomed by the local police, who evidently wanted a brisk chat with someone or other.

Would the boat be impounded and certain people along with it? Whom, exactly? Those of us involved in the mutiny discussed what might comprise the worst possible scenario and decided it might be we buccaneers who were arrested, a simple made-in-Cambodia solution. Piracy charges perhaps? Plans were hastily discussed as to our next move.

The prospect of spending quality time discussing legalities with the local gendarmerie in the local slammer weighed heavily upon my stomach, which had already been tied in knots for several hours, so I headed directly for the loo where I did emergency business. Searching my pockets desperately for paper, all I could find was my $25 fast ferry ticket, printed on glossy paper. I made good and thorough use of the document, an appropriate gesture given the situation I thought, and tossed it down the bog. A rough day under trying circumstances to be sure, but the job's never really over until the paperwork is done.

⊰ ⊰ ⊰

Michael McCarthy is a travel writer who journeys by many forms of transport, although they seldom sink. His work can be found at www.intentional-traveler.com.

EMILY STONE

~ ~ ~

On the Occasional Importance of a Ceiling Fan

An exploration of accelerated intimacy in the U.S. Navy's former bombing range.

CYRIL WORKED AT THE SCUBA SHOP JUST UP THE ROAD from where the ferry docks in Isabel Segunda, one of the two towns on the island of Vieques, deceptively large at about the same size (and roughly the same shape) as Manhattan. The jet set can make the trip from New York in a weekend, but it had taken me days on a combination of planes, ferries, and privately-operated vans called *públicos*. And Cyril was not who I expected to meet.

"I'm not going to leave here for the next five days," I'd told Zore, the manager of the Sea Gate Guesthouse, as she led me to my room that afternoon. I needed a breeze, a beach, a view, silence. The Sea Gate was the cheapest hotel I could find, and it wasn't cheap. I'd arranged for the smallest room, just painted and still giving off fumes, and I only succeeded in knocking $5 off the nightly rate. I'd be all right, I thought, as long as I had my small luxuries—plush towels, a sexy ceiling fan.

The place was dilapidated. Cement walkways had once been painted dreary white, then institutional green, then a makeshift terracotta, and now the ground was crumbling in a way that exposed all three colors. What had once been a basketball court had become overgrown, rusty, and overrun by feral animals. What was the point of the paint job they'd given my room? It couldn't cover up the tacky threadbare linens, the ancient Venetian blinds fit for a nursing home in Florida, the bunker-like architecture. Blow the place up! I thought. Build a courtyard, let the sun in, paint the walls pink.

The beach was someplace else. The empty roads surrounding the property were forbidding. The noise of the local chickens was so obscene that it reminded me of a mockumentary I once watched about a community terrorized by a neighbor breeding roosters against regulation. As soon as Zore's tour was over, I stumbled down the road looking for a new place to stay.

"Where can I find a *público* that will take me to Esperanza?" I asked the first gringos I found, a young guy and an older woman sitting on either side of the counter in a shop, drinking beer.

"Yeah...that can be kind of tricky," the guy told me. He explained that drivers pick people up when the ferry comes in and drop them off when the ferry goes out. The rest of the time, they don't work.

He introduced himself as Cyril. While his skin seemed permanently tanned, his hair was so blond and his eyes were so clear that he looked like he might disappear into himself. He wore flip-flops, board shorts, and a shirt that seemed like an optional part of the outfit. The woman, maybe twenty years older and dressed in a similar style, was Cyril's mom. Cyril had been born in St. John, where his mom had worked as a bartender. Then they moved to Colorado, where Cyril bought and sold a couple of pieces of property before turning twenty-seven and returning to the Virgin Islands. Last year, he bought a sailboat and sailed with his girl to Vieques. After his girl left him, his mom showed up. She'd been here for six months already and she was buying a house. Yesterday, she'd bought a car.

Cyril's mom offered me a ride. She did that by way of telling Cyril that he could borrow her car to take me to Esperanza for a drink. Esperanza, the other town on Vieques, is where the gringos drink beer and eat burgers on the beach. I'd planned to stay away, but that was before I saw the Sea Gate.

"What time do you get off work?" I asked Cyril.

"Five o'clock."

It was already four o'clock, and my guess was the wait for a *público* would be more than an hour. It was a date.

Cyril's mom drove a solid car, an old Jeep that was wide open but nevertheless infested with mosquitoes (she suspected they were hatching out of somewhere near the glove compartment). "You should show her the Bravo Beach Hotel," she said to Cyril.

"Yeah," I said, "I'm looking for a place to stay. Let's go on a tour before the sun goes down."

We took a couple of turns on high-up roads with a view of the sea and parked outside the BBH, proudly the first boutique hotel on the island. After you, Cyril motioned. We found the manager, who slapped Cyril on the back and pointed out two pools, an outdoor daybed big enough for two (or three) underneath a sun umbrella, a restaurant, a sushi bar, and a chef carrying a can of coconut milk. I was about to throw caution to the trade winds and take a room there at any price, but then a breeze picked up that smelled like a bad day at the beach—gasoline and old fish.

The manager ushered us to the bar. "I'd like to buy this couple a drink," he announced.

"I'll have a Cuba Libre," I said, "with dark rum—and have you got some kind of pretzels back there?"

The anthropology student working behind the bar didn't have anything but the booze. I'd been traveling all day and hadn't eaten.

"What if we get a to-go cup and continue our tour?" Cyril asked. He had some snacks at home, he said, and he wanted to change his shirt.

Home was an estate that some Californians were building as an exclusive corporate retreat. Cyril might as well have been from California instead of St. John or Colorado. He talked more like a surfer than a sailor or a rancher: Dude...Yeah...Yeah, dude...

Cyril was stoked to be the manager of the property. But, at the moment, the property was coral floors and bare walls and no plumbing. He offered me the spare bed in the room next to his in lieu of finding another hotel room. I've put myself in many a compromising situation—some good, some bad—in exchange for a nice place to stay on my travels. If there had been running water, I might have accepted.

The only water was in the swimming pool, carved into the cliff below the balcony that held us up. Cyril flicked on the pool lights. Then he opened his fridge: white bread, ham, cheese, White Castle burgers, pretzels with nacho cheese dip made by Keebler. We held onto our drinks and watched the sunset, the pool beckoning us to come down the spiral staircase, take off our clothes and dive in.

I knew this moment—the Cuba Libres, the accelerated intimacy. On my first solo trip—to Guatemala at age twenty-three—this moment had been intimidating. It marked my introduction to a new kind of travel, a new kind of sex.

"What do you want to do now?" Cyril asked.

This kind of thing was safe, I'd taught myself, as long as you knew how and when to get out.

"Let's go to Esperanza," I said.

On the *malecón*, the boardwalk that everyone referred to by the Spanish name, we met a sailor named Jack and a drummer named Carlos. Jack lived on Cyril's boat, a green hull with black masts like a pirate ship, which was visible from where we stood. Cyril told me he gave Jack free rent because Jack had done him a favor. A guy from St. Kitts named Creation who carved coconuts on the beach told me the next day that it was because Jack had kept Cyril's boat from sinking. Cyril called Carlos "Uncle Carlos" and I started calling him "Tío Carlos," slipping in and out of the Spanish I could remember from Guatemala. Puerto Rico has an easy bilingualism that never let me embarrass myself.

"Let's go have a drink at my favorite bar," said Carlos. His favorite bar was an island grocery store where you could fill plastic cups with ice, buy a $5 bottle of rum and a $1 can of Coke, and make a round of Cuba Libres. "Do you like rum?" he asked. "I'll buy this for you."

The four of us—Carlos, Jack, Cyril, and I—sat outside with our drinks and played dominos. I don't know how to play dominos. It's about strategy, the boys told me. There are seven tiles to each number. I'm a card player, and I'm sure I could have figured out the odds if I'd set my mind to it, but I didn't want to set my mind to it. Instead, I looked steely-eyed at my opponents (really, one was my partner, but I kept forgetting which) and laid out my tiles in an entirely random fashion.

"Yeah," said the boys, "she knows what she's doing." We played and talked and drank. The boys joked and philosophized about life and sex and sailing. "You know what I mean?" they turned to me occasionally and asked. "Yeah," I said, "I know what you mean."

That's how I travel. I trade on my wits and my wit. I'd spent years of my life like this, exchanging quips that meant something entirely other than what their language suggested. "Do you know what I mean?" men would ask. And I would always answer, "Yeah, I know what you mean." The realization came kind of late that if I truly understood nothing that they said, they must not have understood anything I said either, must not have known anything about me.

From the grocery store, we continued on to a beach-front bar called Duffy's.

"Do you serve food here?" I asked.

"Yeah, sure we do."

I squinted at the blackboard menu. "How are the fish tacos?" I asked. "Where does the fish come from?"

"Boston," said the barmaid with a laugh. "It's halibut. It's good."

Another man came to join me and the domino players. He stood tall and proud, talking fast. He'd robbed a bank in some Midwestern city, he said. The police had found him, but they knew that if they put him in jail, they'd have to pay to fix up his leg. The wound was patched with skin from his ass, he announced, and bone from his hip. He rolled up his pants to show it to us, and I looked in the other direction.

Tío Carlos glanced at me. He shook his head.

"O.K.," I said.

He shook his head again. "Do you know what I mean?" Carlos asked.

I didn't know. Did he mean stay away from this guy? Or did he mean this guy is full of shit?

Either way, I'd lost interest.

Across the bar, I saw a man sitting by himself. Dark-haired, dark-eyed, sandy from the beach with several buttons undone on a shirt that he might have otherwise worn to the office, he was confident, content and reading an issue of *The New Yorker*. I was transfixed.

Cyril was getting back into the Jeep. He had to go to Al's Bar in Isabel Segunda. I'd had too many Cuba Libres. I asked if he would give me a ride home to the Sea Gate on the way. It was fun, looking for the hotel in the middle of nowhere in the dark.

"How the hell am I going to get back to Esperanza tomorrow morning?" I asked.

"I could drive you," Cyril said. "But I'd have to spend the night at your place."

I conjured up all the bluff I had. "I'm just not that kind of girl," I told him.

I think he said he respected me for not being that kind of girl. He didn't know what I meant.

What I meant was, I'm the kind of girl who will follow you around the world, I'm the kind of girl who will straddle you in the driver's seat of this car, I'm the kind of girl who grabs passion by the throat and pulls it between her legs. But that's when I feel like being in love, and I don't feel like being in love now. I just want a beach and a breeze and a view.

In the morning, I waited quietly for dawn, whose breaking had no effect on the cacophony coming from the chicken coop. I slipped out of the Sea Gate Guesthouse like a lover who neither wants to stay for coffee nor wishes to explain why he doesn't want to stay. I left a note that read: "Sorry, gone to Esperanza, all the best." (In an incredible act of foresight, I'd paid for only one night, in cash.)

I walked to the dock, waited a long time for a *público*, and finally found a nice man who offered to drop me at the *malecón* on his way to work. I took a room at the inn above Duffy's, which was more expensive than the Sea Gate but cheaper than the Bravo Beach Hotel. The walls were painted pink—and green. A ceiling fan pulsed overhead and sun-yellow curtains opened onto a balcony where I could sit and look out onto solid blue ocean, solid blue sky, reading the latest issue of *The New Yorker*.

❧ ❧ ❧

An MFA candidate and a writing instructor at the University of Pittsburgh, Emily Stone is a native New Yorker. Her work has also appeared on World Hum, where this story was first published.

❧ ❧ ❧

That's *Amore*

The hunted have now become the hunters.

"GUYS LIKE THAT ARE BETTER THAN ZOLOFT," CAROL whispers, as we clink glasses at a wine bar off the Campo dei Fiori in Rome. "I know a shrink back in New York who sends women who are suffering from low self-esteem to Italy for a month."

The guy she's referring to is a handsome Italian standing at the other end of the room, who's had his dark piercing eyes fixed on the two of us since we walked in the door. His stare washes over us, blending in with the deep rich taste of red wine, the sharp pecorino cheese, the warmth of the rustic wood tables.

I have to admit it feels darn good.

I flashback to 1976 when I was eighteen and arrived in Rome for the first time, when the flirting game was more primitive, played in the Me-Man-You-Woman-Hubba-Hubba style.

My "American Girl in Italy" experience began as soon as I stepped off the train, just as it was captured in the famous Ruth Orkin photo. There, a young woman walks in Florence while thirteen men—from a guy in a t-shirt on a Vespa to a group of older gents in suits—give her variations of the leering eye. The American Girl steels herself, looking like a frightened doe. The photo was taken in 1951, and that sweltering August back in 1976 things in Italy hadn't changed that much.

"*Signorina, signorina*," men hissed from every corner. They popped out of nowhere, grabbing their crotches, making kissing-sucking sounds, reaching out for pinches. I was fresh American meat in their jungle.

According to my Catholic upbringing this reaction was all "through my fault, through my fault, through my most grievous fault." I was supposed to be behaving and dressing with "Mary-like modesty" so my body would never be an occasion of sin to others.

I felt guilty for wearing a wraparound skirt and sleeveless top, but it was too hot for anything else. I felt guilty for lying to the men who stopped me and asked if I was lost—of course I was, but I wasn't supposed to talk to strangers...right? I felt guilty because I'd read *The Sensuous Woman* and wasn't FRIGID the worst thing a woman could be? I felt guilty because Gloria Steinem had ordered me not to be objectified—should I be kicking these guys where it hurts?

At a loss, I assumed the American Girl in Italy walk, with my mother's "don't encourage them" mantra in my head. This strategy became futile in the Forum when a man who'd been stalking me, hissing behind every pillar, finally lost control at the House of the Vestal Virgins, ran up and slung me over his shoulders in a fireman's carry, squeezing my behind like a ripe tomato. I beat on his back and hollered till he dropped me down and ran off laughing.

I brushed myself off, shaken to the core. Did that just happen to me? Me, the high school drama club geek? Me, the one who stood watching the girls with their flawless Farrah Fawcett hairdos get smooched up against their lockers by the cool guys? I scurried for my guidebook and squelched the confusion by reading about how the vestal virgins served Vesta, the Goddess of the Hearth, by keeping her flame continuously burning and maintaining a vow of chastity for thirty years.

But that moment of being airborne, pinched, and that laugh—especially that laugh—kept playing back. As if it were a grown-up game of tag and I'd just had my initiation.

Thirty years later, Italian men have refined their flirting style to an art form I rank up there with the country's many masterpieces. I've watched it evolve over many years coming here as a travel writer. It's as if they were all sat down and ordered to view Marcello Mastroianni movies, memorizing his looks and moves to perfection. Now what's in their genes, in their historical legacy from the days of Casanova, has come to full flower. Women are adored—from precious baby *principessas* to mammas and everything in between.

And who doesn't adore being adored? Having reached that certain age where attention back home is waning, here in Rome it comes at me with every encounter. The *barista* at the café brushes my hand with a smile as he passes me my morning cappuccino. I get a wink from the shopkeeper who bundles up my postcards. At dinner, a *cameriere* pulls out a chair for me whispering "*Buona sera, signora*," in a low sensuous voice, keeping a firm hand on my back.

When I get back to Los Angeles and report these flirtations to my husband, he comes back with, "Unbelievable! That stuff was beat out of us guys in the seventies. I held open a door for a woman once back then and she read me the riot act. And now with sexual harassment, I could be sued for reckless eyeballing if I turn my head toward a female for two seconds longer than I'm *supposed to* at work."

I ask him to stare at me and he gives it a try, but it just gives us both a case of the giggles. Seventeen-year marriages and the enticing mysteries of the flirting game go together like a bowl of minestrone topped with tiramisu.

So I go to Rome and play the soft, subtle version of the game, now that I've grown from *signorina* to *signora*, knowing the strategy is to not take any of it seriously. It's a harmless way to get a little lift, simply accepting being appreciated for nothing more than being a woman.

Walking along Via del Corso there's so much to admire—from the guy with the slicked-back hair and leather jacket speeding along on his moto who brings back memories of bad-boy high school heartthrobs, to the elegant men who stroll with their suit jackets slung behind them off their index fingers, displaying tempting torsos in crisp white shirts. Mix these visions with church bell gongs, gushing fountains, naked thick-rippling-muscled statues and a street violinist playing "*Besame Mucho*" and I am oh so relaxed as we catch each other's eyes.

I realize my style differs from how other American women play it when I sit with Mario, a bar owner in Positano. Suddenly, a table of women of a certain age having had one too many limoncellos zigzags by to give Mario their *buona nottes*. One of them, a bleached blonde, squeezed into white jeans with silver-studded pockets, turns to present her rear to Mario. He pats and pinches obligingly, sending her giggling away. As soon as she's out the door he rolls his eyes and throws up his hands, "American women! They don't understand the affair is an affair. The European woman, she knows, she takes care of herself. But these Americans!"

Fabio, a boatman (who looks like a darker version of our Fabio) joins in, "I'm exhausted. All summer I bring the American women from here to Capri. We have the sun, the wine...then one of them has a top off, another one a bottom off. I am a man, what can I do? But it's too much, too much—they come here, they expect!"

Back in Rome, the trend becomes even more obvious when I walk by a Piazza Navona café and see a group of females ogling a businessman in a well-tailored suit. He puts his head down, avoiding entanglement. It all adds up to the inverse of Ruth Orkin's masterpiece. Now it's The Italian Boy in Italy who's being leered at by gangs of American women.

Yikes. Is this behavior going to ruin my game? Will the barracudas with their blatant expectations scare off the *signori*? I have an urge to start a campaign to stop this trend, like the Italians did when a McDonald's was opened beneath the Spanish Steps and they started the Slow Food Movement to preserve the country's culinary culture. Their symbol is the snail, posted on all establishments that play by Slow Food rules.

I can see myself plastering Rome with graphics of the Italian Stare, setting up enclaves where none of this breed of American woman tourists can trespass, so that the delicate tradition can be preserved safely, and these men won't become an endangered species.

I finish up my glass of wine and turn to look at the staring man. He raises an eyebrow to add just the right mischievous element, as if beckoning words from the Roman poet Ovid's advice to men in the *Art of Love*: "They may cry, naughty, but they want to be overcome..."

Could he be the one who slung me over his shoulder in the Forum those many years ago?

"*Buona notte*," I say to him, as Carol and I head out the door. And as I toss my scarf over my shoulder, I realize the shock I felt thirty years ago has transformed to a flutter that whispers enchantingly: *We are men, you are women. We are alive! And what a fun game we play!*

≈ ≈ ≈

Los Angeles-based Susan Van Allen is the author of 100 Places in Italy Every Woman Should Go. *She has also written for National Public Radio's "Savvy Traveler," and "Marketplace," CNN.com, newspapers, magazines, websites, and the television show* Everybody Loves Raymond. *She travels to Italy as often as possible, to blend in with the natives, visit relatives, eat and drink well, soak up the culture, and enjoy the flirtations of those handsome Italian men.*

≈≈ ≈≈ ≈≈

Toward Stalin

Evil casts a long shadow through
the years.

WITH TWO OF OUR THREE DAYS IN GEORGIA GONE,
my girlfriend, Anya, and I sat down to dinner
at a large table holding the region's signature offerings,
wine and mineral water, to discuss where we should head
the next day. There was no confusing this place with the
confederate state. We had spent our first two days in the
capital, Tbilisi, and had been moved by the beauty of the
city's crumbling façades, many of which are bathed in
faded, pastel colors that give them great life even as they
decay, and are adorned with precariously tilted wooden
balconies that draw the eye upward to open doors that
offer the promise of a sight or sound of the exotic quotidian life within.

Now we wanted to move from city to country, to see another side of Georgian life. "We could go to Gori," Anya said. One of the men at the hotel had suggested it to us as a day trip, saying simply, "It's the birthplace of Stalin," as if it did not need further introduction or advertisement. Intrigued, and without a better plan, we decided that we would drive to Gori the next day and visit the Josef Stalin Museum, first opened in 1957, four years after his death.

The next morning, Nouri, a large, tanned man given to spontaneous chuckling and worldly philosophizing, met us at the hotel. He had agreed to be our driver for the day. I was excited to move beyond Tbilisi, but as we jumped into his station wagon, I could not shake a dark, unsettling feeling that we were doing something wrong. By my own reckoning, Stalin ranked as one of the most vicious despots of the bloodiest century the world has ever seen. Though a personal narrative was not necessary to confirm this thought, Anya was present in the front seat. A native Muscovite, her great grandfather was one of the thousands of Russian Orthodox priests who were murdered during the purges that began under Stalin in August of 1937.

As we rolled along the highway, I grew more and more disturbed by the thought of spending time and money to go to a museum dedicated to Stalin. I wondered, were one to exist, and should I find myself nearby, would I visit a museum dedicated to Hitler? The idea seemed preposterous. I thought of the conversation that Anya and I had had the night before, which concluded with our agreement that whatever else Gori was, it was a historic place, and for that, and the chance to drive through the Georgian countryside, we would go. In the light of day, our reasoning lacked the conclusiveness it possessed the night before. If they built the museum, I thought, it must pay homage to him. I looked to the front seats. Anya and Nouri were chatting away in Russian. Later I would learn that he was giving her advice about the importance of having babies. I did not understand a word of what they were saying, but realized quickly that it would not make a difference if I did. We were already half way there. Russian or not, we were headed to Gori. At the very least, I hoped the museum would contain some reference to Stalin's destructive political and economic policies, but I braced myself for the worst.

The people of Gori have a unique relationship with their native son. To many in Georgia, Stalin represents the low point of seventy years of brutal Soviet subjugation. In Gori, however, he has been celebrated. In the aftermath of independence in 1991, as Georgians around the country tore down the statues of Stalin erected under Soviet rule, hundreds of people in Gori gathered to protect the city's monument to him. Today it remains in front of City Hall, along with the museum, which includes the tiny, dilapidated house where Stalin was born, and a stretch of railroad track where Stalin's personal railway car, on which he traveled to Yalta, sits, with his bedroom and bathroom still intact, adjacent to the larger meeting room where he would, presumably, take his tea and finger maps along with political leadership as he rolled through the Soviet Union's vast holdings.

Still today, over fifty years since his death, Stalin is, even for many Gori residents who recognize his dark legacy, a source of pride. Without Stalin, Gori is like thousands of other little-known places in the world that have suffered greatly. It is a small, poor, industrial city of roughly fifty thousand people, situated in the middle of a country that has been subject to the will of outsiders almost continuously for the past four hundred years. Because of Stalin, however, Gori is on the map. People who have never set foot in Georgia know of it. And tourists spend time and money to visit it. If one focuses on the fact that Stalin was a world leader, and not on how he got to that position or what he did while there, his life can be viewed as exactly the kind of story of empowerment and success that can motivate and inspire. Many in Gori view Stalin this way, making him the greatest "local boy makes good" tale the city has ever known. As a result, Gori stands alone amidst the Caucasus as a lacuna of historical amnesia, where Stalin's most brutal actions are often minimized, explained away, or forgotten entirely, the narrative of the great rise from humble roots preserved.

Housed on the second floor of a large, two-story structure, the museum is made up of six rooms, each relating to a different era of Stalin's life. As I ascended the stairs after paying roughly $10 to enter, I was instructed by an elderly woman to proceed to the room directly before me, which holds artifacts and memorabilia concerning Stalin's early years, and which contains the only reference in the entire museum to any of the atrocities committed by him: a placard on the wall that bears a quotation from the man himself, asserting generally that though mistakes were no doubt made, as they are by everyone in every time, history would be his last judge. The rest is hagiography. A painting of young Stalin playing with his boyhood friends; a picture of

Stalin studying at the seminary he attended in Tbilisi; a
reproduction of a poem Stalin wrote as a young man that
was published in a local newspaper; a painting of Stalin
exhorting workers in the countryside; the desk Stalin
sat at inside the Kremlin; Stalin's Cuban cigars; Stalin's
favorite cigarettes; behind a glass case filled with Stalin
curios, the pocket watch that Stalin's mother gave him
as a present. In a room by itself, one of the twelve copies
of Stalin's death mask stands alone, held aloft on a white
pedestal that rises from a dark hole cut from a swath of
blood red velvet cloth that extends out a number of feet
and is enclosed in a circular, pillared structure. With
lights dimmed, the dramatic backdrop draws all attention to the spotlighted Stalin. The fat mustache immor-
talized, the cult of personality lives on.

As I walked from room to room, I grew more and
more agitated. I wanted to shout out to the old lady who
showed me into the museum, "What are you doing?
This guy was terrible for your country!" I thought of
Stalin's famous throwaway reference to his homeland,
"that small area of Russia, which calls itself Georgia." I
knew she was just working a job, trying to make a living, but someone, or body of people in Georgia, here,
or in Tbilisi, had affirmatively decided that the Stalin
museum should stand, and therefore was responsible for
an irresponsible shading of the past. The whole attitude
about Stalin seemed like a lingering case of Stockholm
syndrome, amplified by the fact that the hostage taker
had been the victim's son.

Finally, after exiting Stalin's rail car, I sat down, completely disgusted with the whole enterprise and with
myself. Why, exactly, had I waited in Stalin's rail car
bedroom for the tourist in front of me to leave Stalin's

personal bathroom, so I too could poke my head in and see the bathtub where Stalin scrubbed himself and look into the mirror that Stalin saw his own face in each morning as he brushed his hair?

From the rail car, I walked over toward Stalin's childhood house, which stands, covered by a domed Greco-Italianate pavilion, at the head of a public park. A soft, hot wind passed through the park, bending the treetops with it. A few young couples sat lazily in the shade on benches beneath trees, talking quietly. Old men and babushkas walked to and fro with purpose, but without urgency. The sun, softened only slightly by a high haze, beat down strongly, muting and slowing the scene even further as it likely does every August in Gori when the temperature rises. I looked at the house from afar, but did not attempt to enter it.

Anya and I headed back to the car and asked Nouri if he knew of a spot for lunch before our return to Tbilisi. "In Gori?" he asked rhetorically, with an air of big-city provincialism. "Agh, you're likely to be poisoned here." With that, we drove back, past the oil pipeline from Azerbaijan to the Black Sea, which snakes along the side of the road, inexpertly obscured by a man-made mound of Georgian soil. I wondered if my aversion to the Stalin museum, and my time there, would abate or grow, and whether the entire trip to Georgia would recede in my mind, taking a backseat to the many impressions I had already gathered from Russia and would continue to gather in my last three days there before heading home to Boston.

That evening, Alexander Solzhenitsyn, the famed Russian dissident who exposed the inhumanity of Stalin's repression, died in Moscow. Arrested and imprisoned himself, his works, including his Pulitzer Prize-winning book, *The Gulag Archipelago*, in which he chronicled the nightmare of the Soviet gulag system, gave voice to millions, and inspired a whole generation—in Russia and in the West—to hope. I lay transfixed on the couch in our hotel room in Tbilisi and watched CNN International and the BBC report on Solzhenitsyn's epic life. News reports indicated that he would be laid in state at the Russian Academy of Science on Tuesday, and buried the following day at Moscow's famous Donskoi cemetery after a funeral service.

"We should go," Anya said.

Having just come from a museum dedicated to Stalin, Solzhenitsyn's state ceremony seemed like both a chance for expiation and a once-in-a-lifetime opportunity for me, an outsider, to witness a historic Russian tribute to a great man on his home soil. We agreed to find out where the Russian Academy of Science was when we returned to Moscow that evening. In the afternoon, Nouri stopped by to take us to the airport. We drove through Tbilisi and it struck me again how small and impossibly beautiful it was. It is nothing like Moscow, where scale seems to have been of paramount importance in any urban planning that may have accidentally occurred in the past fifty years. In Tbilisi, as in Moscow, construction is ongoing everywhere, but, at least in the downtown area, it is relatively circumspect; new boutiques hide behind small curving roads, and in the shadows of churches that have been standing since just after the Patron Saint Nina brought Christianity to Georgia in the fourth century. Children run through the side streets, ducking in and out of corners, and often down stairs, where many basements double as shops. I knew I was romanticizing the place, but I thought that the people, devout Christians who have endured extensive suffering over the years, seemed happy. Even our guide from the first day there, whose English was terrible, and who seemed, at the time, in many ways hostile to the presence of "tourists and wealthy people," whom she constantly singled out along our walk, seemed a little less cold in hindsight. She had proudly proclaimed that she was related—distantly, but really, why quibble—to the nation's first Olympic Gold Medal winner since it split from the U.S.S.R. Apparently, the Georgians are great at judo. His medal, from 2004, hangs in a state museum for all to see.

Exiting the city, Nouri turned right onto the George W. Bush Highway, which had been rechristened in 2005 after President Bush traveled to Georgia to congratulate the country for its continued Westernization. I remembered that, on the way into the city three days before, I had asked Nouri about what looked like roses affixed to the balconies of the buildings that line the road. He had told us that the government had placed them on the balconies as a welcome to the city, and then paused, and belted out, "They've been there since Brezhnev visited!" and laughed, his enormous belly shaking and pressing up against the steering wheel of the car.

The next day, back in Moscow, Anya and I set out to see Solzhenitsyn. It was a dark, cold, gray Tuesday—as dark and cold and gray as a New England day in February—and rain poured down steadily. With an umbrella in hand, we walked through Anya's mother's neighborhood toward the metro station that had opened within the year. The "new" Russia that the world press is so fascinated by was all around. High-end cars sped by. Large machinery littered the landscape. Workmen busied themselves constructing a forest of highrises. Still, for all its newness, the neighborhood looked worn down. It resembled, more than anything else, a large-scale American housing project. Mangy stray dogs roamed; sparsely adorned playgrounds sat on patchy grass; small, portable, corrugated-tin garages crowded the streets; tired commuters stood waiting at bus stops; men huddled on stoops and drank beer from large aluminum cans. We walked on narrow concrete pathways through a maze of bleak twelve-story apartment buildings, all with balconies that offered views of the center of Moscow, which sat deep in the distance, far, far away, with thousands of apartment buildings dotting the landscape between. The shear size and number of buildings was daunting. It is indeed true. In Russia, everything is done on a grand scale.

When we arrived at the Academy of Science, Anya stopped into a kiosk and purchased a bouquet of six white chrysanthemums to lay at Solzhenitsyn's feet. She informed me that, in Russia, flowers are offered in even numbers on somber occasions, and odd numbers on celebratory ones. The Academy, too, was massive; a top-heavy, Stalinist-era, gilded, white marble building. Though I had not really known what to expect, I had imagined a certain pageantry to the affair, and long lines of mourners. The closer we got to the Academy, however, the clearer it was that, though some pageantry was present, mourners were scarce. We passed a security guard about five hundred yards from the entrance. Steel fences had been erected to control and direct the flow of people, but they contained only a sparse crawl of elderly guests, ambling slowly, many having come from the subway and holding flowers, too.

Before I knew it, I had walked past the press corps, which seemed to outnumber the line of mourners, and into the large, round marble hall where Solzhenitsyn was laid. Massive bouquets of red and white roses populated the room. The faint sound of a classical piano floated overhead. Solzhenitsyn lay in the center of the room, in an open casket framed by an enormous photograph and two members of an honor guard—one on each side of the casket—their backs ramrod straight, eyes fixed firmly on nothing before them, the butts of their rifles placed solidly on the floor. Solzhenitsyn's wife and three sons stood to the right of the casket receiving well-wishers. Not knowing Russian, and panicked that I would appear before Solzhenitsyn's wife as a dumb mute at her lowest moment of sorrow, I followed the woman in front of me and walked to the left, where I paused before the casket. Pallid and diminished by sickness, Solzhenitsyn looked smaller than I had imagined, as is often the case when those who have died from illness are viewed in the flesh. As I looked at him, he seemed further dwarfed by the large portrait just above his head. Nonetheless, he was instantly recognizable. His trademark beard, which had always run wild, giving him the look of a man ready to dissent, had been trimmed neatly, but was still iconic. His head and hair were as I remembered them from photographs, too; a bald dome surrounded by a wave of silver locks, his reticulated temple still showing through the mortician's makeup. He had been dressed in a white shirt, black-and-white tie, and black suit, which seemed appropriate to both the somber character of the day and the wretched weather outside. His hands lay neatly at his belt, completing a perfect picture of repose. Without adequate thoughts to pay respect to him, I dropped my head and nodded, as the babushka before me had done, and tried to reflect upon his courage.

Within fifteen seconds, Anya and I had both exited the hall and were quickly moved out the back door. An hour's worth of travel had led to one brief moment. I was thankful I had seen him. I was also surprised that so few others had shown. Newspapers reported the next day that the number of mourners had only amounted to "hundreds," and noted that President Dmitry Medvedev and Prime Minister Vladimir Putin had both paid their condolences, with Putin leaving the largest bouquet of flowers of the day. The press, it seemed, more than the people, were driving the national reflection on what Solzhenitsyn had meant to Russia. I ran through the potential reasons for the low turnout. It was August, so some people might have been on vacation. It was a Tuesday; many were no doubt working. The cold and rain had surely dissuaded some from going outside for any reason.

These reasons helped to explain the low numbers, but it was also clear that the sparse crowd was a measure of how far Solzhenitsyn's stature had fallen in recent years. Though revered by many older Russians, by the time of his death, a large number of people had come to view him as an old and irrelevant crank. Upon returning to Russia after the fall of the Soviet Union, Solzhenitsyn took aim at both the West, for its moral degeneracy, and the many former Soviet apparatchiks who had so easily transformed themselves into businessmen and democrats as they became fabulously wealthy when state assets were privatized through backroom deals with the Kremlin. At some point along the way, his constant criticisms began to blend into one another, forming, in the public's mind, one long rant that could be pushed to the background of Russian public discourse.

Solzhenitsyn's marginalization could not, however, be explained entirely by a generational divide or his rhetorical excess. In some ways, it had less to do with Solzhenitsyn himself and more to do with Russia's recent embrace of the power and prestige of the Soviet era, and its attempt to rehabilitate the man that Solzhenitsyn had been so critical of. After enduring years of lawlessness, poverty, crime, and diminished international influence, Russia has stabilized itself, buoyed, in part, by the high price of oil, which has helped the economy grow by an average 7 percent over the past nine years, creating a whole new set of middle-class Russians, and a superset of mind-bogglingly rich ones. Violent crime has dropped precipitously. Bribes are still commonplace, but the black market has stabilized somewhat from the 1990s, when access to free markets and opportunity was so new and intermittent that black market prices were often entirely divorced from reality. Now strong and growing, Russia's interest in calling on its grand past to guide its future is manifesting itself both publicly and privately. The Russian government has placed its imprimatur on new textbooks that indicate that Stalin was "the most successful Russian ruler of the twentieth century," who expanded the empire, built a nuclear superpower, and acted "entirely rationally" in engaging in purges of those whom he could not be sure would not turn against him. Putin, for his part, has called the collapse of the Soviet empire "the greatest geopolitical catastrophe of the century," and has presided over a movement to recast the accomplishments of the Soviet Union under Stalin in order to restore national pride.

It seems to be working. In a recent poll, over 35 percent of Russians said that they would vote for Stalin if he were still alive. In late 2006, almost 50 percent of one survey's respondents indicated that they viewed Stalin as a positive figure. In July of this year, internet voters elected Stalin to the top spot in the preliminary round of a television contest to determine the greatest Russian of all time, offering him more than 178,000 of the over 1.1 million votes cast. When I asked Anya's grandmother, whose family was persecuted under Stalin, and who suffered through the indignities of communist rule for most of her life, what she thought of the result, she scoffed, and indicated that she thought that the voting had been marred by a number of zealots who had voted over and over again. While this may be true, interest in celebrating Russia's history and recapturing its past glory is growing, leaving less and less room for those, like Solzhenitsyn, whose thoughts and works reveal the dark brutality of the Soviet system.

The day after Solzhenitsyn's burial, I touched down in Boston and learned that war between Russia and Georgia had erupted with numbing speed. Purportedly about the region of South Ossetia, and subsequently Abkhazia, too, the battle was for much more than that, and reminiscent of Stalinist-era geopolitics. Just as in 1939, when Stalin ordered Russian troops into Poland in the name of endangered Ukrainians and White Russians, whom Stalin insisted needed protection because of the destabilization wrought by Germany's attack from the west, Russia informed the world that it was advancing in Georgia to protect the interest of ethnic Russians in South Ossetia, to whom Russia had provided Russian passports, and who, Russia argued, were threatened by the hostilities between South Ossetia and Georgia.

The war, of course, concerned larger issues than the safety of a few thousand ethnically Russian South Ossetians. Facing threats of EU and NATO enlargement, the westernization and democratization of Georgia and other countries, such as Poland, Ukraine, and the Baltic States, that had, during the twentieth century, always looked east to Moscow, and the prospect of oil and natural gas running directly from Azerbaijan, through Georgia, to the Black Sea and on to Europe, where it would undercut Russia's energy dominance and greatest source of strength, the Russians sought, in a clear, confrontational way, to send a message, not only deep into the heart of Georgia—only forty miles from its capital—but also into the psyche of the West, that it is back, and that it will no longer stand for Western meddling in its "near abroad." In this sense, the war was a battle over the legacy of the Soviet Union, a counterpunch in defense of Russia's past and in aid of its rise as a power to be considered on the world stage, certainly different from its Soviet predecessor, but similarly brash, and emboldened by a strong sense of self—in other words, "the second burthen of a former child." As for Stalin, as the writer Simone Sebag Montefiore recently noted, he stands now to some as a Russian czar, "the inspiration of the authoritarian, nationalistic, and imperial strains in today's capitalistic, pragmatic, swaggering new Russia."

Soon after the Russians took Tskhinvali, the capital of South Ossetia, Russian bombs began falling on Gori, lighting the city afire, destroying many of the ubiquitous drab, concrete, Soviet-era apartment buildings that line the city's streets, killing scores of people, and sending

tens of thousands more scrambling east toward Tbilisi
for refuge. The Georgians, I learned, had set up military
installations in and around Gori, making it a target for
Russia, which was determined to push beyond South
Ossetia, further into Georgian territory. Over the next
days, I spent all of my free time reading newspaper ac-
counts of the war, searching the internet for updates, and
watching news reports about the drama that was unfold-
ing. The pictures of Gori were stark. Old women, sitting
bloodied in the street. Dazed men, shirts ripped, staring
into the distance. Buildings torn in half, flames burning,
seemingly unchecked.

While in Georgia, I had written e-mails to a few
people about my time there. In re-reading them after
war broke out, it became clear that I had described a
place that no longer exists, if it ever did. Though em-
blazoned just days before, my impressions were already
as outdated as a TV manual from the 1950s. And yet, I
felt a closeness to Georgia, and Gori in particular. It is
true that, as a first-time tourist who stayed for only a
few hours and spent most of my time on the grounds of
a museum, I hardly knew the place. At the same time,
having just been there, I knew it intimately, and was
connected, by recent experience, more than most, even
those who knew it well from years gone by.

While there, I had seen the day-to-day life that was
destroyed by war—the birds that were later scattered by
gun fire; the leaves on trees that trembled just days later
as the earth around them shook; the children who had
run in the street without a care in the world who were
later ossified by fear as bombs broke through the air.
They had all seemed exotic at the time, and yet somehow normal, too. Now, having been there and back, but

with war ongoing, they seemed less exotic to me, but hardly normal. Tbilisi, too, had changed dramatically. Gone was the sleepy feel of the pink Parliament building and the charmingly unhurried Rustaveli Avenue that ran in front of it. With the outbreak of war, the stimulants of patriotism and fear took hold. Leaders from the Baltic States and Ukraine descended on the steps of the Parliament to stand with Georgian President Mikhaïl Saakachvili and thousands of mobilized Georgian citizens. Together, they condemned Russia's actions and called for peace where shoppers and tourists had strolled days before.

Facing little Georgian resistance, the Russian troops rolled into Gori soon after the bombing. While there, they set up a security checkpoint 500 meters from the museum, which survives, though damaged slightly by the attack. Reports indicate that, having taken the city, and no longer burdened by the concern of a Georgian counterattack, Russian soldiers began to walk freely about the town, some to the gate of the museum, which, like almost every other commercial establishment in Gori at that time, was closed. Young and in a foreign land, they stood before Stalin's palazzo and snapped photographs, just as tourists had done days before, basking in a job well done, and, perhaps, admiring the leader of the once great Soviet Union—the greatest Georgian from Gori—and, for the first time since setting foot on enemy soil, finding common ground with some of those whom they had been tasked to defeat.

It was, of course, not lost on anyone with knowledge of the region that two days after Stalin's greatest critic passed away, Putin stood in the Southern Russian city of Vladikavkaz, next to the border with Georgia, and presided over the bombing of Stalin's hometown in a campaign that would have seemed very familiar to Stalin himself. It was written earlier this decade that "the sad city of Gori is everything that is wrong with Georgia today, and what is wrong with Georgia today is rooted in Stalin." Sadly, with the city only beginning its recovery, there is still truth to this statement. What is most wrong in Georgia today is war and its aftermath. No place knows this better than Gori, fifty-five years removed from the death of Stalin, and still cursed by the legacy of the son it celebrates.

❧ ❧ ❧

Gabriel O'Malley lives in Cambridge, Massachusetts. Though a lawyer by training and profession, he occasionally fails to object when leading questions are posed. His writing has appeared in The New England Journal of Public Policy, Psychology in Society, *and* Law, Democracy and Development, *among other publications.*

❧ ❧ ❧

Tiger

What fearful symmetry lay behind his gaze?

WE HUNG ON TO THE ROLL BAR OF THE OPEN Land Rover as the driver careened down the dirt track through the thick overhanging trees. Early that morning we had crossed the Rapti River, the boundary of Chitwan National Park in Nepal. We were holding a permit that allowed us to explore only until sundown. We could feel the atmosphere cooling from the heat of the day. The forest shadows were long and the sun dipping behind the jagged snow-covered Himalaya peaks. The river lay four miles ahead and it was vital that we be across it by 6 P.M. sharp.

Chitwan is one of the last tiger sanctuaries in the world, and by order of the Nepalese Army, no one is allowed in the park after dark. We were told that if you are seen in the park after the curfew time, you are assumed to be a poacher and you will be shot. It was twilight, and from the expression on our guide's face and the hard grip of our driver's hands on the steering wheel, we believed this to be no idle threat.

Over the strain of the motor I heard my daughter's voice, a whisper but clear to us all, a call that stopped the wheels of the machine in mid-rotation: "Tiger."

The driver cut the motor; now the buzz and click of the jungle insects were the only sounds. Even the birds were still. Carol stood on the back of the Rover, her finger pointing just beyond the side of the road.

We followed the direction of her hand and there, fifty feet from the path, in the long wheat-colored grass, his back to us, stood the tiger. He was a giant, about half again as big as a male lion. Solitary, he turned, now facing us, and lay his great body down. Like an illusion he disappeared, his stripes a perfect camouflage in the shadows of the forest and the long yellow grass.

We moved from the Rover, and edged to the verge of the road, not daring to go closer. I stayed toward the rear wheels, a little separate from the others who were near the front. We all strained to see, and seemed to blink in unison to try to capture what now seemed like a mirage.

The tiger raised his massive head separating his power from the passive grasses, and turned his gaze toward me, his golden eyes skimming over me, an insignificant intrusion in his world.

Then, he turned again, and studied me, then stared directly at me, into me. I could see the black slits narrow in the amber of those eyes. His body tensed and moved slightly forward, the muscles of his haunches tightened, the skin of his pelt trembled with tension. He held me there by his beauty, and an authority I cannot yet name.

I felt the others move back closer to the Rover. I could not look away from the tiger. I was defenseless, frozen in awe. My legs felt heavy, the backs of them ached, and I knew I could not run.

Unable to breathe, I waited for his decision. It was his alone. Then, the yellow eyes left me, his body relaxed, and he lowered his head. Shaking with relief and afraid to cry, I breathed deeply. We slipped back into the Rover, all silent, as we raced for the river.

I have a tiger's tooth, one that our guide presented to me, now cracked and dull, resting on my table. The tooth is curved, long and ivoried, a scimitar, once sharp and fearsome, bloodied and bared, a symbol of terror to its prey. The majesty is gone, only suggested, now just a small part of a once powerful beast.

How like the tiger's tooth I have become. Once I was strong, in control of my territory, but time has dulled and cracked me. I am a woman camouflaged by age. Younger people, strangers, unbidden, call me "Mom" or "Grandma." They look but they do not see, they cannot distinguish the tiger of my soul, the power that is mine. They glimpse only the cracked tooth on the table.

I smile and forgive them, for I have seen the tiger and he has seen me.

～ ～ ～

Patricia Dreyfus is an award-winning poet and freelance writer who was raised in Compton, California. She is too old to be eulogized as "So young and so gifted." She is the best argument for gun control laws you will ever meet, because if she had her pearl-handled derringer in her purse, some people would be in danger. She spent many years in the laundry room and kitchen in the contemplation of socks and spaghetti. Patricia has raised five outstanding children, who in turn have given her eleven perfect grandchildren. She has traveled extensively, speaks very poor Spanish, and lives in Corona del Mar, California, with her first and favorite husband, Gary.

～ε ～ε ～ε

The Empty Rocker

Lives of quiet desperation are sometimes
not what you think.

THE EMPTY ROCKING CHAIR ECHOED SLOWLY, ITS ARC
poised in mid air. The chair's body still held the
motion of another's warmer body. The seat back and
curved arms molded themselves around the memory of
the weighted flesh by whom they had been hastily abandoned. A rhythmic motion of patient waiting hung in the
air; the chair tipped in anticipation of its owner's return.

Next to it, a soft fringed lamp, still on. A passerby
could see boldly into the window, for the feigned modesty of lace valences fringing the edges were primly
tied back. A confrontational rocking chair, aggressively
empty, its full face turned to the passerby and still moving; a yellow lamp flattering the whitened glare of the
window: emptiness.

Somewhere within, the half-Indonesian prostitute Jung Li was applying her ministrations, rocking and rocking in other, more desperate arms. She flung back her head in mock abandon, then opened her eyes quickly to glance at the clock in the corner. She shut her eyes again, calculating her take. "Again," she moaned. "Again."

It was Christmas in Amsterdam. Everywhere, the naked windows revealed interiors elaborate as Russian Easter eggs: fine filigreed Christmas trees laden with delicate decorations, soft glowing light, round tables in warm-looking rooms. One expected to hear a *clavecin* playing; to see round-bellied women tightly posed, their bejeweled slender hands resting upon those of their fiancées, front vision.

I had traveled from Paris, where everyone shuttered their windows, to Holland, where apparently nobody did. But it was too deceptive, all that bluff Dutch honesty and openness. "Nothing to hide." I wondered what lay beneath.

The canals were bright, iced over, and a happy drunken jollity hung in the breath-fogged air. Strong, ruddy men gestured to me and my friend Candy as we walked together, passing the many bars that gleamed beside us, warmly wooden and gold in their interiors. "Come in, come in! Have a drink with us. Don't be afraid," they urged. "It's Christmas, after all, Happy Christmas!"

Candy waved back at them as she pressed my arm, hurrying me past. "You just won't believe the sex shops," she said. "I want you to see them."

Our breath was freezing in the freezing air and she urged me away from the wistful warmth of the pubs and toward the icy bridges spanning the canals. We were hurrying away from safe conviviality toward the seamier parts of town. "You've got to see them. You just won't believe it."

I must have looked back longingly—the Dutch men seemed so welcoming—or perhaps one in particular had caught my eye. Candy grabbed my elbow harder, impatiently hissing through her teeth, "Come on, come on. They make me sick!"

Earlier that day, after Candy had met me at the train station, we had taken a trolley toward her apartment on the outskirts of Amsterdam. The trolley trundled slowly along its icy tracks. As we sat crammed together in wet wool camaraderie, Candy suddenly insisted that I change seats with her. She gestured urgently. There was a young, blond, hearty-looking Dutch man sitting next to her, trying to make conversation with what he perceived to be a vivacious American woman. He overheard us talking. "Are you American?"

"Here," Candy grunted, getting up and shoving me into her seat. "*You* like them; *you* talk to him."

The man fell silent as I moved over into her seat. Candy, now standing in the aisle, proceeded to bounce from the strap, exclaiming as she looked out the window at the snowy scene the bus traversed. "Whoopee whoopee, look at that!" She added a few words in Dutch to impress me. "Hey, we're in Holland. Right, white girl?"

Since moving to Amsterdam from Paris, Candy had been studying Dutch. "I guess I plan to stay here," she said. She chanted her new words nonstop, repetitively showing off for me. And I was totally impressed. She seemed to relish that comic-sounding glockenspiel language. In her hyperactive way, Candy, bouncing and swaying and chanting Dutch words for "toilet" and "sausage" and "thank you" while cheerfully commenting in English on the passing snowy scene—"Colder than a witch's teat," she caroled, top voice—kept the whole trolley car entertained. The young man next to me, amused and fascinated, couldn't keep his eyes of her.

"Don't look at me," she warned him. "Look at *her*, not me."

"Men, I can't stand 'em," she muttered to me in a loud stage whisper. Impossible Candy.

Candy! How did anyone so sour get to be named something like "Candy"?

Most likely she had named herself, ironically, in defiance against the sugar of the concept. For the woman herself was vinegar-sharp, tarragon by nature, with a bite to the person, an independent tough-guy butchness concealing her generosity and vulnerability. She was small, built like a little tank, and sported denim bibbed overalls and Muslim embroidered caps.

Candy, antithesis to sweetness, was a woman who, it seemed to her friends, had completely reinvented herself. What did we know of her? She told us many stories, perhaps lies. She was the last of twenty-three children. She had been brought up by a grandmother. She had lived her whole life in orphanages. She went to college and grad school, became a psychologist, moved to Oakland, California. There, if we were to believe her, she counseled AIDS patients. Though Candy was such a nonstop talker, so agitated and energetic, so filled with hyperactive advice, that it was hard to imagine her sitting still long enough to counsel anyone, let alone someone who was dying. But perhaps someone dying would be too sick to notice their therapist bouncing from a bus strap, saying "How ya' doin'?" happily to everyone around her, and in Dutch.

Although a black belt in karate—"No motherfucker's going to get near *me*."—the 1989 earthquake in California frightened her enough that Candy resolved to sell her house in Oakland—"And it was *beautiful* honey, and I'm talkin' *millions!*"—to break with her lover of twenty years—"Girl, that's one thing I *ain't* talkin' about"—and to take her life savings and move to Paris. "The U.S. is dead. Europe is where it's happening."

Candy's older brother was the famous trumpeter Charles Stone. He'd moved to Paris, too, twenty years earlier. Now he was there permanently, buried in the cemetery Pere Lachaise. "A heart attack," Candy said. The other musicians who had known him mourned his departure, but said little. Charles was an idol, an icon, second only to Jim Morrison in the drawing power of his tombstone in this crowded City of the Dead. His grave was more famous than that of Frederic Chopin. On Sundays, groups of young black men could be seen lolling about his tombstone, passing weed from hand to hand, while the punk white American kids with shaved heads, boys and girls, with their pierced nostrils, all wearing black leather and high tops, their surprising shafts of green and red mohawks like plumage, smoked herb on Morrison's gravestone by the opposite cemetery gate. Oh Charlie! Oh Jimmy! The visiting Americans made their pilgrimages to their heroes.

So Candy came to Paris because "Charlie liked it here." Soon taken up by the musicians who revered her brother, she found a little room on the Isle St. Louis and started to study French. That's when I met her. "I'm takin' a rest from the States, honey. How 'bout yourself?"

It was a winter of driving rain. Candy turned up everywhere, making cheerful trouble wherever she went. She attended an erudite lecture on "rascism" at the Sorbonne and told me afterwards, "I was the only woman, the only black woman, the only American, the only lesbian, and the only one stoned." She was indignant. "They wouldn't even let me talk, those *men*." But of course she had talked plenty.

The next fall a friend offered her an apartment in Amsterdam and, disillusioned with Paris, Candy moved. "They've got plenty of racism there," she said optimistically as I took her to the train. "Holland is definitely where I need to be. Yup. I'm goin' to organize those motherfuckers *good*." She looked small, vulnerable, lonely despite her bravado, a person who drifted from one catastrophe to another. "Come visit me, girl." I hugged her, trying to give her energy and warmth, and promised I would.

Now here it was, Christmas break, and relieved to have a place to go, and a friend to visit, relieved that I did not have to spend Christmas alone, I kept my promise.

"These sex shops have *got* to be seen." Candy was tugging my arm, hurrying me impatiently against the freezing wind, a round squat figure in her overalls and down jacket. We passed furtive bands of men who, prowling wolves, looked over their shoulders at us, the only women out on the cold street so late. "Candy," I said nervously, trying to stall.

"Honey, these people ain't interested in *you*," Candy hissed cheerily, dragging me deeper and deeper into the seaminess of the town. "Here, get a look at *these*."

She clutched my elbow in a karate warrior's grip, hauling me to a stop in front of a store window. Embarrassed, I tried not to look, averting my eyes which were stinging and tearing in the cold. "Hey," she cried enthusiastically, "will you look at *that*! Look at the size of that dildo!" Candy was ecstatic.

"How'd you like to try *that* out, girl?" Candy regarded the window with a fascination reserved for Lourdes. "And lookie here, right next door!" She dragged me a few feet down the street.

Oh Lord, why don't the Dutch have the decency to shutter their windows? The street was festooned in yards of pink extruded plastic, enormous fleshy penises, vibrators, and huge inflated dolls with unmistakable cunts. Everything was larger than life, including the leather objects draped over the plastic models, the underwear, the corsets and chastity belts, whips and clever instruments of sexual titillation.

I turned away, unwilling to look. But Candy, talking volubly, kept trying to draw my attention to one large pink object after another. "Will you look at *that*! The *size* of it! Girl, isn't that just about one of the most beautiful things you've ever seen?"

As I waited for her on the deserted freezing Amsterdam street I wondered why I was here. It was Christmas; bloody Christmas, I was reminded through Candy's eyes that I was hopelessly white, heterosexual, and an utter prude. As Candy enthused about dildos and vibrators I would have given anything to be anywhere else, even back in Paris, alone in a small dark room, far from home and family and friends, drawing the covers over my head while every French person relaxed inside closed doors, embraced by familial warmth and delicious food and drink. I would have preferred to be walking self-consciously alone beside the freezing Seine in front of monstrous Notre Dame, looking out at innocent bridges and thinking vaguely melancholy thoughts. Candy might be American, she might seem familiar, but standing with her on Christmas eve while she went on and on about sex shop windows was the most painfully foreign experience I could imagine. A few stray men passed us, then re-crossed the cold span of bridge to pass us again, staring, challenging, all the while.

"Candy, come on," I managed to say, tugging at her padded sleeve. But she didn't seem to care. "Let's go inside," she said. "I want to get me some of those things."

"Not me," I answered quickly. "You go ahead if you want. I'll wait here."

Chortling to herself, Candy disappeared inside. I could imagine her hyperactive glee.

The moments I waited for her in the icy wind were the longest imaginable. I stood, back resolutely turned to the window display, dropping my eyes at the aggressive looks of the men who passed and avoiding the occasional lone man who dared to accost me. What to do? I was trapped between the warmth and vulgarity of the sex shop interior, and the wait beside a frozen canal, my feet blocks of ice, at a prostitute pick-up stop that no prostitute would ever choose on a cold Christmas night like this one. I faced outward, feeling my face freeze disapprovingly, a prudish intellectual bluestocking from Boston, Massachusetts, and told myself that this was an interesting travel experience, one that I would never have had to endure had I comfortably stayed home. I wish: my adventurousness had once again gotten me into trouble.

Candy emerged, stuffing a package into her pack.
"Come along," she said, "I got someone I want you to
meet." She was humming as she walked, our footsteps
squeaking on the thin layer of ice crystals that lay sparkling under the street lamps. On the canals, tethered
barges strained against their ropes and groaned in the
frosty air. "I'm dreamin' of a White Christmas," Candy
hummed. She was pleased with herself. It was almost
two in the morning and from various parts of the city
church bells started to peal. "A White Christmas...."

"You know, girl," she interrupted herself, "if you
hadn't come up here to visit I'd *never* be walking around
like this." I was surprised. "Well, I had this breakdown
in Paris after Suzy threw me over. Too much, after
the earthquake back home and all. A real breakdown,
honey. I knew it was coming. All those sick people, my
friends, dying of AIDS. Yes siree, dying like flies in
old Candy's arms. I just couldn't take it anymore." By
now she was humming, whistling through her teeth,
and talking, all at the same time. "White Christmas..."
She poked me for emphasis. "Bet you didn't know that
did you? About my nervous breakdown, I mean. Why
honey, by the time I came up here to Amsterdam I was
so bad I couldn't leave the apartment by myself. Just
couldn't get out, couldn't see anyone, didn't want them
looking at me, see. Not enough black people up here.
Everybody stares." Her isolation had lasted over three
months, she told me.

Three months. I calculated quickly; from her arrival
just up to my visit. "Come on, Candy," I protested, "it
can't have been that bad."

But by now Candy was humming again and whistling and saying "Hey sport" and "Merry Christmas" in

Dutch to whatever lonely guy we passed, also looking
for a bit of Christmas cheer.

Now we stood side by side in front of a window on
the street of prostitutes. An empty room, a rocker still
moving. "They're the lucky ones. Jung Li works here.
Some of the other girls, I got to know them, too." Many
little houses, many softly lit, barred windows like the inside of a chocolate box. What lay behind the visible part
of this town, I wondered.

"AIDS," said Candy. "This town is full of AIDS." She
was surprisingly silent, watching and waiting. "Lousy
with it. They bring these girls out here and then they
just dump them," she said. "These men. They come here
as workers and then they bring their women and then
they can't support them. What can they do?"

The fragile figure that was Jung Li came to the window. She looked severe and pretended to ignore Candy
and myself as we stood outside.

"Watch her," Candy breathed excitedly. "She'll pretend
not to notice us. They lose their jobs if they move."

The woman placed herself carefully in the rocking
chair whose embrace surrounded her as if she were
home. A quick furtive rearrangement of a strand of
hair, one ankle crossing the other: now the woman,
the tableau, was stilled. Jung Li folded her hands upon
each other and stared into the dark, somewhere far
beyond us.

"It's supposed to be legal here," Candy said. "They
pay off the police. They get medical inspections
every week."

Not wanting to offend the prostitute by my too direct stare, I allowed the whole street to enter my vision.
The street was full of naked windows, with women

waiting motionless in Flemish interiors. Fat women, thin women, women in all shades of color and costume. Women who looked at us with hard aggressive eyes. Women who did not even twitch. I could see their weariness, their bad skin, malnourished collarbones, could smell the perspiration from all their stale toil.

"Well, what else can they do? They're stuck here, working on their backs. And these are the lucky ones. The others, the ones whose johns don't pay enough, they have to work outside." She took my arm, walking me away from this section of town, then waved a passing taxi to a standstill.

The women were motionless, holding themselves as much like embroidered dolls as possible, receding as we pulled away from them.

"They had a conference about AIDS and sex workers," Candy told me. By now we were back in her apartment, warming our hands around mugs of steaming tea, our frozen garments unstiffening themselves on the backs of chairs.

"You want to sleep in my bed?" she asked abruptly. "Or do you want your own mattress on the floor?"

I was thawing out, looking out the window, admiring her view of frozen trees that loomed darkly beyond the kitchen. The dark had a purplish light to it: not really early morning, but instead that headachy three A.M. glaze when one is too nervous and cold to get to sleep.

"O.K., the mattress," said Candy, not waiting for my answer.

I lay down on the mattress, fully clothed, not even taking off my boots, and pulled her down sleeping bag over me. Would I ever get warm?

"Want some music?" Candy turned on the radio full volume. "Want some hashish?"

"No, just to sleep now."

Candy took out a corncob pipe from the drawer, tamped it down, and stuffed it with weed. "I got my suppliers," she winked. "You can get anything you want here. *Anything*. We'll go get some more tomorrow."

"Candy, I really need to sleep, It's been a long day." Apologetically.

"Well, honey, don't mind me. I never sleep." Candy settled herself into her rocking chair and sucked contentedly on her pipe. The radio blared full volume and I lay at her feet, pulling the sleeping bag over my ears.

"Listen," she said, turning the radio up further. "Christmas carols!" The song "Silent Night" in Dutch paradoxically shattered the air. "Ain't that somethin'?" Candy said, smoking. She shook her head. "Holland!"

"You know..." she continued dreamily. The hash was slowing her down. "They aren't allowed to use condoms, those whores. Well, they're supposed to, but if they do, the men beat them. Won't have anything to do with them. And if the girls insist, the hotels and bars won't let them work there either."

"But don't they know they might get sick?" I was sleepily trying to carry on my side of the conversation now that Candy seemed to be slowing down enough to actually *have* one.

"Of course. But what can they do? Those whores need work as much as anyone else. They know to use those safes, but the johns will just go to somebody else."

I drifted to sleep as Candy was telling that in her opinion a man and woman together was the most disgusting and sexually exploitative arrangement known to the human race. The creeping warmth of the sleeping bag, the inevitability of her words, and the *creak, creak* of the rocker as she sat there smoking and talking somehow soothed me.

It was a restless sleep. I'd never in my life slept through a radio so loud, and I woke from time to time in the cold dark thinking of the women forced to screw without condoms, knowing all along they were bound to get sick, the police "protection," the medical exams not picking up disease until it was too late—a whole refugee nation of women brought to and abandoned in Western Europe with no skills and no future. The rocking chair tipped and muttered in the dark and when I briefly opened my eyes and shut them I could still see the glowing bowl of Candy's corncob pipe as she inhaled, could hear her humming, could make out her stocky overalled figure and her little embroidered cap.

I woke finally with a splitting headache and the sense of not having had enough sleep, to a gray sodden northern European light that managed to leak through the windows from the park outside, insinuating dirt and grime in its wake. That light, even thinking about European light in winter, gave me a migraine. It was late morning and I remembered that it was indeed Christmas, the darkest most depressing day of a winter calendar full of despondent moments. Christmas!

In their smug well-lit homes the Dutch were no doubt being jolly in a red-cheeked Santa sort of way. I thought of my family back home in the Untied States and then was quickly, piercingly grateful that I had escaped the burden of creating enforced jollity by choosing to be miserable and lonely in Europe instead. But I hadn't escaped the headache.

Stirring a bit, pressing my exploding temple, I noticed Candy. Now in a long white nightgown, her feet tucked under her, the corncob pipe still in her mouth, she was sitting and smoking reflectively on the edge of my mattress, watching me wake up.

I closed my eyes again. "What time is it?" I asked. I wanted to ask: "How long have you been sitting there watching me?" but didn't.

Instead of answering, Candy puffed on her pipe, looking exactly like Mammy Yokum in *Li'l Abner*. She took the pipe out of her mouth. "Want some?"

I shook my head.

"You know, girl," she said, "you are the first *white* woman and the first *straight* woman I have ever let stay at my apartment." This in the tone of conferring a great honor.

Although I am white, I may be more bent than Candy was aware of, but I was not about to shatter her moment of magnanimous tolerance. "Awful white of you to let me stay here," I murmured, and took her hand. She cackled.

"Merry Christmas, honey," she said, and thumped her backpack onto my feet, drawing from it a large suspicious package. "Have I got a Christmas present for *you*."

"Oh no!" I remembered the sex shop of the night before. Candy smiled wickedly. I drew the stiff pink thing out of its tissue paper wrappings. "No, Candy!" I had brought her a pair of delicate filigreed pearl earrings as my Christmas present to her.

"Girl, girl, don't knock it till you've tried it." She handed me the pipe full of glowing hash, its odor sickly sweet in the room.

A huge Christmas mother-longing overcame me, and I wanted to put my throbbing head down onto her wide lap and have her rub my temples.

"You know," she said, pensively, "I went to a meeting of those whores we saw last night. They were trying to organize themselves. How do you get a john to use a condom? One of them demonstrated how to put it on so the man doesn't even know that's what you're doing. You practice maybe three months with your teeth, putting safes on cucumbers, till you can do it in your sleep. Imagine that."

Her voice trailed off. We spent a quiet Christmas. We were careful around each other, gentle with differences.

How was anyone to know that six months later, Candy would be dead. Heart attack, some said, or drugs, or high blood pressure. Whatever the reason, she lay three days in her Amsterdam flat before anyone found her. Did she call for help in English? In Dutch? Smoking her weed alone, so far from home?

⚜ ⚜ ⚜

Kathleen Spivack is the author of six books of prose and poetry. Her most recent book is The Moments of Past Happiness. *Essays have appeared in the* Atlantic Monthly, Kenyon Review, The Harvard Review, *the* Virginia Quarterly, The Massachusetts Review, North American Review, *and in many anthologies, including several of the Best Travel Writing collections. She is currently working on a personal literary memoir about Robert Lowell and his circle: Sexton, Bishop, Plath, etc. She teaches in Boston and in Paris.*

Papa's Ghost

The writer catches a last glimpse of what was.

I HAD HEARD RUMORS OF HEMINGWAY'S GHOST APPEAR-
ing from time to time around Paris, Key West, and
even Oak Park, Illinois. For a long time I had the notion
of being the first writer to record the great man's spec-
ter in Cuba—a kingly phantom on the ramparts of El
Morro Castle. As the drawbridge of diplomacy creaked
down and I was at last granted permission to travel to
the workers' paradise, I made a pilgrimage to the island
haunts of my literary idol.

Perhaps there, walking the same cobblestones, gazing at the same sunsets, falling through the same holes
in the sidewalk as the master, I would find, to quote
Hamlet's father, a "spirit, doomed for a certain term to
walk the night."

~~

Hemingway fell in love with Cuba when he first went there during a 1932 fishing trip with his buddy Joe Russell, owner of Sloppy Joe's Bar in Key West, Florida. From Russell's cabin cruiser Hemingway caught nineteen marlin and three sailfish and was, well, hooked.

Two years later he bought his own boat, *Pilar*, and over the next several years popped over to the big island when the spirit moved him, which—given the deteriorating state of his marriage to second wife, Pauline—was more and more frequently. When not on the water, he stayed at the five-story Hotel Ambos Mundos, near Havana harbor.

In 1939, Hemingway's girlfriend, writer Martha Gellhorn, visiting Cuba for the first time, persuaded Hemingway to abandon his bachelor quarters at the hotel and rent a home. She found, and he rented, Finca Vigía—Lookout Farm—fifteen miles from central Havana. In 1940 he divorced Pauline, married Martha, and bought the farm, so to speak.

For the next two decades he lived in the house overlooking the countryside. When he wasn't entertaining celebrities, getting wasted, writing masterpieces and duds, he and his first mate and blood amigo, Gregorio Fuentes, would set sail on his beloved *Pilar* from the nearby fishing village of Cojimar to hunt marlin and, sometimes, submarines. In the mid-1940s, outfitting *Pilar* with armaments, they prowled the Caribbean for German U-boats—which, thankfully for literature—they never encountered.

In 1960 he left Finca Vigía and Cuba for the last time, without packing much. Some offer that as proof that he

intended to return when things settled down there, but
an Idaho shotgun had other plans.

In Old Havana, swaggering distance from my hotel,
El Floridita restaurant pulses like a matador's heartbeat,
its huge neon sign visible, I suspect, from Pamplona. It is
a clean, though not well-lighted, place, noisy, crowded,
and upscale. Despite this being a country where pesos are
less valuable than toilet paper, where the one is no doubt
used for the other, at Floridita you'll find white-linen
tablecloths, candlelight, a menu to rival the trendiest
bistros in South Beach, and, as in every other venue in
which Hemingway lived, ate, drank, or relieved himself,
plenty of photographs of Papa and his entourage: Gary
Cooper, Spencer Tracy, Ingrid Bergman. Hemingway,
whose attitude toward trendy was the same as a ham-
merhead's toward chum, would not have approved. But
then, of course, there are the Floridita's daiquiris: Hem
proclaimed them the best in the world. And he was a
man who knew his cocktails.

Squeeze past the beautiful *señores* and *señoritas* and
belly up to the runway-length mahogany bar where, on
its far left, you can catch a glimpse of the great man's
favorite stool, enshrined behind a velvet rope. My reaction was, like his favorite cocktail, mixed. On the one
hand, my breath came up short as I gazed at the very
leather on which the maestro hatched some of his most
famous fiction and infamous grudges. On the other, I
felt like telling him to do the world a favor and quit
pickling his brain.

Nevertheless, I ordered a daiquiri—reputedly of
the same formula as in my hero's time—and braced
myself for ghostly nirvana. The drink wasn't bad, but

apparitions evidently did not get clearance to land. So I ordered another and another still, staring at the master's chair until, amoeba-like, the ivory-colored leather seat doubled and doubled again. If this was where Papa's spirit hung out, the old man's protoplasm must have been fishing, because the only specters that materialized were my own retinal floaters, drifting across my blurry corneas. All right, it was only my first night and it was a big town. Banshees had to be lurking somewhere, and in the meantime I got to take home three nifty El Floridita cocktail stirrers. Perhaps Papa's poltergeist turned in early these days. He was, after all, 102.

The next morning, I ate a hearty breakfast of some-thing-or-other with ham (in Cuba you cannot eat without involving pig parts; not a pork lover, I forti-fied myself by remembering that Hemingway not only would have eaten the oinker, he would have shot it—in that order). Then I wound my way through the nar-row, cobblestone, canyon-holed streets of Old Havana, past peeing dogs, cigar-smoking *señoras*, and enterpris-ing urchins wanting money for "milk." Once-grand buildings had weathered to the color and consistency of matzo, their arabesque façades dripping with corbels and laundry, their amputated fountains hidden in dreary courtyards pulsing with state-sponsored TV—slouched and faded beauties whose insides were rotting, the way nightly rum eventually rots your guts.

On tapeworm-thin Empedrado Street, I found La Bodeguita del Medio and would have walked right past the narrow storefront had it not been for the clot of fellow pilgrims posing beneath the hand-painted sign for photos of themselves in front of this other famous Hemingway watering hole.

I decided that here, unlike the Floridita fern bar, is where a ghost of true grit would hang out. Here you read the daily specials, which apparently had not changed in years, on a wall, not a damn menu. In this sardine-packed bar, every centimeter of wood is carved with someone's initials or death threat. There is so much beer on the floor, locals come just to preserve their shoe leather. This was, and still is, Hemingway's kind of bar, where each trip to the men's room brings an exponential increase in the risk of emphysema, and the toilet is broken in any case, so you make do with what you have. Yes, del Medio is where I would find my elusive wraith.

"Mojito?" the bartender asked, and before I could answer, he was crushing a mint branch into a glass. Maybe my Banana Republic journalist's vest with pen in every pocket was a giveaway. Never mind, the mojito—rum, lime, sparkling water, lots of sugar, dash of bitters, and aforementioned fresh mint— felt as refreshing as a summer cloudburst. Hemingway is said to have claimed, "My mojito in La Bodeguita, my daiquiri in El Floridita." Judging by the working-class crowd, pestling me against a photograph of Papa and sailfish, this is where I was most likely to find the phantom of the ever-raucous Ernesto.

Unfortunately, though, unlike the earth for Robert Jordan and Maria in *For Whom the Bell Tolls*, other-worldly dimensions did not move for me. Nary a quiver.

All right, it *was* the middle of the day. Metaphysically or not, Hemingway had to write sometime. And I knew exactly where. Off I weaved, several sidewalk-canyons-of-death up the street, to the bustling Ambos Mundos, Papa's home-away-from-Pauline, at the wide, sunny corner of Mercaderes and Obispo.

In the premier corner of this renovated five-story Spanish-colonial beauty, a lovely young docent motioned me into Room 511. The small room was like any hotel overnighter, except that it had once been occupied by the greatest American literary talent of the twentieth century. There were a couple of things you don't normally find in a Motel 6: an Underwood typewriter under glass, a guest book, and obligatory wall photos of Papa and Fidel.

No ghost, though. On his taut-sheeted bed no crater betrayed an invisible man, as it had in the movie starring Claude Raines. At the open window, I gazed over rooftops of the sunlit, shadowed city and squinted at El Morro's tower, trying to imagine Papa's ghost, head in hands, pacing its catwalk. But the only scary vision was a tubby tourist smoking an oversized cigar.

It occurred to me that, as Hemingway had first come to Cuba to escape the tumult of notoriety, perhaps now his incorporeal self had decided to ditch the noise and hubbub of Havana. If so, surely it was to retire in seclusion at his tranquil Finca Vigía. Who's to say phantoms don't appreciate their peace and quiet like the rest of us? Maybe for Hemingway's ghost, it was a weekend-weekday thing.

The next morning dawned gray, dismal, and gloomy, just the right chill, drizzle, and fog to invoke the supernatural. I took a taxi, a 1955 Buick, to Hemingway's hilltop home, fifteen miles from downtown Havana. After paying an admission fee at the gated entrance, my driver chugged up a quarter-mile, tree-lined driveway to let me off at front stairs as wide and white as the writer himself.

At the top of the stairs, a vacuous-eyed young docent welcomed us to Museo Hemingway. She had made her spiel a thousand times, and it showed: *Can't go inside. No flash photographs. Exactly as the writer left the house in 1960. Wrote* For Whom the Bell Tolls, The Old Man and the Sea, *and other famous stories here. Entertained many Hollywood stars and starlets. Recorded his daily weight next to the scale on the bathroom wall.* Pilar *on exhibit around back. When he left he donated the house and boat to the Revolution.*

Say what?

"Donated the house to the People's Revolution," she repeated with a straight face.

The house is a one-story, off-white, stucco villa, not very big—about two-thousand square feet, if you don't count the imposing tower, La Torre Bianca, that Papa's fourth wife, Mary, built for him to write in and that, apparently, he couldn't write in (maybe the view was a distraction).

The claim that the house was exactly the way the Hemingways had left it the day he "donated it to the Revolution" didn't ring entirely true. The whole deal looked pretty staged to me. On his bed lay his fishing cap; shotgun shells stood at attention on his desk; bullfight paintings lined his walls; half-filled Campari bottles decorated nearly every room, as did the heads of the African beasts to whom Papa had just-a-little-too-generously given "the gift of death." (The disembodied trophies had actually been brought in when they turned the house into a museum. I'm guessing a lot of Papa's books—reputedly 9,000—were, too. No one man could read all those, not even in the days before cable TV. You can either entertain Hollywood starlets or you can read, but you cannot, ahem, do both.)

In turn I stared at Hemingway's desk chair, his bed, his sofa, his toilet seat, trying my best to conjure a vaporous,

grizzled hulk. But as in downtown Havana, no appari-
tion made itself known.

I followed a slippery, moss-covered, inclined path
past the empty swimming pool, past the graves of
Hemingway's favorite dogs, to a covered, fenced-off
pen, where *Pilar* was waiting stoically for her sailor—or
his deathly shadow—to return. A little irritated now at
my hero's absence, I bribed the guard to let me climb
over the barrier and into Hemingway's fighting chair. I
knew Papa wouldn't take kindly to this sacrilege, but I
was in a sacrilegious mood. Perhaps he'd reveal himself
to box my ears. When the only vision-from-beyond was
the guard tucking my dollar into his guayabera, I strode
back to the house, stuck my camera through the bathroom window, and took a flash picture of the wall on
which Hemingway had recorded his soaring weight.

On my way back to town, I began to wonder if one of
the infamous Hemingway grudges included the whole
damn city of Havana.

Maybe if Fidel had given the Campari to the peasants,
if he had distributed those 9,000 books to libraries across
the land, if he had converted Finca Vigía into a neighborhood clinic, it would not have been so bad. But the
truth is, although the writer had welcomed the flushing
of Batista's filth off the island, Hemingway, son of Oak
Park Republicans, was about as keen on communism as
a bull is keen on picadors. That his property, which he
"donated to the Revolution" in the same sense that a bull
donates his ear, would now be laid out like the stucco
equivalent of Lenin's corpse; that his beloved boat would
be plattered like a stuffed pig for public consumption,
must have been galling. That the virile young writer-

sportsman so full of optimism in Paris in the 1920s had ended up having his ballooning weight visible to any gawker for the price of admission, must have been, to a wandering but proud soul, insufferable.

As funked out as Hemingway had been after reading the reviews of *Across the River and Into the Trees*, I wasn't expecting much, spook-wise, when, the next day, I visited Cojimar, the home of Papa's friend and *Pilar*'s first mate, Gregorio Fuentes—amazingly, still alive at 104. Keen on my new insight, I now had reason to suspect that my hero's ghost no more haunted the fishing village than it had bedeviled Havana. Still, I had come this far...

Gregorio Fuentes came to Cuba at the age of eight when he was orphaned on a ship on which his father, a Spaniard, had been a cook. He first met Hemingway in the early 1930s while escorting *Pilar* through Cojimar harbor in his own boat. The macho writer and the rugged boatman hit it off right away. Hemingway saw something of himself, perhaps, in the Canary Islander's penchant for riding out hurricanes at sea, in his love of cigars, rum, and *señoritas*. Gregorio told his new friend, "Don't worry, whenever you're in Cuba, I'll take care of you." And for the next two decades he did, accompanying the writer on hundreds of fishing trips as helper and confidant. On land they hung out together in local tavernas, exchanging tales of adventure.

Cubans believed—and still do—that in *The Old Man and the Sea* Hemingway pretty much just transcribed one of Gregorio's stories. The writer, always eager to find a slight, must have bristled at this impugning of his creative power. In truth, although Hemingway was dissipated by the mid-1950s, this last great work, which helped him win the Nobel Prize in 1953, could have been written by no genius, pickled or otherwise, but himself. Still, the rumors must have stung.

After Hemingway's suicide in 1961, Fuentes and Cojimar faded into obscurity. Then, in the 1990s, when Americans started returning in dribs and drabs, Papa's favorite Cojimar bar, the seaside La Terraza, spruced itself up, hung plenty of photos of you-know-who, and gave Gregorio his own table (and free meals and rum) from which to regale customers with stories of Hemingway Past.

By then Fuentes was firmly established, by tradition and economic necessity, if not fact, as the certified model for the fictional fisherman, Santiago. To anyone who would listen, it was now Gregorio himself who had gone too far out to sea, Fuentes who had caught the magnificent marlin, Fuentes who had futilely thrashed at the marauding shark. For an extra dollar or two, you could take your picture with the true and authentic old man of the sea.

Even after Gregorio became wheelchair-bound with cancer, cranky and reticent—perhaps it was painful to speak—one family member or another would wheel him into his living room to greet, nod at, shake hands, and take pictures with busloads of tourists. Payment was not required but appreciated. One certainly could be excused for having the feeling that his family, with no argument from the state, was propping the old guy up. It's a wonder they didn't strap a tin cup to the chair.

To a man like Hemingway, after a lifetime of lip service to dignity, there surely would have been something unseemly about his old friend, far beyond a serviceable existence, being wheeled out to meet motor coaches and shake hands for a buck.

As I trudged up a hill to find his house, I wondered how Gregorio could have strayed so far from macho grace. Call me old fashioned, but I believe that after a certain age—say, oh, 101—if you know with reasonable certainty that you're never going to open a topless table-dancing club in Vegas, it is entirely within your rights and possibly your duty to excuse yourself from the next HavanaTur bus, retire to the bedroom, get comfortable, and will your heart to stop.

In searching for his home, I was struck by how the vil-lage—a string of cottages hanging like tarnished pearls down the coastal road—had not changed from the old photographs on La Terraza's walls. It was as though someone had turned off a giant switch in 1960 and had yet to flick it back on—a village and city and nation sus-pended in time, an ancient insect fossilized in amber.

Up a side street I found the small, one-story bunga-low with teal trim and clay-tile roof that matched the bartender's description. When I knocked, I half-hoped no one would answer. A moment later, though, a mus-tachioed man of about forty came to the door.

"I'm a writer," I said, realizing how stupid it sounded.

The door opened wide. "Yes, yes, come in. There have been no visitors for a while. I am his grandson. Wait here. I will bring him."

The living room was clean and uncluttered. On one wall hung a paint-by-numbers-grade painting of Gregorio and Papa. On the floor stood a swordfish sword carved with fishing scenes. The carpeting was sculpted and olive, like my grandmother's in the mid-1960s. All that was missing was a swag lamp.

"Here he is," said my host, as he wheeled in his shrunken grandfather.

It's tempting to say that, like Hemingway's Santiago, "Everything about him was old except his eyes and they were the same color as the sea and were cheerful and undefeated," but it would be a lie.

Gregorio was shriveled and rumpled and dazed and miserable-looking—folds of jaundiced, mottled skin hanging on a bent and brittle frame. His ears, which had not shrunken with the rest of him, drooped like beagle ears. His eyes, nearly shut with skin flaps, were not in the same solar system as cheerful. The back of his hands were black with moles. His head hung at an unnatural angle, much too heavy, not worth the effort. Tumors clung to him like mushrooms to a tree stump, sucking out the last of its nutrients. On the left side of his neck a four-inch bandage partially fell away, revealing a huge bleeding knob.

I wondered what more Gregorio wanted from this earth. Papa would not have thought much of the freak show either.

"I told him you're a writer," the younger man said.

"From...Illinois," I stuttered, not knowing what else to say.

The ancient mariner awoke from his far-off dream. The light caught the slits of his eyes. *"Como?"* he muttered, perking up a little.

"A writer from Illinois," his grandson repeated in Spanish, letting the old man read his lips.

Gregorio raised his head, held it straight, dignity trying to inject itself into his dissolving spine. He held out his hand, and I took it, not prepared for its strength.

Even after his grandson took our picture, the old man would not let go of my hand. His eyes open wide now, the folds of skin willed aside, he gazed into my soul and said, in a deep, strong voice: "Ernesto?"

I glanced at the grandson, who seemed as perplexed as I was.

I turned back to the old man. After another long beat, I whispered, "Sí. Ernesto."

"You came back," Gregorio said in faltering English. "You came back," he muttered, releasing my hand and falling once more into his waking dream. But as the younger man wheeled him back into the shadows, Gregorio's smile remained.

When the grandson returned, he seemed a little unsettled. "That was strange, no?" he asked with an embarrassed laugh. "He thought you were someone else." He looked me over. "That has never happened before." Again, a nervous laugh. "You don't resemble Señor Hemingway at all."

No, I do not. I am short and thin. I do not fish. I boxed in high school but did not like it much. I get seasick. I've never shot a living thing and hope I never will. Alcohol upsets my stomach, and the only military combat I ever engaged in was on my computer. I've been married only once, to an unfathomable woman who rules my roost, and I never won a single literary prize. My hair is still brown, I've never grown a beard, and none of my prose has ever excited the imagination of my poker group, let alone the Nobel Prize committee.

No, it's not easy to mistake *me* for you-know-who.

But for some strange reason, that withered, tumored, weary-beyond-endurance old man, who even at the impossible age of 104 was still waiting for God-knows-what to call it a day, thought he saw something in a certain visitor, possibly his last on earth, that Cojimar afternoon, something that brightened him for a moment—a phantom, a ghost, a memory—before he lapsed again into his dream.

A clear case of mistaken identity.

The next morning the old man did not wake up. But he waited a few more days to die. Perhaps he spent that time, impenetrable to visitors, savoring the memory of the reunion for which he had waited so long.

We writers are an insecure lot, searching for validation where we can, roaming ramparts for the spirits of dead idols who might assure us that we're not fakes. So it's tempting for me to make something profound and self-assuring out of the old fisherman mistaking me for the greatest writer of the twentieth century.

But the truest sentence I can write is that one old man with longevity in his veins lived to the point of dementia. He might well have mistaken a broom for Hemingway, or me for a broom. He would have died on that day whether I was in Cojimar, Cuba, or Mundelein, Illinois.

When someone once asked Papa what Pauline died of, he reputedly said, "She just died, that's all, like everyone else, and now she's dead." No pussyfooting with profundity in this joint, pal.

Still, as I look over the photos of my pilgrimage—me in *Pilar*'s fighting chair, me sitting at Papa's table at La Terraza, me crouching next to Hemingway's old man as he breathed his final breaths—it's easy to forget, for a little while at least, that there are no such things as ghosts.

꙳ ꙳ ꙳

Gary Buslik doesn't have the faintest idea how to make an honest living. When he wrote for travel magazines, he discovered that by tossing around insincere promises he could get hotels and restaurants to give him free rooms and meals and so managed to forge a useless profession into a rewarding lifestyle. These days he writes novels, short stories, and essays and, in case the government should ask any questions, teaches literature and creative writing at the University of Illinois at Chicago—which isn't quite an honest living, but you work with what you have. He windsurfs and plays softball. He does not play golf. You can visit him at www.arottenperson.com, but please do not ask him to play golf. It will just irritate him. He is the author of A Rotten Person Travels the Caribbean, *from which this piece was excerpted. If you'd like to see a photo of Buslik with Fuentes, possibly the last ever taken of Hemingway's "Old Man," e-mail Gary at: arottenperson@earthlink.net.*

❧ ❧ ❧

Shopping for Dirndls

Such mysteries abound in clothing and the minds of women.

"JILLY, LOOK AT THIS ONE," MY FRIEND SIMONE SAYS, stroking the fabric of a pale, pink dress. We've just entered a weird little Viennese storefront and I'm having a Laura Ashley flashback circa 1973.

"Oh, my friend, I don't know," I say. There's something about the rose shade that reminds me of a doll I had when I was four.

Simone has planned this day for months, ever since I first visited Austria to work on my master's thesis. She is insisting that if I am to attend the Jaeger Ball in Vienna, I must wear the required *trachten* attire, which, much to my horror, resembles the getup on the St. Pauli Girl beer label.

This quaint establishment, located in Vienna's fashionable First District, is regarded as one of the finest dirndl shops in Vienna. I cannot even pronounce the name properly. "Dern dull," I say without rolling the "r" in that sexy way my Austrian friend says it.

"O.K., start trying some on," Simone prods. I get the impression by her crossed-arm stance this whole dirndl selection process should take about ten minutes.

Suddenly, amidst the cotton and chintz, a flashback hits me: I'm twelve, shopping for my first junior high prom dress. Ah, that memorable night where nobody asked me to dance and I burst into tears when my dad picked me up afterwards. I shoved that tear-stained peasant dress with the ivory lace trim in the back of my closet, damned for eternity.

There are countless dresses wedged onto rack after rack. Each dress looks more juvenile than the next. *Oh, here's one with embroidered farm animals and cowbells. Great, I'll tinkle as I walk. That'll come in handy should I go missing at the ball.*

These dresses come in a myriad of colors, mostly pastels and muted tones. Being American, when I think "evening wear," I think "little black dress." By comparison, some dirndls have vertical stripes that remind me of pajamas with feet. Some have decorative bows or tacked-on appliqué. *Are they kidding me? This is what a grown woman wears to the Jaeger Ball?*

I envisioned the traditional attire would be more classy and sophisticated. I pictured Empress Elisabeth's famous portrait donning that ethereal white gown, how she wore those sparkly stars in her long mane of chestnut brown hair. Where were *those* dresses? The

Jaeger Ball is held in the Hofburg *Palace* for God's sake, not a barn.

Overwhelmed by the choices, I struggle to slide the dresses along the clothes rack. *Does it even matter which one I choose? I'm going to look stupid no matter what.*

"Jilly! What color apron do you want?" Simone asks sensing my hesitation.

Apron?

"I think maybe I just won't wear the apron," I say. Her face drops. Without realizing it I've insulted my friend's cultural fashion tradition. It was as if I'd asked the *Sex and the City* girls to go barefoot to a cocktail party. And if the apron reference isn't bad enough, I keep referring to the dirndl as a *costume*—until my friend finally snaps back, clinging to a mannequin's green plaid skirt, "*This* is an elegant dress, not a *costume!*"

I try to save face. "I think I want to wear a *red* apron," I say.

"Oooh," she reacts smiling again. "The color of *danger*."

Yes, I am in danger here. Danger of paying the equivalent of a laptop computer for some traditional Austrian garb I'll probably wear once. I just can't see it. When I think "ball gown," I think "Red Carpet Fabulous" not the wardrobe from *The Sound of Music.*

When I show Simone the black dresses I've chosen, she looks at me like I've just announced an interest in transgender surgery—but I stand my ground, determined not to give in to anything resembling an Easter egg or a Scottish kilt.

A portly sales woman waddles over with a forced grin. Simone takes over and soon she's speaking in German, probably telling the woman I'm an American virgin dirndl shopper and to please excuse my ignorance.

There's nothing worse than being under or over-
dressed for a big night out. And, even though I may not
be Austrian, I feel intrigued by these odd dresses. It sud
denly occurred to me that which color I chose could set
me apart at the ball. This was my moment to create the
perfect Americanized version of the dirndl.

I gather up a few dresses and enter the dressing room.
Simone hands me a slip and a blouse over the door and
says, "Don't forget these."

I am aghast by the blouse's white puffed sleeves with
billows the size of eggplants. I put it on. *I'm wearing
Raggedy Ann's bra.*

Next, I step into the white cotton slip. The bottom is
jagged with thick, white lace. The reveal has to be just
right to peek out from under the dress's hemline the
exact length, I'm told. This is much harder work than
I'd anticipated. Most American evening gowns are one
piece. The dirndl is four separate garments: the bodice,
the blouse, the slip, and the apron.

I'm drawn to a black dress that has tiny embroidered
flowers in pink and red around the surprisingly low
neckline. The workmanship displays painstaking effort.
I throw the heavy garment over my head and begin
fastening the hooks and eyes that connect the bodice
together. My waistline increases in mere seconds, en-
gulfed by the massive folds of material that gather up
the waist.

"Is this right?" I gasp. Surely I need a larger size.
Can't breathe.

I fashion the apron around what once was my waistline. I've even remembered to tie the apron's bow to the
left to alert the men at the ball I am single. (If you're
married, the bow goes on the right.) As I step out of the

dressing room the sales woman immediately instructs me to bend over, making strange gestures with her hands. Seeing that I am baffled by what she's asking of me, the sales woman moves toward me and places her plump fingers underneath my chest and hoists my breasts upward. She's not shy about readjusting my girls to spill out even more than they already are atop the corset of pain.

I glance down and see unfamiliar cleavage.

"Fabelhaft!"—*fabulous!*—Simone shouts, knowing it's the only German word I know apart from a couple of cuss words. My C cups have transformed into double Ds. I cannot stop staring at my own chest. I grab hold of my apron, twirling around singing, "I am sixteen, going on seventeen." Simone and the woman laugh hysterically.

I finally understand the allure of these dresses. The dirndl is the peasant version of the naughty schoolgirl outfit: youthful, innocent, with just a hint of easy bar-maid. I'm guessing not many Austrian girls choose this color combination, but I like the sharp contrast. I want to wear it out of the store. I feel like yodeling.

Tomorrow night at the ball, I'll play their Austrian game.

～ ～ ～

Jill Paris is currently a graduate student at the University of Southern California in the Master of Professional Writing program. She holds an MA in Humanities and has taught at the university level. Her writing has appeared in In the Mist, Galavanting, *and in the Style section of* Los Angeles *magazine. Her personal motto is: Live, Laugh, Love, Drink, Travel.*

ROLF POTTS

Up Cambodia without a Phrasebook

Communication doesn't require language—
but it sure helps.

I AM FIFTEEN MINUTES INTO MY HIKE DOWN THE MUDDY little stream when a tree carving captures my attention. Sticky with sap and arcing brown across the bark, it seems to have been made recently.

I drop to my haunches and run my fingers over the design. After three days of living in the Indochinese outback without electricity or running water, I feel like my senses have been sharpened to the details of the landscape. I take a step back for perspective, and my mind suddenly goes blank.

The carving is a crude depiction of a skull and crossbones.

223

Were I any place else in the world, I might be able to write off the skull and crossbones as a morbid adolescent prank. Unfortunately, since I am in northwestern Cambodia, the ghoulish symbol can mean only one thing: land mines. Suddenly convinced that everything in my immediate vicinity is about to erupt into a fury of fire and shrapnel, I freeze.

My brain slowly starts to track again, but I can't pinpoint a plan of action. If this were a tornado, I'd lie face down in a low-lying area. Were this an earthquake, I'd run to an open space away from trees and buildings. Were this a hurricane, I'd pack up my worldly possessions and drive to South Dakota. But since I am in a manmade disaster zone, all I can think to do is nothing.

My thoughts drift to a random quote from a United Nations official a few years back, who was expressing his frustration in trying to clear the Cambodian countryside of hundreds of thousands of unmarked and unmapped mines. "Cambodia's mines will be cleared," he'd quipped fatalistically, "by people walking on them."

As gingerly as possible, I lower myself to the ground, resolved to sit here until I can formulate a course of action that won't result in blowing myself up.

For the past decade, northwestern Cambodia has been home primarily to subsistence farmers, U.N. de-mining experts, and holdout factions of the genocidal Khmer Rouge army. Except for travelers headed overland from the Thai border to the monuments of Angkor Wat, nobody ever visits this part of the country.

If someone were to walk up right now and ask me why I'm here, who I'm staying with, and how I got to this corner of the Cambodian boondocks, I could tell them truthfully that I do not exactly know.

Technically, I was invited to come here by Boon, a friendly young Cambodian who shared a train seat with me from Bangkok to the border three days ago. Our third seatmate, a Thai guy who called himself Jay, knew enough English for the three of us to exchange a few pleasantries along the way. Our conversation never amounted to much, but as we got off the train at the Thai border town of Aranyaprathet, Boon asked through Jay if I was interested in staying with him and his family once we got to Cambodia. Eager to explore a part of Cambodia that had been a notorious Khmer Rouge stronghold only six months ago, I accepted.

Jay parted ways with us at the train station, and that was the last time I had any real clue as to what was going on.

Perhaps if I hadn't forgotten my Southeast Asian phrasebook in Bangkok, I would have a better idea of what was happening. Unfortunately, due to a moment of hurried absent-mindedness shortly before my departure to Aranyaprathet, I left my phrasebook languishing on top of a toilet-paper dispenser in the Bangkok train station. Thus, my communication with Boon has been limited to a few words of Lao (which has many phrases in common with Thai, Boon's second language) that I still remember from a recent journey down the Laotian Mekong.

My *Lonely Planet: Southeast Asia* guide also provides a handful of Khmer words; unfortunately, phrases such as "I want a room with a bathtub" and "I'm allergic to penicillin" only go so far when your hosts live in a one-room house without running water.

As a result, trying to understand the events of the last three days has been like trying to appreciate a Bengali sitcom: I can figure out the basics of what's going on, but most everything else is lost in a haze of unfamiliar context and language. In a way, this is kind of nice, since I have no social expectations here. Whereas in an American home I would feel obliged to maintain a certain level of conversation and decorum, here I can wander off and flop into a hammock at any given moment, and my hosts will just laugh and go back to whatever it was they were doing. At times I feel more like a shipwrecked sailor than a personal guest.

The majority of my stay here in Cambodia has been at Boon's mother's house, in a country village called Opasat. Boon's wife and baby daughter also live here, as well as a half-dozen other people of varying age, whose relation to Boon I have not yet figured out.

My first morning in Opasat, Boon took me around and introduced me to almost everyone in his neighborhood. I don't remember a single name or nuance from the experience—but everyone remembers me because I kept banging my head on the bottom of people's houses, which stand on stilts about six feet off the ground. Now I can't walk from Boon's house to the town center without someone seizing me by the arm and dragging me over to show some new relative how I'm tall enough to brain myself on their bungalow.

After five minutes of paranoid inaction in front of the skull and crossbones tree, I hear the sounds of children's voices coming my way. I look up to see a half-dozen little sun-browned village kids strung out along the stream bank. Suddenly concerned for their safety, I leap to my feet and try to wave them off.

Unfortunately, my gesticulations only make the kids break into a dead sprint in my direction. I realize that the kids think I am playing a game I invented yesterday, called "Karate Man."

The rules behind Karate Man are simple: I stand in one spot looking scary, and as many kids as possible run up and try to tackle me. If the kids can't budge me after a few seconds, I begin to peel them off my legs and toss them aside, bellowing (in my best cartoon villain voice) "I am Karate Man! Nobody can stop Karate Man!" Caught up in the exaggerated silliness of the game, the kids tumble and backpedal their way twenty or so feet across the dirt when I throw them off. Then they come back for more. It's a fun way to pass the time, and it's much less awkward than trying to talk to the adults.

At this moment, however, I'm in no mood to be surrounded by a field of exploding Cambodian children. "No!" I yell desperately. "No Karate Man!"

"Kanati-maan!" the kids shriek back, never breaking stride.

As the kids charge me, I clutch them to me one by one, and we sink to the ground in a heap. Convinced that they have just vanquished Karate Man, the children break into a cheer.

I stand them up, dust them off, then make them march me back the way they came. Thinking this is part of the game, the kids take the task very seriously. We walk in single file, the kids doing their best to mimic my sober demeanor. Nobody blows up. By the time the buildings of the village are in view, I begin to relax again.

Once I arrive back at Boon's house, one of the kids is immediately dispatched for a sarong. This, I have learned, is the signal that it's time for me to take a bath.

I've already bathed once today, but my hosts seem to think it's time for me to bathe again. This could have something to do with the fact that I'm sweaty and dusty from the hike, but I suspect that my hosts just want an excuse to watch me take my clothes off.

Since there is no running water at Boon's house, all the bathing and washing is done next to a small pond out back. The first time I was hustled out to take a bath, I didn't realize that it would be such a social undertaking. By the time I'd stripped down to my shorts, a crowd of about ten people had gathered to watch me. Since I'd never paid much attention to how country folks bathe in this part of the world, I wasn't quite sure what to do next. I figured it would be a bad idea to strip completely naked, so I waded into the pond in my shorts. A gleeful roar went up from the peanut gallery, and a couple of kids ran down to pull me out of the murky water.

In the time since then, I have learned that I am supposed to wrap a sarong around my waist for modesty, and bring buckets of water up from the pond to bathe. Since I have very white skin, my Cambodian friends watch this ritual with great curiosity. My most enthusiastic fan is a wrinkled old neighbor woman who is given to poking and prodding me with a sense of primatological fascination that would rival Jane Goodall. When Boon took me over to visit her house two mornings ago, she sat me down on her porch, yanked off my sandals, and pulled on my toes and stroked my legs for about five minutes. At first I thought she was some sort of massage therapist, until she showed up at my bath this morning and started pulling at the hair on my nipples.

This afternoon, Old Lady Goodall manages to outdo herself. As I am toweling off under a tree, she strides up and starts to run her fingers over my chest and shoulders, like I'm some sort of sacred statue from Angkor Wat. If this woman were forty years younger and had a few more teeth, it might be a rather erotic experience; instead, it's just kind of strange. Then, without warning, Madame Goodall leans in and licks the soft white flesh above my hipbone. Comically, furrowing her brow, she turns and makes a wisecrack to Boon's mother, who erupts into laughter.

I can only assume this means I'm not quite as tasty as she'd expected.

By nightfall, I know something is amiss. Usually, my hosts have prepared and served dinner by early evening, and we have cleaned up and are playing with the baby (the primary form of nighttime entertainment, since there are no electric lights) by dark. But this evening there is no mention of dinner, and a group of a dozen young men from the neighborhood have gathered at Boon's place. They gesture at me and laugh, talking in loud voices. I laugh along with them, but as usual I have no idea what's going on. For all I know they're discussing different ways to marinate my liver.

About an hour after sundown, Boon indicates that it's time to go. I get up to leave, but I can't find my sandals. After a bit of sign language, a search party is formed. Since my size-13 sandals are about twice as big as any other footwear in the village, it doesn't take long to track them down. One of the neighbors, a white-haired old man who Boon introduces as Mr. Cham, has been flopping around in my Tevas. Mr. Cham looks to be about

sixty, and he's wearing a black Bon Jovi t-shirt. When
Boon tells him that he has to give me my sandals back,
Mr. Cham looks as if he might burst into tears.

Finally ready, I hike to the village *wat* with Boon and
the other young men. The *wat* is filled with revelers, and
has all the trappings of an American country fair. Dunk
tanks and dart-tosses are set up all along the perimeter,
and concession tables selling cola, beer, noodle soup, and
fresh fruit dot the courtyard. A fenced-in dancing ring has
been constructed around the tallest tree in the *wat*, and a
sound system blasts traditional and disco dance tunes.

Boon nods at me and sweeps his hand at the courtyard. "Chaul Chnam," he says. "Khmer Songkhran."

Songkhran is the Thai New Year celebration, so I
gather that Chaul Chnam marks the Khmer New Year.
As with Thai kids at Songkhran, Cambodian children
run roughshod over the Chaul Chnam celebration,
throwing buckets of water and pasting each others' faces
with white chalk powder.

I suspect that Boon's young male friends have brought
me to Chaul Chnam so they can use me to meet girls, but
I am surrounded by little kids before we have a chance
to do any tomcatting. Apparently, my reputation as
Karate Man has spread, and now I can't walk anywhere
without a gaggle of Cambodian kids trying to tackle me.
Not up for a night of getting mobbed like a rock star (or,
more accurately, a cast member of *Sesame Street Live*),
I manage to neutralize the children by shaking hands
with them in the manner of a charismatic politician.
Since I can only shake hands with one kid at a time, this
slows things down a bit.

Boon ultimately rescues me by taking me to a folding
table, where he introduces me to a fierce-looking man

called Mr. Song. Mr. Song has opted not to wear a shirt to the Chaul Chnam festivities; his chest is laced with indigo tattoos and his arms are roped with taut muscles. He looks to be in his forties, which inevitably means that he has seen some guerrilla combat over the years. Given our location, I wouldn't be at all surprised if he served his time in Khmer Rouge ranks. When I buy the first round of Tiger lager, Mr. Song is my buddy for the rest of the evening.

Although I am tempted to jump into the dance ring and take a shot at doing the graceful Khmer *aspara*, I end up holding court at the table for the next three hours. When Boon leaves to dance with his wife, Mr. Song becomes master of ceremonies, introducing me to each person who walks by the table. Everyone I meet tries to make a sincere personal impression, but it's impossible to know what anyone is trying to communicate. One man pulls out a faded color photograph of a middle-aged Cambodian couple decked out in 1980s American casual-wear. The back of the photo reads: "Apple Valley, California." Another man spends twenty minutes trying to teach me how to count to ten in Khmer. Each time I attempt to show off my new linguistic skills, I can't get past five before everyone is doubled-over laughing at my pronunciation.

It comes as a kind of relief when the generator suddenly breaks down, cutting off the music in mid-beat and leaving the *wat* dark.

On the way back to the neighborhood, Boon pantomimes that Mr. Song wants me to sleep with his family. Once we arrive at his house, Mr. Song lights some oil lamps, drags out an automobile battery and hooks it up to a Sony boom box. After a few minutes of tuning, we listen to a faint Muzak rendering of "El Condor Pasa" on a Thai radio station. This quickly bores Mr. Song, and he walks over to the corner and puts the radio away.

He returns carrying a pair of AK-47 assault rifles and four banana clips of ammunition. Motioning me over, he sits on the floor and begins to show me how the guns work. Three of the clips, he indicates, have a thirty-round capacity, and the fourth holds forty bullets. In what I assume is a gesture of hospitality, Mr. Song jams the forty-round clip into one of the rifles and hands it to me. I get a quick lesson on how to prime the first round, and how to switch the rifle to full automatic fire.

Mr. Song doesn't appear to realize that this is a doomed enterprise. Unless we are attacked tonight by Martians, or intruders who wear crisp white t-shirts that read SHOOT ME, I won't have the slightest idea how to distinguish a bandit from a neighbor. For good measure—and not wanting to sully his macho mood—I hand Mr. Song my camera, and indicate that I want him to take a picture of me with the AK-47. From the way he holds my camera, I can only conclude that this is the first photo he's ever taken.

When I finally fall asleep, I dream that I am renting videos from a convenience store in outer space.

Not wanting to overstay my welcome, and largely exhausted by my local-celebrity status, I tell Boon of my intention to leave Opasat the following morning. Boon indicates that he understands, and sends for a motor-cycle taxi to take me to the overland-truck depot in the city of Sisophon.

To show my appreciation for all the hospitality, I give Boon's mother a $20 bill—figuring that she will know how to split it up among deserving parties. As soon as the money leaves my hand, I see Mr. Cham run off toward his house. When he returns, he is carrying a travel bag, and he's traded his Bon Jovi shirt for a purple polo top and a brown porkpie hat. Boon confers with him for a moment, then apologetically indicates that Mr. Cham wants me to take him from Sisophon to Angkor Wat. Not wanting to seem ungrateful, I shrug my consent.

When the motorcycle taxi arrives, I make my rounds and say my goodbyes. I save Boon for last. "Thanks, Boon," I say in English. "I wish I could tell you how much I appreciate all this." He can't understand me, of course, but he returns my pleasantry by bringing his hands together in a traditional Khmer bow. I give him a hug, knowing that I will probably never know why he invited me to come and see his family, or even what he does for a living.

I get onto the motorcycle between the driver and the eccentric Mr. Cham, and we take off in a flourish of dust. Opasat disappears behind me in a matter of minutes, and my thoughts move on to the sundry details of finding an overland truck and fulfilling my tourist agenda at Angkor Wat.

I am still not exactly sure what has just happened to me, but I know that I rather enjoyed it.

This will not stop me, however, from buying a new phrasebook the moment I see one for sale.

※ ※ ※

Rolf Potts is the author of Marco Polo Didn't Go There: Stories and Revelations from One Decade as a Postmodern Travel Writer, *from which this piece was adapted, and* Vagabonding:

An Uncommon Guide to the Art of Long-Term World Travel. *The former Salon.com columnist is best known for promoting the ethic of vagabonding—a way of living that makes extended, personally meaningful travel possible. His work has appeared in* The New York Times Magazine, National Geographic Traveler, The Best American Travel Writing, *several Travelers' Tales books, and on National Public Radio. Visit his web site at www.rolfpotts.com.*

DAVID GRANT

~≈ ~≈ ~≈

I Hold High My Beautiful, Luminous Qur'an

How do kids in a West African village manage to "get krunk" with each other in a Muslim culture that doesn't allow dating, or even holding hands?

I N MID-NOVEMBER, 2006, MY COUSIN DAVID Agbemabiese and I visited Ghana's Mole National Park. My agenda for this first trip to Ghana had been unbelievably rich and deep, so this expedition up to a game preserve in the savannah of the far, Muslim north had been only tentatively penciled in…something I'd try to pull off if it didn't interfere with my primary business. I was here in Ghana because, through DNA-based gene-alogical research, I had just recently found and connected with the African family from whom my father's line had been separated since slavery—a very big deal, indeed.

And I had just dived head first into the writing of both a weekly blog and a book about the experience.

This fantastic bit of serendipity had turned my first, long-anticipated trip to Africa into something even more special and emotional than I had ever dreamed. I had found a large group of blood relatives here in Ghana, separated from my family in the U.S. by an ocean and about three hundred years of history. And they were anxious to meet me and see, if after all this time and distance, there was anything at all about us that might still make us identifiable to one another as family. We had discovered to our surprise, joy and delight, that yes, indeed, there was. Incredibly, strong physical resemblances had survived; shared interests; attitudes; a dozen different little recognizable traits of family character. Amazing. And there was *so much* family to meet. Patriarch John Kofi Agbemabiese had, over his long, successful and highly interesting time on earth, sired forty-one children with seven wives. I spent a couple of very intense weeks being escorted around the ancestral Volta region, Accra, and Kumasi, getting introduced by one group of relatives to another. In between, I stole time to write, and occasionally, to be a tourist too.

My cousin David had recently lost his job. When another relative told him of my desire to visit Mole Park, he'd jumped at the chance to accompany me. I was paying, and he had the time. "We don't do enough internal travel," he said. "We have so much beauty here, but we Ghanaians, we hardly ever get the chance to see and enjoy our own country." Travel in west Africa—even in a country like Ghana with much better than average infrastructure—is hard. And it's not cheap, in a society where the economy just limps along and almost everyone is chronically underpaid.

Mole had held a special allure for me, ever since I first read about it in the process of preparing for this trip. I'd loved every minute of my time on the coast, the hill country; the rain forest. But so much of my long-imagined Africa had always been about the savannah, too—the land of baobab trees, mud houses, and mud mosques; the Sahel region at the edge of the great Sahara—the home of magical, mythical towns like Timbuktu and Djenne. And the *other* savannah; the home of big game and the safari. Mole is one of the only places in all of west Africa where visitors can have that quintessential *east* African experience of close encounters with some of the big, endangered animals with which Africa is forever linked in the popular imagination. And this is a place where you don't need to rent a guide and an expensive four-wheel-drive vehicle to see the park and its animal life. At Mole, as at some parks in east Africa, you can do your safari as part of a small group led by a ranger, *on foot*. You can also explore some of the park's miles of trails by rented bike. The prospect was much too good to resist.

The hotel at Mole is nice. Clean, sunny rooms, but no frills, and the water is only on for a few hours each day. But it's safe to drink. And there's a pool. And a decent restaurant with a bar. And just down from the pool, there's an observation deck, perched in a perfect position for guests to sit and watch the action at the two watering holes on the wild, species-rich savannah below the escarpment on which the hotel sits.

That next morning, just after sunrise, David and I enjoyed a three-hour hike with park ranger John, and

a very pleasant retired German couple enjoying their
second holiday of the year. Our "safari" didn't disap-
point. We got close...almost too close, to elephants and
crocodiles. We were treated to close-up encounters with
three different species of antelope and numerous species
of birds. And later in the day, a mere stone's throw from
our hotel door, we watched dozens of baboons and wart-
hogs, as well as green and patas monkeys, go about their
daily business as if we weren't even there at all. Great
stuff. I shot a lot of photos and video.

But the most memorable part of our stay happened
during the night hours, when all kinds of activity is
going on in the park, invisible to all but those who have
a great hidden perch and night-vision glasses. David
and I lamented the fact that we didn't have these. But
fortunately for us, these are not necessary for night
people watching.

Early that evening, a staff person made the announcement that at 6:30 there'd be a graduation ceremony just
up the hill in the park rangers' quarters for several new
rangers, and that any guests who wanted to come were
very welcome. As soon as we heard, David and I knew
we were going. We wanted to support the new rangers,
just out of principle. In a region where few good jobs are
available, these are good jobs. And local guys like these
new graduates are precisely the ones who have the best
chance at convincing old friends, family, and neighbors
not to poach on park grounds; to participate in making
this area safer for all the endangered animals and more
tourist-friendly at the same time.

I had another reason for wanting to come. The music
of this region has always spoken to me in a special way.
My CD collection at home is full of the Islamic-flavored

music of the Sahel: Salif Keita, Thione Seck, Ba Cissoko, Oumou Sangare, Ali Farka Toure, Sekouba Bambino, and Issa Bagayoyo, among others. Wandering through the rangers' quarters that afternoon, I'd heard intriguing bits and pieces of northern pop music in the air: the music kids were dancing to while they played, blaring from radios their mothers had placed in windows so they could listen while hanging laundry; wafting out from kitchen doorways while they began work on the evening meal. It was wonderful—melodic, complex, flute- and voice-driven, with rolling base lines and undulating percussion underneath—and I wanted to hear more. And since every African party is a dance party, I was pretty sure that tonight, at the graduation, I'd get my wish.

When the announced start time of 6:30 rolled around, David and I were the first guests from the hotel to arrive...the *only* guests for a while. We watched as a couple of local women turned up, matronly, but like butterflies in their brightly colored party best. As they got the punch bowl and some refreshments arranged on a side table, the DJ set up his turntables and his soundboard, fiddling endlessly with the mix on the microphones that would soon be used for speeches. He started messing around with the speaker mix for the music, and the four nervous ranger graduates got up to shake off their growing anxiety about soon being the center of attention by dancing with one another—tentatively at first, but then with more energy. Soon, a few kids from the rangers' quarters turned up and began to dance too, around the edges of the outdoor employees' canteen where the festivities were being held. Before long, they were joined by a growing number of kids who came by bike, on foot, and by motorbike from the nearby town of Larabanga, and other smaller villages a little farther up the road. A couple of young European backpackers had wandered up there by now as well, but other than David and I, they were the only ones who'd responded to the repeated entreaties to come join the party that had been broadcast down to the hotel over the P.A. system.

An official from the park leaned over the table to speak to the DJ, and within moments, the music came to a crashing halt. Without further ado, the formal program began. It was brief. The four graduates received their diplomas to much applause. Then the music was cranked back up, but this time, it was serious. Now that the obligatory speeches and ceremony were done, it was time to dance.

David excused himself, reminding me not to stay too long because we had to get up well before the sun to catch a 4 A.M. bus into Tamale the next morning. I said I'd be along soon, but I'd been anxious to hear some more of this music, and now, here it was.

The dancing, which had been confined, except for the graduates, to the outside perimeter of the open-air canteen area, now took over the entire space. Anyone who's ever been to Africa will tell you, there's no such thing as a wallflower at a party. Even non-dancers with their amateur anthropologist hats on like me will eventually have to get up and dance. In my case, it was young Latif who called me out. He'd seen me smiling at him and some of the other youth as they warmed up to take the floor, and they'd been curious about where I was from. After I gave them a good laugh with my spirited but Cosby-esque gyrations on the floor, we talked—shouted at each other—over the booming, compelling sounds of the pop music of their native land.

It was a big deal to them that I was from the U.S. Huge. When they asked me about my work and I told them I'm a writer, mostly a screenwriter and playwright, they got *really* pumped. Now, the excited, rapid-fire inquiries were all about who I know. "Damn," they were thinking, "Brotherman must know all *kinds* of incredible people we've heard of." I hemmed and hawed...and it hurt me to watch creeping disappointment suddenly dull the bright, expectant sparkle that had lit up all their faces just moments before. I was losing major cool points by the millisecond. I rattled off a few people they might know, before the well ran pretty dry. I had to dig deep for stories from friends and associates who have at least been *in the same room* with some of the people they've heard of. This did the trick. Very quickly, joy returned because, just like that, the huge space between them and the epicenter of all things cool had shrunk considerably, and they were basking in the glow of how it suddenly felt to be a mere two degrees of separation from Tupac, Snoop, Jay-Z, J-Lo and Oprah.

As my official host, my new friend Latif had just scored major cool points too, and I could see it in his eyes as he drank in their admiration—especially the awed expressions of the girls on the periphery of the action here. An already pretty good party was suddenly much fuller of intriguing possibilities for him. He spoke mostly in rapid fire Dagbani, but the sense of it was easy enough to understand. "See, I told you he was cool," he was saying.

And as I scanned their beautiful, sparkling faces, it hit me like a ton of bricks—about a third or more of the people gathered there were female, but so far, between the graduates, the emcee, the DJ, and the dancers, it had been an *all-male* show. The grown women had been in the background applauding the speeches, serving food, watching the kids. But in the dark fringes of this outdoor café turned party room, they had literally become invisible now. And the girls—all in *hijab*; all in colorful party clothes—they'd hung together in a pack, in their own space out on the edge of things, their eyes on the boys they knew, watching their moves, tittering back and forth with each other about them like birds on a wire.

Suddenly, my eye caught something else that turned my attention entirely away from them. Into the party walked a lanky youth whose t-shirt sported a very familiar face.

Back in Accra, I'd seen several sidewalk stalls that silk-screen images onto plain white "Ts" for you. It seemed to be the same basic choices everywhere. You could get white Jesus, brown Jesus, Nelson Mandela, Bob Marley or, interestingly, Osama Bin Laden. I'd been thinking, if I had a spur of the moment opportunity, that I'd buy that brown Jesus. No lame, schlocky t-shirt Jesus, he, with his deep, beautiful eyes. And he wasn't merely the white Jesus, but tinted brown, either. He had his own face; his own impressively deep persona. So...brown Jesus, Nelson Mandela and Bob Marley, I was thinking. One of them for me; the others for gifts. I'd had yet to actually see anybody sporting one of these shirts, so ubiquitous at the street stalls. But now here came Osama, big as life, rippling like a limp flag on the chest of this gangly, dust-covered kid from the village.

Before he could advance even a few steps from the entryway, Latif shot like a bolt to his side and pushed him up against the fence. I was alarmed. I stood up to see what was going on back there where almost no light managed to seep over from the dance floor and the area around the refreshment table. But it didn't feel like a fight. Nobody back there seemed to feel it was necessary to separate them. All I knew for sure was that Latif was speaking to him very urgently about something, then gesturing back towards me. And then I watched Osama remove his shirt, turn it inside out, and put it back on. Latif seemed satisfied and returned to the area near where I'd been sitting. Now I understood. Latif was looking out for me. He hadn't wanted me to feel offended by the sight of a local kid sporting a Bin Laden t-shirt.

I caught Osama's eye and called him over. Now, in the light, I could see something that I'd only caught a tiny glimmer of when I'd first spotted him in the near darkness of the entryway. It was the way he moved. It wasn't just the awkward gangliness of an adolescent who hasn't quite grown into his suddenly larger frame yet. He seemed to me now an oddity of nature—someone whose every joint is not merely double, but entirely elastic—a rubber man. As he approached, I smiled broadly at him. "Hey, kid, your t-shirt's on inside out. That the new style or something?" He grinned sheepishly and looked down at his feet. "I saw you have Osama on your shirt." He looked confused. "Osama...Bin Laden. I saw you have his picture on your shirt." Latif spit some terse words at him in Dagbani. "Oh," said Osama. "The shirt. You saw."

"Yeah, I saw. You a big Bin Laden fan?"

Osama shrugged. "He fight for Islam."

"Hmmm. Well, there's all kinds of ways to stand up for your faith without killing folks, don't you think?"

He nodded slowly, his eyes never rising to meet mine.

"And him and his kind, they don't like music and dancing, you know? If they ran this town, they'd never allow it."

He looked a little sheepish and shrugged. I got it. I wasn't going to break this kid's balls over his damned t-shirt. It occurred to me that for kids in this part of the world, wearing a portrait of Bin Laden on your chest *might* mean you want the world to know he's your personal hero, but I'd bet my last dollar that for most, it's probably much more about wearing a big "F.U." on your chest...a way, like anywhere else on earth, for a kid to wave the flag of rebel youth in the face of every adult who crosses his path, the point being to offend or piss off as many people as possible. Osama was no heavily-politicized young jihadi. He was just a kid who likes to dance, looking for a little action on a Friday night in a place where there's generally little action to be found.

"You like to dance, huh?"

For the first time, he gave me his eyes, and they sparkled. "That's why I'm here."

"Let's see your moves then," I said. "Let's see what you're all about."

He cracked a wry grin. "Let's see yours first."

"I already did mine," I said. "You missed it."

Latif backed me up. "He was funny."

The DJ was into a furious mix now; wonderful stuff; and the crowd was eating it up, girls in their corner and the guys in theirs—parallel universes—a guys' party and a girls' party, sharing the same space, but, at least on the surface, only tentatively connected to and aware of each other. Yet all were dancing, on fire, to the same relentless, throbbing beat.

Watching them made me think of other kids in other places on earth on this Friday night, eagerly looking, even within the mannered confines of a well-chaperoned dance, for the hot, electric thrill only a little proximity with the opposite sex can give.

From time immemorial, when men and women have partnered up to dance, dance has been a metaphor—a meditation in motion—encompassing every aspect of our relationship with one another: communication, both spoken and unspoken; nurture; longing and desire; sex. The European tradition is full of slow, courtly dances which leave a lot to the imagination. Subtlety is the point. Boys and girls taught to dance in this tradition learn, literally, to turn slow, cautious circles around each other as they take their first baby steps toward deciphering the deeper mysteries of intimacy between men and women. Generations of youth have taken some of their most important and memorable steps toward adulthood as they promenaded awkwardly onto the floor with a partner at a middle school dance, watchful adults in the wings making sure that all major body parts remained a respectable distance apart.

But Africa, the original Land of a Thousand Dances, is the home of the beat that created rhythm and blues, rock and roll, and jazz, and funk. The dances people do to this music are more primal and leave a lot less to the imagination. Some are an exuberant and unapologetic celebration of sex and desire. Just as changing beliefs and understandings about sex in western culture gradually freed love-making from the insanely limiting confines of "the missionary position," dances eagerly adopted in the West from the Afro-Caribbean-Latin tradition have

profoundly energized and underscored a liberated con-
sciousness that there are, indeed, many, many wonderful
ways to make whoopee.

Yet even with their evolution into styles which are, at
base, a celebration of all things carnal, the dances which
have sprung from this tradition have still left at least *something* to the imagination. But lately, as any adult who's
recently chaperoned a dance will tell you, one popular
style, even with the middle-school set, is nothing more
and nothing less than just raw, simulated sex. No matter
where parents find themselves between the extreme right
and the extreme left of the culture wars continuum, there
is, generally, a feeling that this trend away from at least a
thin veneer of subtlety has drifted too far.

So, I was intensely curious about how this concern
over what is widely perceived as a coarsening of world
youth culture might play out in a rural village where
fundamentalist Islam holds sway. How much would
these kids care to mimic the styles they see in American
and European hip-hop videos? How far would their
adult chaperones let them go in a culture which forbids
both close dancing and dating as we know it?

It dawned on me, as I strained to hear and understand
the lyrics of the music being played that a big part of
what made this dancing *halal* (like saying "kosher," or
theologically acceptable) was the lyrical *content* of these
songs. I speak very little Hausa, and no Dagbani, the
languages of many of these lyrics, but as I listened, the
chorus of my favorite song of the evening so far seemed
to be saying, "Whatever I do in this life, I know I'm alright as long as stick to my glorious Qur'an." I checked
this out with one of the new ranger graduates when he
passed my way to grab himself another cup of punch.

"Yes, yes, exactly so," he said. "It says, 'I know I can never stray too far in life as long as I hold high my beautiful, luminous Qur'an.'" As I surveyed the enthusiastic dancers, many of them were singing, some shouting this chorus. So, that was it. As long as the sentiments being expressed by the music were not only innocent, but positively righteous, and the boys and girls were not dancing together, the dancing could be whatever the kids wanted and needed for it to be. And the style they were into was furious and intense.

As the kids with whom I was sitting and I watched, the competition on the floor between the boys was heating up. The dynamic that revealed itself was that one boy or man would make a move toward the center of the pack and then, all eyes on him, he'd bust his best moves, holding the floor for half a minute before fading on back into the pack.

Some of the boys who'd been holding it down on the floor began to look at Osama expectantly. He and Latif gave each other a look, and then rose in unison, heading straight for the center of the action.

They were both really, really good...fluid, athletic, artful. But Osama's odd body type gave him another whole set of tools, and he used them well. What he was doing out there is hard to describe, simply because I've never seen a human being move like that. It was urgent; crazy...like what *krunk* strives to be, but isn't quite. His moves were like a rapid-fire ritual in which his purpose was to remove his own skin, not out of some tragic and bizarre self-loathing, but out of sheer joy—as if he wanted to say, "Hey, y'all ain't gonna *believe* what I got inside of here! Now, watch; I'm'a show you. Stand back!" Like *that*.

As he danced on into the next song, neither he nor Latif faded back into the group to let someone else step up into the center. It didn't feel like a selfish choice on their part.

It was as if the collective mindset of the entire male group was, "Hey, the competition's over, and we all know who won; let's just dance." And dance on, they did, letting these two bring the energy of the whole group up to a fever pitch while the chorus of the current tune raved on, "*Allahu akbar! Allahu akbar!*" (God is great), their arms flailing; fists pumping skyward to accentuate the words.

I glanced at the time on my cell phone and frowned. The evening was young yet, but I had to pack, and try to get some sleep before rising at 3 A.M. to catch that 4 o'clock bus to Tamale. I waded onto the dance floor, gamely shaking my rump, shouting to my new friends that I had to leave.

Night falls early and hard in this part of the world. I stumbled and twisted each ankle more than once as I made my way back down the pitch dark gravel road to my room. I washed; I packed, and then I fell heavily onto my bed. It had been a very good day, and the party had provided a perfect ending. Now, there was a knock on my door. It was my cousin David, saying he'd come wake me at 3:15 if he didn't see my light on. We wished each other a good night, and I settled in to catch some sleep.

Some other time, in some other place, the insistent *thump, thump, thump* from up on the hill would probably have felt like a real irritant right about then. In fact, I'm sure I would have been lying there feeling more and more pissed off by the minute. But not tonight. Despite the fact that I desperately needed to catch some sleep, the music just made me smile. I pictured the kids I'd met still at it up there; the DJ expertly plying his trade under that glorious velvet-black African sky full of stars.

But instead of lulling me to sleep, those thoughts kept me awake...kept urging me up out of bed and back outside. That jet-black African sky, for instance. "When, ever again," I was thinking, "am I going to have a chance to gaze at stars in a sky like this?" I'd noticed on the way back down to the hotel that there was an area by the side of the road almost completely free of the little bit of light pollution thrown up by the hotel and the rangers' living quarters. In fact, gazing up at the glory of it as I walked back down was at least half the reason for my twisted ankles. That thought alone got me halfway out of bed. But the clincher came only moments later, when, faintly, behind the sound of the music from up on the hill, I could hear the muezzin's call for evening prayers from the mosques of Larabanga. Soon, the music came to a dead halt; there were a few announcements over the P.A. system...then silence, except for the final chorus of the call to prayer.

O.K., that's it, I thought. Party over. And now, the call to prayer will be my lullaby, and I'll get some sleep. Perfect. But within what seemed a span of just a few minutes, I heard the party music start back up again. And this time, it was different. Faster; harder. An Afro-beat/techno/rave thing going on. "Now, *this* is interesting," I thought. If most of the adults and some of the youth had all gone down to the mosque to pray, leaving only the die-hard dancers and the DJ up there, what were they into now? Had some of the dynamics on the dance floor changed now that things might be a little

looser? Would boys and girls dare to dance together
with their chaperones gone? I had to know. If it meant
getting through the next hard day's journey on even
less sleep now, or perhaps no sleep at all, I was curious
enough to risk it.

I threw on a few clothes and headed back up the hill.
The first thing I saw was all the hands waving in the air,
in unison. The dancing had more heat; more sensuality.
And then, as the DJ skillfully mixed the next song into
the foreground, I noticed the big difference between
what he had played earlier in the evening and now. This
was an all-instrumental set. I got it. If you're a DJ up in
this country, this is how you get around social stricture
when you run out of the music with the pious lyrics. You
create a hot mix that has no lyrics at all.

I took a seat on the far perimeter of the action. Only
the colored party lights were on now, and as far as I
could see, no one had noticed my return. This suited me
fine since all I wanted was just to perch here for a little
while and satisfy my curiosity.

The boys and the girls were still very much apart,
but the dynamic between them had, indeed, changed.
It was subtle, but there it was. What had seemed before
like almost completely separate parties had become one.
The boys and the girls were still dancing in separate
packs, but they seemed to be dancing *for* each other
now—showing off for each other; flirting across the
space that divided them. I couldn't help but be struck by
the sweetness and the innocence of it all.

There's a strong tendency in the West, especially
with regards to the cultural traditions of the Islamic
world, to look with a jaundiced eye at such anciently
cherished social conventions—an easy readiness to judge

them pathologically backward and old-fashioned. But as I watched the big fun these kids were having, I had to wonder, "Is it a bad thing to preserve a little mystery and innocence about male/female relationships and sexuality for young people making their first tentative steps toward adulthood?" If a culture's dance traditions reflect in some larger way the dynamics of relationships between men and women, is it a bad thing to dance in a manner which affirms the fact that men and women live most of their lives in intimately connected but parallel universes? At the end of the day, is this really so very different from how things are between the genders in the West?

The dancers and the DJ took a break and headed for either the bathrooms or the punch bowl. Latif spotted me and excitedly made his way over to where I sat.

"Ah, *Daddy*, you camed back. You camed back to us!"

"Yeah; I couldn't sleep. And you know I love the music."

"Yeah, it's good, yes?"

"Very good."

I nodded toward the girls. "Who have you got your eye on over there?" He looked at me blankly.

"I mean, of the girls over there, is there one who's special?" His eyes lit up.

"Ah, yes...my love, my wife, Aisha."

"Your *wife*? Get outta here, man, you ain't married yet. Does she know? Does she know that's how you think of her?"

"Yes."

"And does she approve?"

"Yes."

I was dying of curiosity, of course, so I asked him to point her out. She was a real beauty, with a magnificent

smile and bright eyes that could light up any room. I
grinned at Latif and slapped hands with him.

"*My* man. She's the most beautiful girl here, no
doubt."

"Smartest, too."

She spotted us, obviously talking about her, and
headed our way with another girl in tow.

"How long have you known you were made for
each other?"

"All our life. Since we are five years old. Our families approve."

As Aisha and her cousin Maryamu approached, he
introduced us. We sat down on a bench, the girls on
my left, and Latif on my right. I was surprised at how
close Aisha sat by my side. It was like being treated as a
favorite uncle might be, even though we had just met. I
guessed that Latif's obvious affection for me and the fact
that he'd taken to calling me Daddy was good enough
credentials of my trustworthiness for her.

"Latif is real proud of how smart you are," I told her.
"So, you're a really good student I'll bet. What's your
best subject in school?"

"Science."

Maryamu shook her head. "Maths."

"Science *and* math, yes, I like them both."

"And what do you plan to do with your education?"

"I'll be a doctor, *insh'allah*. The kind that works with
children."

"I'm going to study for electrician," said Latif.
"We'll get married, and then I'll support us while she
goes to school."

"No children 'til I'm done with school."

"Just one," said Latif. She shot him a look.

"After school."

She nodded, satisfied. "Then, I will support us while he takes his second degree."

"I go for electrical engineer. Then, we have one more child, but just one. With only two, we can give them the best of everything and see well to their education."

It was like talking to two grown folks. I've never met a sixteen-year-old couple with such a clearly thought out game plan for their lives. Nor such complete faith in it.

Before long, the music started up again and it was hard to hear ourselves talk over it. I bid the kids farewell, and watched as they took the floor once more.

I made up my mind to linger only another minute or two. I had to try and get some sleep. As I surveyed the dance floor one last time, I suddenly had a stunning revelation—something my outsider's eyes had missed when I first returned to the party. Yet, it was so clear to me now. These boys and girls weren't dancing *for* each other, they were dancing *with* each other. Just as water will find its way down a hill, young love will find a way around whatever social conventions may restrict its path. With respect for tradition, but with great creativity and force of will, I saw that these kids have figured out how to use intense eye contact and body language to shrink that twenty feet of space between them down to what must feel more like two inches. Or less.

It was crystal clear when I watched Latif and Aisha. I thought I'd test the premise with Maryamu. She hadn't mentioned a boyfriend, but did she have one here? I did my best to trace the eye contact she was making straight into the crowd of male dancers...and sure enough, there he was. Young Muhammad, a friend of Latif and

Osama's whom I had met earlier in the evening, was making strong eye contact back at her, his movements synchronized with hers in every way.

I searched the crowd now for Osama. Did he have a mate here somewhere? *This* would be interesting. I didn't see him. Maybe he'd already left. But just as I turned to leave, there he was, alone, still dancing like a madman; like someone who'd caught the Holy Ghost. His body jerked rhythmically to and fro, his eyes rolled back up into his head as if he were dancing at a party in yet *another* parallel universe...located someplace where the rest of us couldn't follow.

I finally turned to go in earnest. As I made my way back down the hill, I noticed that a gorgeous crescent moon sat low on the horizon over Larabanga, painted pink from the red dust raised by the early-arriving Harmattan wind. And in the darkest part of the road, my eyes drank their fill of starlight too. The music was still playing up on the hill, but as I walked on, I was suddenly startled to realize how razor-sharp *all* my senses felt, especially my sense of hearing. I knew that, as busy as the savannah is during the day, when all of us diurnal critters are out and about, it's actually much busier at night. I couldn't see any of this activity that takes place in the deep and dark, but I could hear and feel it all around me...I smiled to myself, relishing the thought that I must surely somehow have caught a little bit of Osama's Holy Ghost, because all of this sounded like music to me now—the rhythmic throbbing of the insects; the shriek of a small animal only yards away who'd just become someone else's late-night meal; the frantic, urgent beating of bats' wings; the breeze, like someone's soft breathing, in the long grass.

And even though I was only walking, it felt like dancing, because I was dancing in my head. And I stopped worrying about launching into a long, hard day's travel on only two hours sleep. I felt good. The day would be fine. I walked down the hill to my room, fully surrendering into the embrace of this good, velvet-black African night.

～～～

David Grant is a Minnesota-based screenwriter and playwright who loves to travel. He is currently collaborating on creating two shows for basic cable TV: one aims to explore interesting, little-known corners of the African diaspora in the New World, the other will shine a light on grassroots efforts throughout the developing world to get sustainable energy projects up and running. Both programs are guaranteed to keep him on the move to the kinds of places he finds most interesting. He is also at work on a book about the recent experience of having found, through incredibly good luck and DNA-based research, the African family from whom his father's line was separated by the transatlantic slave trade.

~❦~ ~❦~ ~❦~

Antarctica Concerto

The beauty of life trumps death and destruction, again.

Except for the gangway's frenzied chunk-chunk against the flank of the anchored ship, the Antarctic blizzard furies around us in eerie silence. The captain of our converted icebreaker has sought shelter in the flooded caldera of Deception Island, an ancient volcano north of the Antarctic Peninsula. Despite this safer anchorage, the *Polar Star* rolls and heaves in the five-foot swells.

Feeling for the gangway's ice-skimmed steps with clumsy, insulated boots, I inch my way downward. Below, a zodiac bucks at the end of its frozen tether. Other photographers and naturalists, waiting their turn to go ashore, press against the deck railing above me, faces shielded from the stinging snow by Darth Vader facemasks.

For a split second the base of the gangway comes level with the zodiac. Gloved hands grip my wrists. One, two...THREE, and I land like a diving sea bird among six other passengers hunched against the gale. The outboard guns us forward. Almost immediately the storm envelops us. We can see nothing but a tight circle of black water inches from our backsides.

Wilderness has always been a magnet for me. It offers something that eludes me in my modern-day life, a fast-paced world given over to anthropocentric power and control. To stand in a place where nature, not man, runs the show, and has since earth's beginnings, is, to me, a miracle in action.

Antarctica is the largest wilderness on our planet. Yesterday, as the *Polar Star* cruised past the sheared-off abutments of glaciers creeping towards the sea, we saw layers of pumice and ice centuries old. I look at the beaches and try to stretch my imagination around the slow-motion pulverizing of volcanic rock that took eons to form their black sands. Even more amazing is the image of this continent as a once-upon-a-time tropical land whose plants and trees turn up as fossils buried in those black sands, a land from which sections detached and sailed away to become South America, Africa, and Australia.

Here in today's Antarctica our ship skirts icebergs sculpted by wind and water into blue caves hung with stalactites, turrets clear as glass. Seals and penguins hitch rides on their glazed surfaces like commuters on public transport. Whales glide under our zodiacs, large and pale as the bottoms of pools.

On our daily landings we step around skeletons picked clean except for inedible flippers and claws. Our guides

gauge every ripple of air as a possible overture to gales
that will hold us hostage on shore for hours. To keep my
fingers from freezing I learn to press the shutter of my
camera without removing my insulated gloves.

Try to play God here, and you're bones on the
beach. In wild places like this, where life evolves at
its own pace, according to its own mechanisms, I can
slow down, think, regain my balance. The stark reality
pushes aside my own nonessentials and zeroes me in on
the best in myself.

As our zodiac hurtles across the snow-shrouded sea,
I have the sense of a more recent past coming to life.
Our invisible destination is a pebbled beach that, along
with multiple other Antarctic locations, witnessed an
epic slaughter of marine wildlife between the late 1800s
and the mid-1960s. Here rest the rusting remains of
machinery that processed the blubber of thousands of
whales and, when the whales ran out, seals, sought in
earlier years for their fur. Ultimately, even penguins
became victims, feeding the hunger for oil destined to
light lamps and lubricate newly invented machinery
in faraway countries. The animals were taken in such
numbers that many, thick in the water for centuries,
reached the point of extinction in less than fifty years.

Straining our eyes, we begin to make out a blurry
shoreline. Gauzy scarves of snow stream from figures
bent against the wind, passengers and guides who left
the ship on earlier zodiacs. The boat crunches onto
volcanic rocks that emerge slick and glistening as we
swing our booted feet into the surf and stagger onto
the beach.

Through the snow flinging itself across the landscape,
swaybacked wooden structures and spires of shattered

machinery appear and disappear. To my right loom
three rusted tanks the size of small buildings, against
whose shelter we lay our backpacks. Monuments to the
butchery, these stored the oil.

The base of the farthest tank reveals a recently chis-
eled opening and through this all fifty of us make our
way, one by one, into the gloom of an enormous interior.
Cylindrical walls rise to a ceiling far above our heads,
its fluted-umbrella shape pockmarked with points of
luminescent snow-light. We fumble across a floor criss-
crossed with pipes, at one time filled with steam or hot
water to keep the oil from solidifying in the cold. I feel
dizzy trying to fathom the number of slaughtered animals whose oil would have filled this one drum alone.

We are gathered in this place for a reason that I find
deeply disturbing. A passenger, blessed with an operatic
voice who enjoys performing before fellow voyagers
when he travels, has suggested that he sing for us within
the oil drum. The acoustics are said to be phenomenal. To
transform this memorial into a theatrical showcase seems
to me to belittle the desecration that occurred here.

Layered in sweaters under a sky-blue windbreaker,
the singer mounts a heap of burlap sacks. Wind, amplified within the hollow space, thunders against the drum,
shakes and rattles sections of loose metal. We, the audience, ankle-deep in mud and pipes, wait.

The man holds aloft a tiny Walkman, pushes a but-
ton. From it issues a sound, dreamlike in this environment, the thin voices of violins barely audible above the
storm's din. Despite my disapproval, goose flesh prickles
my neck and spine.

The soloist hits "stop" and begins to sing. Into the
huge echoing chamber pours the beauty and tenderness

of de Crescenzo's "Rondine al Nido." The man's tenor voice is rich and mellow, a meditation within the storm's chaos. Next comes Giordano's "Amor ti Vieta," its loveliness threading through the howling wind. Softened by the drum's half-light, the singer's self-importance fades, revealing dignity and passion. Tears run down my cheeks.

The concert lasts less than five minutes. Its effect on me is both unexpected and remarkable. With the storm stripping away attitude, the music has emerged as more than entertainment. It is an element that springs from something magnificent and unmarred in humanity, a beauty of spirit that has transcended centuries of ego and aggression.

As the other passengers and I make our way through the blizzard, heading for the zodiacs that will take us back to the *Polar Star* and, ultimately, to our far-off cities and towns, I carry with me a reminder that within mankind exists a force that is capable of shining a light into all corners of the world, the radiance of the human soul.

~ ~ ~

Cecilia Worth is a writer who lives in Homer, Alaska. "Antarctica Concerto" won the Gold Award for Cruise Story in the second annual Solas Awards for Best Travel Writing.

DEBORAH FRYER

❦ ❦ ❦

A Vast Difference

Summer camp is the first adventure
for many a traveler.

Like many kids, I went to summer camp to learn
to sail and ride a horse and tie a bowline. I whittled
green boughs into perfect marshmallow-roasting sticks
and stayed up way past bedtime reading by flashlight on
my top bunk. I sang raunchy songs and played capture
the flag, got poison ivy and carved my initials into the
cabin wall. I kissed a boy for the first time. He had blonde
hair and braces and pimples, and he was as nervous as I
was. We held hands for a week, and then one day on the
way to dinner, he leaned over to kiss me. His wet lips felt
like a slug. I was grossed out. I told him we had to stop
seeing each other. Sleep-away camp presented an exhila-
rating opportunity to explore nature and first love and
independence and homesickness. I did all that, and took

lots of mediocre pictures of everything with my Kodak instamatic. The photos eventually yellowed and curled around the edges. All but one. In my mind, one image grew darker and sharper over time. It was scarier than falling off a galloping horse, and harder than righting a capsized boat. It burned worse than a bee sting and was more confusing than calculus. Thirty years later, I am still stunned and amazed at what we did at camp, for it wasn't child's play at all. It was a dress rehearsal for death.

"Who here has ever been to a funeral?" asked Max, picking flecks of potato chips out of his beard with his tongue. Max was the big, jolly camp director. His beard was like a Navajo blanket—gray and brown and white and red—thick in places and threadbare in others, prickly, and full of crumbs. We had just finished lunch—a dairy meal of tuna salad sandwiches, potato chips and brownies. I received my Jewish education at camp. My parents were secular Jews. They had a season subscription to the symphony and ate lox and bagels on Sunday. We didn't have a television, but we had a piano and a house full of books. My religious education was left to the camp counselors, who taught us about keeping kosher and celebrating Shabbat, singing prayers of blessing before and after meals, and thanking the creator for the beauty all around us. Little did my parents know when they sent us off that summer that we would also be forced to learn about the Jewish rituals surrounding death.

"Anyone ever seen an open casket?" Max queried again. We were a group of ten and eleven year olds. The idea of death seemed as far away as Mars to us. "A tisket, a tasket, I saw an open casket," my bunk-mate Mindy started to chant, wagging her head side to side like a rag doll. "That's not funny, Mindy," Max said sharply. "This is serious business." Little spit bubbles sprayed from his mouth when he talked because he was so animated. We all looked down at our high tops and shook our heads. None of had ever been to a funeral, much less seen a dead person. The wind blew through the birch trees, giving us a momentary respite from the heat of what Max was asking.

"Today we are going to learn about the Jewish ritual of death," he said, making eye contact with each one of us to be sure we were paying attention. "Oh, Gawd," Jane mumbled under her breath and rolled her eyes. "We do not use the name of Ha Shem in vain. Please." Max was stern but gentle, if not a little twisted. Jane was contrite. "Sorry, just kidding," she muttered.

"Now girls," continued Max, "today we are going to hold a mock funeral. Yes, that is what I said. A burial. We are going to learn the Jewish tradition. And what better way to learn than to experience it yourselves?" I was a little bit in shock. But Max had bought my grandparents' grand piano so I thought he was sort of a family friend who could be trusted. What an irony that was: my parents were getting a divorce, and I was burying a 300-pound man in a refrigerator box at Camp Hope. Talk about the elephant in the room. There was not a lot of room for hope in my brain that summer. It was more like clinging to the sweet smell of rain and the curling tails of the clouds that swept across the lake every night, praying that I might just get picked up accidentally and harmlessly transported to a distant shore where people were nice and loving to each other and there were no mosquitoes.

"The reason you all have never seen an open casket is that Jews don't believe in open caskets. We don't believe in embalming either," Max explained. "We believe that when you die, G-d breathes your soul back into the One." We nodded seriously in agreement. "Now," continued Max, "listen carefully. I have something in my pocket. Can you guess what it is?" He fished his plump hand into his pocket and you could see his fingers squirming around in there like a mouse inside a snake's belly. "A $100 dollar bill?" someone said. "A yarmulke?" someone else said. "An apple?" "A stone?" It looked like he was trying to wrap his hand around something round and hard. "Nope." He wrested his hand free from his pocket. Something was going to rip, I was sure of it. Then we saw a Spice Islands jar, with two waterlogged raisins and some spaghetti floating in pee-colored liquid. He held the jar out to the light, turned it around like it was some rare specimen he had recently caught. We gaped. We squinted. We moved in to get a closer look.

"Do you know what this is?" What was he getting at, asking us if we had ever been to a funeral or seen a dead person? Obviously this was something dead, but what creature looked like that? "I am going to pass the jar around and you take a guess." While we were examining the mysterious contents of the bottle, Max told us that according to the tradition, a Jew was supposed to be buried with all his or her body parts. "For example, let's say you lose a limb, you are supposed to keep that limb so that it can be buried with you. When you return to G-d, he takes you back whole, so you need to have your whole body with you."

"That's weird," said Jane. "Go take a walk," said Max. "Come back when you are ready to be respectful." Jane stomped off. I wanted to get away too, but I wasn't sure how I could escape without getting into trouble. Mindy passed the jar to me. I held it close to my face. I peered through the light yellow liquid. It had a funny smell, a little sickening and sweet, like vanilla and ammonia all mixed up. The two whitish things floating in the liquid bobbed like dead fish eyes, only bigger.

As the jar was making its way around the group, Max asked, "Now girls, who knows what this is?" "Some moles you had removed?" said one girl. "The ends of your toes from frostbite?" another guessed. "No." Max shook his head energetically. His beard created a breeze all its own. "This," he held up the jar proudly, "this," he repeated, turning the Spice Islands bottle just so, so the sun shone through reflecting in diamonds and making pretty prisms on the ground, "this is my vas deferens."

A hush fell over us like an avalanche. No one moved. No one breathed. We did not know what to do. We didn't know if we should be scared or impressed so we just stayed really, really focused and quiet because he was telling us something that was clearly important to him, and he was the camp director and we were the campers. I felt sorry for Max with the crumby beard and pudgy fingers carrying around his sickness in an old bay leaf jar like it was a rare butterfly or something. "What is it?" I whispered to my sister. "I don't know," she whispered back. "Looks nasty though. Raise your hand and ask him." "I'll get in trouble," I said. "No, you won't. Just ask him."

"What are you whispering about?" Max looked at me. I looked at my sister and she shrugged. "Deborah has a question." "What *is* that?" "Speak up," said Max. "I'm sure everyone wants to hear you. "What IS that?" I asked louder this time. "What is your vast difference?"

When Max smiled, his teeth looked yellow and waxy like cheese. "Ask your parents," he said, like he was trying hard not to laugh. Then he got all somber again. "This was once a part of my body. Jewish law tells us that when we die, we should return to G-d whole. So I had this part surgically removed, but I kept it so that it could be buried with me."

"But what is it?" I asked again. "Is it a tumor?" I knew about tumors. I had had bad dreams about getting tumors. My mother's best friend had tumors in her abdomen. I knew they could kill you if they were not removed in time. My grandfather had died from stomach cancer. They tried to get all the cancer, but they couldn't, and then one day he died on his way to the bathroom. Just fell over one day, clutching his stomach, and never stood up again. I already knew two grownups who had had tumors removed from their bellies, so I was pretty sure that that was what Max was pickling in the Spice Islands jar. I hoped he would be O.K. The tumors looked pretty small and his stomach was pretty big, but maybe there was a lot more cancer hiding in there and it would be hard to find. I was worried until he said, "This is part of my penis. I had it cut so my wife and I don't..." but we never heard the rest of his sentence because we girls were doubled over with laughter, covering our mouths as though we could keep the embarrassment from getting down our throats and choking us. How could he say that word in public with a straight face? I laughed so hard my stomach hurt, and then I remembered what I thought was in the jar and I thought about my grandfather clutching his stomach at the end of his life and I thought about my mom's friend whimpering through her abdominal pain and I became solemn again.

"In the Jewish tradition, we are buried in what is called a *kittel*, a white robe spun of pure cotton," Max went on. "This is so we can return as naturally to the earth as we came into it." Max furled a white sheet around his body like a toga, and knotted it with a white belt, the kind you get in karate. "It is traditional to be buried in a *tallis*, a Jewish prayer shawl," Max instructed, "so I am going to use mine. This is the one I wore when I had my bar mitzvah thirty years ago." He wrapped the blue-and-white striped cloth around his shoulders, and curled the fringes around his sausagey fingers.

"Jews are traditionally buried in unvarnished, un-painted plain pine coffins with seven holes in the bottom," he continued. "We are going to pretend this refrigerator box is a coffin, O.K.?" He fished a Swiss Army knife out of his pocket and cut seven diamond-shaped holes into the cardboard. Right through the word AMANA so it looked like it said A MAN. Then, he did something even weirder than showing us his privates pickled in a spice bottle. He got into the box and lay down.

"Now girls," his voice boomed from inside the box, "there are some shovels leaning against that tree. Start digging until you have a nice pile of earth." I knew deep down that some day I would need to know how to have a Jewish funeral. My parents were both alive and healthy but this was getting really freaky and I figured the sooner we started, the sooner it would all be over.

With twenty girls shoveling, it didn't take long to amass a sizeable pile of dirt under the tree. "Now what?" we asked. "Grab a handful, and sprinkle it on the corpse," whispered Max from the box. Was he out of his mind? "On me," Max clarified. "Sprinkle some dirt on me." He was asking us to bury him alive. With his wiener swimming in a bottle of formaldehyde right beside him. This was even grosser than kissing the pimply boy with braces. "Just a handful or two," he said. "That helps the deceased begin to return to earth. And this act is your connection to the deceased. One day we will all return to earth. This lesson teaches us that death is part of life and life is part of death."

I let the other girls go first. I stared up at the sunlight smiling down at us through the trees. I let my focus drift across the lake to the distant shore. Clouds were gathering. I loved the Minnesota thunderstorms. I loved the electricity and the green color the sky turned just before it began to rain. I loved the smell of the earth after it received the rain. I pushed my bangs out of my eyes and noticed my fingernails caked with dirt. Ten matching black parentheses. I squeezed two fistfuls of earth together and dropped them on top of Max, whose eyes were now closed. He had taken off his glasses and fallen asleep.

Summer was over. The sky was still pink from the setting sun and the fireflies had just come out when there was a knock on the door. It was our neighbor, Mrs. Kelley. "I am so sorry to ask you this, but…" She put her hand on her temple like she had a headache. "But is Delilah at home?" Delilah was the family dog, a miniature white poodle with black ears who slept at the foot of my bed. "Delilah?" I called. "Delilah-berry?" I listened for that familiar jingle of head lifting from sleep. Nothing. I ran upstairs. No familiar pounce of paws hitting the floor from a height. I ran downstairs. I looked in the garage and the backyard.

The tears came before the bad news. We found her by the side of the road, her tongue hanging out like a piece of bologna. Her eyes were open. She had looked death right in the face, but she hadn't seen it coming. I gathered her in my arms. She was still warm. Her legs were splayed out as if in sleep, but she was stiff.

I was crying so hard I couldn't see, but I didn't need to. I knew what to do. I was guided by some force outside of me. I moved in slow motion. I wrapped Delilah in a white sheet and carried her to the backyard. My sister and I dug a hole under the crabapple tree. We put her in the hole, and sprinkled earth and our tears and some dog biscuits for good measure on top of her body. We knew the right prayers because we had just learned them at camp. So that is what we were practicing for. Max was right. Death was part of life.

Bad news always comes in threes. Delilah was just the beginning. A week later, my grandmother died. My parents had snuck me into the hospital, where she was "resting." "Being watched," they said. She had a heart murmur. Something was not normal. The doctors were going to do some tests to find out what was wrong with her heart. She died in her sleep before they ever found out. On the day of her funeral, I wore a tie. "Girls don't wear ties," my aunt scolded me. "Go home and put on a dress." "But then I will miss the funeral," I said. "I have to go to the funeral." "You are too young to go a funeral," my aunt said, all purse-lipped and stern. "No, I'm not," I said. "We practiced this at summer camp and I know all about it. I want to go." "O.K.," she said, "but take off that tie. You can borrow a dress from your cousin."

I changed my clothes, and I believe on that same day, my grandmother turned into rain. They put her body in the ground in a pine coffin with seven holes in the bottom, but her spirit rose like mist from a pond. Eventually, she would form a cloud, and then she would rain down on my face, again and again, so she would always be near me. I knew this was the truth. I had seen it that day at the lake when we were pretending to bury Max and I saw the clouds hovering over the trees. I knew that everything was connected. Max, Delilah, my grandmother. They were all my teachers, all forcing me to face what inevitably would happen to me one day. I couldn't have asked for better training wheels for mortality.

When I was eleven, the doctor told me I needed an operation to take my tonsils out. Now it was my turn. I was not surprised, but my mother was very afraid. She had heard a story of a little girl who had an allergic reaction to the anesthesia and died on the operating table. "We have to put your daughter to sleep to do this operation," the doctor said. "There is no other way to do it." My mother paced and fretted. She was sure she was going to lose me. But I knew that if I died, I would get to be with my grandmother and Delilah again. We would all become one really big cloud, and we would create rainbows and cause flowers to bloom when we rained. That didn't seem scary to me. The doctor described everything that would happen; they would give me a shot, and then have me count backwards from ten to one, and then I would fall asleep. They would take out my tonsils—which were rotten—while I was sleeping. And then, when I woke up, I could have popsicles and ice cream. "You won't remember a thing and it won't hurt," he reassured me. "This is a very routine operation. Don't worry. Everything is going to be fine." He was a nice doctor, and I believed him. "Now, do you have any questions?" The doctor put his hand on my arm. I did have one concern. How could I be whole if they took out my tonsils?

"Yes, I do," I said. "Can you please save my tonsils for me? I need to keep them so they can be buried with me." I felt very brave and wise for my years. The doctor looked amused. "We learned at camp this summer that you need to be whole when you return to G-d," I explained earnestly, "so I need my tonsils."

The surgery was uneventful. I healed well. We got a new puppy. I graduated from high school. I kept my tonsils in a Spice Islands jar on my windowsill for many years. They reminded me of that summer on the lake when I first learned how we are all connected. They reminded me of mad Max and my old dog with her limp bologna tongue and my own fragile mortality. I eventually threw them away because I felt weird saving my rotten body parts for posterity. I don't need the physical proof any more. The experience of interconnection is hardwired into my brain by now. I don't think kissing is gross any more but I still know how to tie a bowline. Every time it rains, the earth smells delicious and sad and I feel my grandmother's love in my hair.

≈≈ ≈≈ ≈≈

Deborah Fryer is a freelance writer and documentary filmmaker living in Boulder, Colorado.

KEN MATUSOW

❧ ❧ ❧

The Long Red Road

Many years ago, a cultural creative found
himself immersed in another reality.

I T WAS WITH THE PYGMIES THAT I WOULD FIND MY
connection with Africa.

Although the path to reach them was long and ardu-
ous, the route was easy to follow. It lay at the end of the
long red road.

The red road stretched a week into the future and
two weeks into the past. It was made of clay the color of
crushed red roses. Our truck, a converted old Bedford
carrying a dozen or so Westerners, rumbled eastward
at a walking pace, slipping and skidding on the slick
mud, occasionally tumbling into immense potholes. The
intense green of the central African rainforest bracketed
the road, creating the impression of an eternal emerald
tunnel, while innumerable butterflies colored the deep

green of the forest like a storm of multicolored raindrops. The road was as wide as the truck, no wider.
There were no side streets, nor turnoffs or open fields.
As Dorothy was forced to follow the yellow brick road
to Oz, so were we trapped on a rose-red road that eventually led to Rwanda.

Occasionally we would come across a village. We
would stop to take a break, or buy half-rotted vegetables
for lunch or dinner. Village kids would invariably run
to our truck and surround us. They wore tattered t-
shirts, leftovers from college bookshops advertising the
University of Texas or, more often, a Mormon school.
Their bellies, bloated by malnutrition, poked through
shredded fabric. With shy eyes, bright with delight, they
would stare at us, smiles painted across fly-covered faces.
If we happened to stop for a number of hours, perhaps to
stay the night, our circle of equatorial kids would often
begin to sing, offering up a friendly group hello, a timid
invitation to begin a conversation. The songs acted as a
magical incantation, a spell-breaking mantra that lifted
the barrier that separated the Western invaders from the
local population.

The villages were the only way off the road. The dense
rainforest allowed no exit. If we didn't come across a village near sunset, we would simply stop the truck in the
middle of the road and set up camp. We would erect our
tents between the truck and a crude, homemade barrier
of jerry cans, dead branches, and other assorted flotsam.
This gave us a semblance of protection in the unlikely
event a truck came down the road as we slept. Even as
Westerners we were not spared the overpowering aroma
of African fatalism. We had no free will. We could only
move forward down the long road.

Once we came to an abandoned village. Even though it was only mid-afternoon, we pulled off the road to set up camp. We spread out, savoring the privacy and the space. The village was spacious, dotted with attractive huts. Yet its emptiness was both eerie and suspicious. Why did the villagers leave?

Although we always enjoyed interacting with the locals we met along the way, it was nice for once to be free of the eternal task of communicating with people with whom we bonded emotionally, but struggled to connect with culturally. As with much in central Africa, our apparent good luck turned out to be illusory. In the middle of the night I crawled out of my tent to take a piss. As I walked I noticed the ground felt strange. My flip-flops seemed to slip with each stride. The earth felt curiously spongy. I shined my flashlight at my feet. Rather than the usual red dirt, the ground was black and seemed to move in waves. I felt a sharp sting on one of my toes. I was walking on a sea of army ants. The mystery of the abandoned village was solved.

A rush of adrenaline instantly cleared my mind and jump-started my heart. I flew into my tent and zipped everything up tight. I had read stories of killer ants, ants that could strip an elephant of its flesh within minutes. I heard a soft patter, the kind of noise rain makes as it strikes the sides of a tent. "Hey, I yelled," rudely waking up a couple in the next tent. "Do you hear it raining?"

"No, go back to sleep and let us be."

The rain-like noise was caused by an uncountable number of ants crawling over my tent. Thoroughly panicked, I squatted on my heels, flashlight in mouth, flip-flop in hand crushing any ant clever enough to slip through the zippers and flaps of my defenses. Ten minutes later the noise petered out. I calmed myself and crawled back into my sleeping bag. I drifted off to sleep as voices from the next tent broke the silence. "Ken, you know, I think it is raining." It was easy to imagine the fear of the phantom inhabitants of the village as a swarm of ants entered their flimsy huts.

As we traveled the red road, layers of history and culture peeled back as if we were cutting through the concentric rings of a tree searching for the heartwood at its center. Each mile took us closer to the core. The world simplified into primary colors of red and green. The journey ended at a village with the strange name, Station de Capture D'Epulu, or in English, Village Where the Okapi was Captured.

Situated deep within the boundaries of the Ituri rainforest, Station de Capture D'Epulu hosts a small French-run research station, the only place on the planet where the mysterious okapi may be seen in the wild. Standing up to six feet high at the shoulder, an okapi looks like a cross between a zebra and a giraffe. It wasn't until the twentieth century that this large and bizarre mammal was first discovered by Westerners. Such is the remoteness and isolation of the Ituri Forest.

As a village, Station de Capture D'Epulu wasn't very impressive. There was, of course, the tiny okapi research station, overseen by a couple of French scientists. Supporting this forlorn scientific outpost was a dirt floor restaurant that also served as the local bar. An ersatz food shop was next door, its shelves empty but for a half dozen cans of pilchards, large sardine-like fish. A few wooden buildings surrounded a small outdoor market. In the market seven or eight local women sat quietly chatting among themselves, waiting for

nonexistent customers. Each woman spread a colorful
shawl or blanket in front of her, upon which she placed a
few bundles of manioc, the staple food of the area, along
with small carefully arranged piles of onions.

The Ituri Forest was also home to the Mbuti
Pygmies.

The Pygmies were as different from the ordinary,
Bantu-speaking villagers as we Westerners were from
the villagers. There was no common language or culture
that linked Pygmies and villagers, even though they
shared the same forest. The very genetic makeup of the
Mbuti is distinct and shares little with the rest of the
human family. Only the San, or Bushmen, of southern
Africa enjoy any similarity to the Pygmies. Both enjoy
the distinction of being a kind of proto-human, modern
manifestations of the original blueprint that eventually
evolved into the private equity bankers of Manhattan
and the flute players of the Andes.

The Bantu-speaking villagers live in a central African
domain of fear and fatalism. Ghouls and ghosts live
deep in the forests laying traps for the mortal inhabitants of the villages. The villagers cling to the red road,
staying clear of the forest, as the forest is a place of
darkness and evil.

In contrast, the Mbuti Pygmies see the forest as the
great nurturer, a vast playground where they hunt and
romp. In the eyes of the Pygmies, the forest is benign
and benevolent. They have a common term that refers
to both forest and mother. It is a partner that provides
food and shelter.

A number of us wanted to explore the world of
the Pygmies. We had taken turns reading a tattered
copy of Colin Turnbull's, *The Forest People*, a classic

exposition published in 1961, of the life of the Mbuti Pygmies of Central Africa. Turnbull describes his life among a Pygmy tribe that lives near Station de Capture D'Epulu. He wrote of an idyllic world of small people who lived in a land of harmony and peace. Although controversial, and perhaps a bit over-romanticized, *The Forest People* remains the definitive work on the Mbuti Pygmies, the context from which all other content is based. We wanted to experience a small glimpse of the world described by Turnbull.

An Mbuti Pygmy called Kenge was the protagonist of the book. As described in *The Forest People*, Kenge befriended Turnbull and over the course of a year or so gradually unveiled the world of the Pygmies to him. It was through Turnbull and his friend—and some think lover, Kenge—that the life and culture of the Pygmies was first exposed to the outside world. Kenge guarded the entrance to the world of the Pygmies in the same manner the mythical ferryman Charon guarded the entrance to Hades, an underworld of mystery and darkness. Wanting to take a brief look at this other African reality, we decided to try to find Kenge and convince him to give us a glimpse into the society of which he played so central a role in *The Forest People*.

Through the French scientists who ran the okapi research station we were able to find a local interpreter who spoke French as well as the Mbuti language. A couple of inquiries established that Kenge was still living in the area, and indeed, was currently staying in the village. After a bit more effort we found Kenge and asked if he would spend a day or so acting as our guide to the Pygmies. After a small fee was negotiated, he agreed.

As we completed our negotiations, Kenge, through our interpreter, indicated he wanted to introduce me to one of his uncles who had moved to the village. He led me to a building where we climbed a set of wooden stairs and entered a small room. The walls framed a wooden door and two unpaned windows. The only furniture in the room was a chair on which sat Kenge's uncle. Kenge attempted an introduction, but as he did not speak French, let alone English, the attempt was futile. After indicating that I should sit on the floor, Kenge left.

Kenge's uncle looked old, perhaps in his seventies. His actual age could just as well been thirty. There was no way to tell. Short curly hair framed a wizened face. His large smile was unforced, comfortably resting amid the wrinkles of his body. On one leg rested his grandson, a lad of two or three years. On his other leg laid a five-foot long marijuana pipe. He was at ease and unperturbed, but clearly interested in my presence. Occasionally he would try to speak to me, and, of course, I would respond to the indecipherable question in equally indecipherable French, the flow of the words more important than their meaning. All the while he would be puffing on his pipe, never offering any to me. After fifteen minutes or so he pointed to his grandson, looked him in the eye, and sang to him "kitchy kitchy koo," apparently a universal phrase of endearment. In an instant, the other-worldliness and familiarity of the situation were overlaid. I was looking at my own grandfather, somehow oblivious to the exotic setting.

Early the next morning, with Kenge and our interpreter in the lead, we left the red road for the interior of the tropical rainforest. We hiked along a well-defined trail. The trail was relatively wide and easy to follow. Like most mornings, the air was surprisingly cool, and as always, damp. There was little underbrush, as the thick forest canopy blocked the most of the light. I was reminded of countless hikes I had taken in the redwood forests of northern California. The walking was easy. This was not the impenetrable jungle I had expected.

After an hour or so we came to a clearing that held an Mbuti village. It was small, with perhaps half a dozen tiny mud and twig huts that together housed twenty or so people. Kenge introduced us to an Mbuti family: father, mother, son, and dog. As expected they were very short. Pygmy men rarely stand more than five feet, Pygmy women often less than four. Their hair was tightly curled, complexion dark, almost black, and their faces glowed with an easy-going self-assurance that accentuated seemingly dark blue eyes and perpetual smiles.

As we casually strolled around the village we met up with a young girl, perhaps twelve or thirteen. She held a small baby in her arms. As did all the Pygmies, the girl wore only a simple bark loincloth. She smiled at us and strolled over to a patch of forest that held a number of plants. She carefully examined the vegetation and gently pulled one up by its roots. With a few deft moves she quickly stripped the plant of its exterior covering and tied a knot, creating a loop. She slung the loop over her shoulder creating a kind of sling into which she placed the child.

Kenge had organized a hunting party. Before the hunt could begin in earnest, specific preparations and protocols needed to be observed. We gathered around a fire where the hunters, all men, sharpened arrows and applied poison to their tips. Plants were placed in the fire creating a pungent, dense smoke. As the keepers of the fires chanted, we were instructed to breathe in the smoke and to try to get the smoke to saturate our clothes. The incense would hide our human odor, while the chanting would placate the forest spirits, increasing the likelihood of a successful hunt.

Once again, Kenge led us into the rainforest. The men went first. They had a serious demeanor as they grabbed their spears, bows, and knives. The women giggled and laughed while carrying large bundles of nets. When we arrived at the hunting grounds the nets would be unfurled and strung along the game trails. Once they were set in place, the hunt would begin in earnest.

All the tools and other artifacts we saw were handmade: the arrows from special hardwood sticks; the bows from carefully articulated branches; the arrow quivers from woven reeds; and the nets from handcrafted grasses. The Mbuti loincloths were made from pounded bark, decorated with simple symbols. The loincloths were kept in place with elaborately macramé grass belts. Daily life was distilled to a set of essentials. Everything made, everything said, everything acted upon, was for a specific purpose. There were no wasted efforts.

With casual efficiency the hunt began. The men took the nets and strung them out through the rainforest, making sure that all game trails converged to the one nestled within the confining circle of nets. They then carefully positioned themselves for the coming hunt. The women silently formed groups and hid about a hundred yards from the nets. The Westerners, including myself, were led to a spot where we could see the hunt unfold. Then we waited silently.

Without warning the women began a frenzied run towards the nets. They whooped and yelled, laughing and leaping. We saw movement in the underbrush. A dash of gray-brown. Then the men started running. All was chaos. We also ran to the nets. We found a hunter unwinding a small antelope, a dik-dik, from the net. No larger than a good-sized house cat, the small creature looked pathetic as it tried to escape from its snare. Once free of the net, but still firmly grasped by the hunter, a quick slash of a knife slit the throat of the animal. A brilliant smile lit the face of the hunter as he held up his prize for all to admire, a small trophy for a momentary victory in the daily game of survival. After hours of preparation, the actual hunt lasted only a few moments.

An exuberant band of Pygmies and Westerners hiked back to the Mbuti village savoring the success of the hunt. When we arrived, the women who had stayed behind were already hard at work preparing the victory meal. However, our day with the Pygmies was over. We were not invited to participate in the celebration. After quick goodbyes, led by our interpreter, we walked back to Station de Capture D'Epulu.

While trekking back to the red road, I noticed the overpowering darkness and conformity of the rainforest had disappeared. Central Africa and the Ituri rainforest no longer smothered me with fear and deadening fatalism. For a few hours I lived in an alternative Africa, an Africa governed by a quiet glee and an innocent love of nature.

A few days later the long red road came to an end. We quickly gained elevation as we neared the Ruwenzori and Virunga Mountains that defined the border of eastern Zaire and Rwanda. The claustrophobia that had enveloped us for weeks eased as we slowly climbed out of the central African rainforest. The world opened up. The soaring peaks of Karisimba and Nyiragongo framed fertile fields of maize and giant cabbage. We stopped our truck for one last look at the rainforest. A sea of dark green stretched to the horizon, seemingly unbroken by road or river. We knew that somewhere amid the green lay the Pygmies of the Ituri Forest. That day, as they have for millennia, the women would gather their nets, the men their bows and knives, and with high spirits all would head deep into the rainforest to find their daily meal.

᪲ ᪲ ᪲

Ken Matusow is a Silicon Valley entrepreneur. Between technology startups and consulting contracts he usually takes off to explore the developing world, often for months or years at a time. He also works as a volunteer to assist technology companies in remote parts of the globe. Working with groups such as Geek Corps and the International Executive Service Corps, he has assisted and advised technology companies in Bulgaria, Mongolia, South Africa, and West Africa. He lives in northern California with his wife, Barbara.

In a Place of Wind

She found a path that has no name.

ICOME UP THROUGH THE PASS OF GIANT WIND-FORMED rocks and blue light. The elevation is an illusion. Only two thousand meters up and I am walking in the sky. Blue, not a cloud, a wind-filled sphere. Always the wind, like food, a drug. I am never tired.

Fifty-thousand hectares of mountain steppe and somewhere the ancient horses the Mongolians call *takhi* or spirit, are threading their way. I have been here a week. Already my prints are overlaid with theirs.

Far behind is the Mölt camp where we spent our day off. The other eco-volunteers have gone in the van. I cross over into birch groves, little white trees snaking towards the light, but honed and stunted by the blasts of wind, nothing like the trees of home. The biologists have said these forests are dying. Global warming. Fallen

trunks and branches lie ghostly in the thick grasses
among blue irises.

Light shimmering across another valley, another
mountain, the high whistles of a hawk. I am not sure
where I am, climbing the rocks above the trees and
woven nests. The wind is rumbling at my back, makes
me turn to see a dark cloud front moving in fast. A cuck-
oo's soft "*hu-hu, hu-hu*," and everything stills. Ahead the
land drops and rises in waves on an endless sea to the
far-off specks of white of the tourist camp.

I begin my descent, legs shaking, rocks scattering.
Winds flood the channels; clouds are blowing in like
night. Nowhere to hide, nothing but open. How can
you tell if the world is ending? End of time? My time?
As a child I used to run in storms through the forests of
home, like those shamans pulling in the whirls of energy, letting the hairs rise on my arms, at the back of my
neck. Grasses blowing like seas before a boat, the rain
rushing and I can no longer see. Now lightning opens
the sky, searing threads burn into earth and up again.
The sky collapses, shuddering in the bones. The entire
thing came out of the blue. I am running, uttering desperate prayers.

The *ger* attendant, Toma, has brought a candle, and
commended the fire I lit in the stove with kindling and
sheep dung old as turf. She throws in another mound
and the fire sparks at her hands. My clothes steam from
the ceiling poles. Rumbling sonic sounds like airplanes
careening out of control mix with the high-pierced
whinnying of horses. Rain and hail rattle through the
broken panes of the skylight. We run out to yank at the
horsehair ropes, pulling the felt flap over. I can see the

camp horses at the tethering post, hanging their heads, and beyond the rush of wind and white where I came out. Was I released or blessed? Born again?

I lie back in my little white tent round as the moon, with a giant black vulture feather stuck into the ceiling above my bed, and the perfect lower jaw of a horse skull on the table, a knucklebone, shinbone, hoof. In the warmth of my sleeping bag I can feel the storm blowing everything to submission, ravaging the heart, stirring up every emotion, every sensing string with painful precision, firelight flickering on the tent wall on my left side, like light on water. I am home.

Gruff old Haska drives us from the research center, far along the sand tracks at dawn. Five volunteers: elder Maggie, sailor and botanist from Devon; young moody Pierre, amateur photographer from France; cool eighteen-year-old traveler Marika; Liv, mother and veterinarian from Holland; and me, wandering writer.

We are searching for those elusive sand-colored horses with black dorsal stripes, brush manes, zebra-striped legs, the ancestors, the ones painted twenty thousand years ago in ochre and charcoal on cave walls.

The radio crackles and hisses, "Haska-Haska-Haska."

"*Té!*" Haska yells. "*Amar baḥuu? Hangaï baḥuu?*"

The rangers are calling in on horseback from somewhere out on the land, the harems' personal bodyguards. They sleep under the stars, keep guns in their packs, ready for the wolves, camouflage cloth sewn onto their saddle seats. They always know where the horses are.

We are let off one by one along the land with only glimpses of our assigned harems in the distance. We walk

out, trying to keep a straight line in the wind, the bum-
bling volunteers, with our packed lunches, our observation sheets and tools, keepers of the coordinates, wind
velocity, weather patterns, pathways of wild horses.

Blowing morning up in the clouds. Hangaï harem has
found a wall of bushes to lean into, warm and sleepy, all
turned towards me, shrouded in the fog coming through
the pass. They disappear and appear again while I
crouch behind a few spindly bushes on the bare slope,
shaking with cold. One of the little white foals stands
bravely with his back to the wind.

They've forgotten me. When I raise my head they
think I'm some kind of wolf, dressed in green rain cape,
with strange hanging things around her neck, binoculars, GPS, anemometer. They escape through the bushes
and up over the rocks. But I know them now. They're
on the southern slope. The sun has come out. I nestle
in among the rocks on the warm black turf, above a
glowing birch forest and a cliff grotto where a flock of
red-beaked crows come dancing, playing on the ledges,
and two kites, light glancing off their wings. The horses
doze in a line down the rocks, all twenty of them, hazy
blue valleys below, foals lying like white cloths at their
mothers' feet, ears flopped back, eyes half-closed.

The blue research center howls with wind. A swallow
is caught in the upper library. Teabags lie on spoons on
the kitchen table to be reused, the stove ticks, a cauldron
of savory mutton and noodles is bubbling away. I watch
the young Mongolian biologists, wrapped in sweaters at
their computers, deep in grasses, water, wolves, winter,

evolution, in this great experiment: keeping the last of the wild horses alive. They were hunted, collected, lost in European zoos, inbred, on the brink of extinction, and saved by Dutch and Mongolian foundations. Eighty-four were flown home in the 1990s. Now, they are hovering at 180, in eighteen harems.

I imagine the winter, solitary on horseback, continuing the work, tracking in drifts. What is it like to live in a place of wind? I have been an observer all my life, but what if I had been a biologist instead, protecting the wild things? The wildlife biologist, Uskuu, sees me gazing out the windows.

"I think your silence is expensive," he smiles.

He thinks I'm in love with someone. But it's the place.

Gale winds yank the little painted door out of my hands, making me hit my head on the low door frame as I am thrown out of my *ger*.

"Force eight winds," cries Maggie, thinking of the sea.

The volunteers have paid to be here. The Mongolians think maybe we are glorified tourists, based at the tourist camp, among charter buses and day-trippers. But where we go they can never follow. We take what we need. Maggie discovers her youth, reading the clouds, finding flowers. Transient Marika sniffles with a bout of malaria and reads novels in far-flung meadows, the horses listening to the tick of her alarm clock. Pierre is the loveable fool, who takes pictures of stallions mounting mares and loses his yellow GPS in the yellow grasses. Liv has lost her mother to dementia and turns to her sketchbook, considers a change of career. I have left a man, left my heart in so many places, my words on pages speckled with rain, dust, sweat, and insects.

There is a ceremony on Ikh Ovoo, highest peak in the reserve. Red deer are running. A ranger's two little boys run with their hands above their heads, gestures of antlers. We see three *takhi* in the distance. Ravens float above. The women must stay behind on the summit with the vans and motorcycles; even the horses go up with the rangers. The men are carrying a cooked sheep on a board, bags of yogurt, thermoses of salty tea, soft and hard cheeses, candies, up the last path through the bushes to the rock peak and the *ovoo*, sacred altar, tattered blue banners loose around its spires. All that comes down to us are fragments of voices caught on the wind, the lamas chanting, blessing the land and the horses, and praying for rain.

The horses are retracing an ancient memory, remembering how to be free. I have blown from place to place with the same need. How to be free and still be held?

Amar harem is shimmering in heat waves, coming off the peninsulas of hills to the open grass sea of the Tuul River valley. There is the foal with the gash in its hindquarters, attacked by wolves last week. The biologists chose to intervene with glucose and antibiotics. There is the newborn foal, tender-footed, spidery legs and twitching tail. A ranger has come galloping on a chestnut horse. He swings off and while his horse grazes he squats down, a foot on the long leather rein. He looks through one eye of his binoculars, holding them vertical, checking on the foals. He sits back, yawns, regards me, not a word. In a moment he is gone. Beyond the horses I can see the river valley and specks of *gers*, the rangers' homes.

On the sunlit pass above the Jargallant valley, a little white foal is standing in the center of our ring of rangers, biology and scholarship students, Nanda, the volunteer coordinator, and me. The rangers found it this morning, after a commotion they saw on the cliffs. No one was sure what happened. Maybe the foal had been stuck in the rocks. The mare turned back for him but the stallion kept herding her away, so she left and joined the herd.

They bring us down the valley on motorbikes, with the foal across Nanda's lap, and leave us at the stream-bed: one lost foal, a Canadian writer, and Nanda, who happens to be doing her thesis on the behavior of foals.

The beauty of the foal, days old, little speckled nose on our skin, breathing our smells. He follows us, nickering, tiny hooves stepping on our heels. We dowse him gently in the stream and feed him sugar water from a baby bottle. He makes us laugh, nudging at our shirts looking to suckle, lying down to sleep at our sides, lifting his head to make sure we're still there. He lays his head on my foot. I look into the large dark eye with pale lashes. It is a gift to touch a wild thing, like touching the wind, some of it comes off on you. The sun burns across the sky. We cover our faces and sleep.

At evening we make our escape, creeping away from the sleeping bundle and up the hill to hide behind rocks. We can see him through the binoculars, still sleeping. His harem will be coming through soon, stopping at the stream. The ranger, somewhere to the south, calls in on the radio. They're on their way. The biologist and the scholarship student are up on the mountain behind us.

Burning sun, the sweat streaming down our faces, the
crackle of Nanda's radio. Now, in the south, the shapes
come running across the slopes. Amar harem. It seems
to take forever for them to arrive, but they do, dipping
hooves into the streambed, tossing their heads, bending
to drink, not thirty feet from the foal.

"Come on, wake up," we whisper.

The foal lies sleeping. The mare is grazing near the
stream.

"Wake up."

The mare lifts her head, catches something on the
wind. The herd is moving off. If she doesn't find him
now, she will never accept him later. The foal lifts his
head, trying to get up. He flops down again. The mare
bolts, returns slowly, shaking her head, grunting. She
knows his smell. Can she smell us? She goes up, circles
him. Horses whinny in the distance.

"Come on. Come on!"

The foal staggers to his feet. The mare sweeps up to
his side. He bobs alongside her, moving shakily to the
stream and across and up the other side, as the herd
moves off across the grass, golden in the long sun.

High on a rock fortress we are crouched in the blasts
of wind, holding down our papers. The wolf biologist,
in ruffling army jacket, is holding onto his hat while
clenching the radio-tracking antennae, pointing it southeast. One collared wolf, male, W5 ID 1538035. The sonic
beeping like a heartbeat, sometimes a double beat.

"He's moving."

The sun burning the earth at our feet, we remember
the tawny shadow moving across the face of the open
hill this morning. The rangers want the wolves dead.

But this boy has never killed an animal. I saw him trying to catch butterflies to study at camp, the elusive white ones, tossing his shirt into the air. He had a hedgehog in a box from his girlfriend. And when we first met he came bareback on a red horse and held out his hand, a silver bracelet with Buddhist inscriptions sliding down his left wrist.

We are all sweating in the conference hall at the awards ceremony. The biologists in suits and gowns, the rangers, poised in their beautiful tunics, golden and copper, metallic earth-green, black with luminous blue embroidery, thick engraved leather belts, studded with silver medallions, cowboy hats soft as velvet or suede, and gleaming knee-high Russian boots. They were always among us, but rarely seen, a glimpse of a motorbike, a lone horseman, their voices coming through the radios, protecting our harems.

We are met at the dining room with a tray of vodka shots in little paper cups, cool to the touch, and a buffet of so many salads and meat plates, and the "hortog" specialty, dripping with grease. The three sheep had been tied to the fence days ago, eyeing us as we came in from observations. They were cut open and loaded with hot rocks and tied up again with rope and left to bake.

The audience sits on chairs in the grass. A DJ-magician walks on a bed of colored glass and swallows fire. A boy in silver suit sings the traditional "Long Song," with the voice of a crooner. A bird flies into Marika's hair beside me, and as she shakes it away it lands on my shoulder and touches my face with its wing. Traveler to traveler.

The Mongolians waltz the night away, young and old to the DJ's synthesizer. Haska, Best Driver for

thirty-five years, has a bottle of Red Label from someone, held to his chest, a trophy. Best Dancer, in tweed cap
and dark suit, spins the women across the darkness. The
volunteers are getting drunk, wind-weathered, forever
altered. Somehow we have been left to our own devices.
No one has asked us to dance.

Smell of burning in the air. Somewhere, hundreds of
kilometers away, forests are on fire. In the dappled light
of a birch grove at 1,700 meters Hangaï harem is nosing
among the roots. Some are scratching against the trees.
Once in a while a dead trunk comes crashing down and
the horses dart like fish through the trees.

The brown mare lags behind and her little brown foal
runs back and forth, nickering for her to hurry. I slip
across the grasses, becoming trees and rocks. Sometimes
they pass so close I could reach out my hand and skim
their hides, the ribs, the tattered winter coats.

They take me right up, over Jargallant valley, Tuul
River valley, all the valleys of silver-weaving threads,
lit grasslands, blue veils, wind-shaped temples. It is not
so much a place as a country, sanctuary for the last wild
horses on earth.

The hours I spend with this harem. The others think
maybe I'm being possessive. An observer should not
get attached, but I am fond of them. They live on the
farthest shore of the park. The stallion, Hangaï, never
picks a fight and never loses his harem, even when he
goes off to play with the roaming bachelors. I see the
foals startled by marmots and picking at the grasses with
delicate noses. I touch the stones they have worn down
and shaped by the rub of skin. I have fallen asleep with

them, scented my boots in their dung, caught the same thistles, been stung by the same bees and horseflies.

The horses are standing in the rock grotto, faces to the cool stone naves. I look down from above as if through a hole in the roof. I can see the marks on their skin, the dorsal stripes, burrs in their tattered tails. I hear stomachs gurgle. I can smell the grass on their breath.

I found the claw of a raptor and was afraid to take it because with this hand life was snatched from the earth, and it in turn was taken. The law of the land. I want to stay, but I must go. Will I pass unseen? Or will I return? I stand high on the rock formations, seeing the tourist camp two valleys and one mountain away. Distance seems so close and yet impossibly far, like you dream when you walk here and suddenly you are miles into the sky.

The winds keep me up at night, blowing heat across the earth, lighting up the fires, blowing through my mind, but I am moored to this earth by long horsehair ropes.

❧ ❧ ❧

Erika Connor is a painter, writer, and art teacher from rural Quebec, Canada. She has a BFA in studio art and creative writing from Concordia University in Montreal, where she also won The Irving Layton Award for Fiction in 1991. She has traveled extensively in West Africa and Mongolia, and recently returned from Rajasthan, where she worked at an animal shelter.

PETER WORTSMAN

⤝ ⤝ ⤝

Confessions of a "Born-Again" Cowboy in France

At home in the U.S., the author is more Woody Allen than John Wayne, but to his adoptive French family, he's "The Man Who Shot Liberty Valance."

A FUNNY THING USED TO HAPPEN EVERY TIME I SET foot in France. Striding down the dusty tarmac at Orly Airport back in the days of cheap charter flights, the sweat-soaked seat of my jeans clung to my limbs like a second skin, my face felt leather-like, a mask tanned taut by sleep deprivation and in-flight tippling. Jet-lagged joints crackled as my compact five-foot-five-inch frame realigned ligaments and cartilage, converting to metric. I pursed my lips and primed my tongue, preparing to converse with the natives.

And then it hit me, that deliciously unsettling sense of displacement, like I'd stepped out onto the wrong movie set. Everything was strangely elongated and set at an odd tilt and timbre, the caps on the heads of the baggage handlers, the muffled rumble of the bus waiting to take me to the terminal. I scanned the bleak suburban scape where aircraft roamed like mechanical cattle and factory smokestacks loomed like giant Gauloises cigarettes. The dislocation was complete. I was ready to saddle up. This was my post-modern Monument Valley and I was the Marlboro Man sans cigarette.

A curious metamorphosis, I admit, for a short, intro-spective New York Jew of distinctly sedentary habits, whose mount of choice is an ergonomic desk chair, his six-shooter a PC laptop. A guy who rides rough saddle on the IRT and ropes yellow cabs at high noon—I'm more Woody Allen in *Bananas*, for Christ's sake, than John Wayne in *Big Jake*! But travel fosters a fluid iden-tity, like the character with interchangeable faces and bodies in the split pages of a children's flip-art book.

It all started when I met my French wife-to-be at a New York party. A petite professor of bookish bent and girlish figure, she asked me what I liked in life. "Sex, food, and travel," I frankly confessed in drunken French, as I never would have dared do in sober English. In the early days of our experiment in international relations, we would rise at odd hours (a compromise on time zones) and stumble naked to the kitchen wrapped in a single blanket. She craved her nightly dose of chocolate and I my Coca Cola, though I have since converted to Calvados.

To the folks in her ancestral French Alpine village, my beloved second home for twenty years and counting, I am still affectionately referred to as "*l'Américain*." My first appearance on the scene is the stuff of local legend.

Gathering to welcome me way back when, the family was half expecting me to ride up on horseback, when a rented Renault 5 rolled in, a vehicle so small the Duke wouldn't have been able to fold in his knees, let alone fit his ten-gallon hat. This being my first experience with a stick shift, I promptly stalled on the village square disrupting a game of boules (a Gallic cousin of bowling). As I swung myself out of the driver's seat, the entire village blinked as one—not unkindly, just a bit bewildered, clearly wondering if I hadn't left half of me behind. Compact Americans seldom made it to the silver screen. "Get you a little whiskey, you'll be all right!" a guardian angel growled in my ear. Then and there, as if reading the subtitles in my mind, Uncle Joubert, since deceased, to whose memory I shall forever be grateful, took me in hand. Popeye's spitting image, this pint-sized, frog-throated, retired seaman from Marseille pulled out a bottle of Johnny Walker and filled his special whiskey glasses to the rim, the kind that when drained dry dissolve the bikini off the bathing beauty at the bottom. "*Eh, Américain!*" He winked and we clinked.

The family took me in with open arms. To these most gracious country folk, hunters all by avocation, I am automatically linked to their trusty Remingtons and prized Smith and Wessons. Raised on G.I. liberators and John Ford Westerns dubbed in French, they cannot help but superimpose the myth on me, and I am happy to oblige.

For whereas, at Paris cocktail parties, I have on occasion been ribbed for tacit complicity in the seemingly unstoppable spread of McDonald's, Disney, and bio-engineering—all my protests notwithstanding—to my adoptive southern French family, I am The Man Who Shot Liberty Valance and helped run the bad guys out of town and give France back to the French.

Am I an imposter? Perhaps. But what a liberating alias it is!

In New York, I was strictly an "indoorsman," all work and no play. In France, I let loose, rode horseback, and shot target practice with my late father-in-law. "Ripped it to pieces, the American did!" he boasted to his brothers with a semi-serious grin, holding up the target I'd riddled with holes. And in my heart of hearts, I longed to one day join the men of the clan in their annual wild boar hunt.

The real payoff came at our outdoor feasts of venison and boar prepared, as per ritual, by the hunters themselves, the ribs stewed in a rich *civet* of blood and wine; the head severed, sliced and simmered, topped with a rich *sauce gribiche* flavored with brains; the tusks passed out as trinkets to the kids. Davy Crockett and Daniel Boone would have felt right at home!

Hardly kosher! you say.

From my mother, whose family ran a poultry stall in the marketplace in pre-War Vienna, I learned how to pick fresh chickens. Contrary to my squeamish contemporaries who purchase their pullets pre-parted and under plastic wrap, I have no qualms dissecting my dinner, cooked or raw, though I do draw the line at buying it live in Chinatown.

French and Americans, we are literally of the same cloth. Let us not forget that the paradigmatic emblem

of the American West (and by extension, of contemporary Western Civilization) was stitched together on
American soil out of French fabric and Jewish thread.
Levi Straus—the peddler, not the anthropologist—
turned a ream of tough material from Nîmes (*de Nîmes*,
"denim" for short) into the iconic American garment
that would later bear his name.

A born-again American cowboy in France, I have
gladly returned the favor. With my French in-laws, we
traveled Out West. Together we trekked through the
real Monument Valley, the unmistakable setting of every
Western worth its whiskey, from *The Searchers* to *Thelma
and Louise*, not to mention the popular French cowboy
comic strip, *Lucky Luke*. We gazed in awe and wonder
at the towering red fingers of rock and, elsewhere, stared
breathless at forests of cacti, and true to our shared cel-
luloid dreams, went gaga when we pulled into a roadside
saloon to find a serious poker game in progress. On another trip, this one to Texas, we bowed our heads (I, with
tear-filled eyes) before the fabled Alamo.

Surely I'd been training for the part since early childhood, when I wouldn't have been caught dead outdoors
without my holsters packed with six shooters and a rubber Bowie knife stuffed in my belt for good measure.

But there was a hiatus.

John Wayne, I owe you a posthumous apology! I who
shamelessly appropriated your persona as the key to the
heart of my Gallic in-laws, betrayed you in life. I was
there in the crowd, back in 1974, when you rolled into
Harvard Square in an army tank to accept the "Brass
Balls Award" of the Harvard Lampoon. I did not come
to greet you, but to stare at the tarnished symbol of
warmongering you represented. They pelted you with

snowballs. And though I did not join in the jeers, it was fear, not conviction, that held me back, lest you leap out and throw a punch.

How strange to see the Duke again on T.V. years later, still scanning the horizon with the same deadpan squint, but with all the feistiness dubbed in French! About to laugh out loud, I wiped a tear from my eye.

Going to France to find yourself is a long-standing American tradition. From Benjamin Franklin to Josephine Baker to Ernest Hemingway to Levi Straus jeans, we've buffed our image on the whetstone of French panache and style.

After twenty years of annual hegiras, the exotic edge of France has worn off a bit. I drive a stick shift, play boules, drink pastis, and swear like a native. Last year I even accompanied the clan on a wild boar hunt, though our elusive target leapt by in a flash and the only shot I took was with my 35-millimeter Minolta, and that one I missed. Still, the thrill lingers. My French and American personae have evolved a free-trade agreement: I let a little Gérard Depardieu into my Woody Allen, with a glass or two of Bordeaux at dinner to lighten up and cut my cholesterol, and keep my John Wayne primed for sunset gallops in the Alps. My venison civet, prepared according to my father-in-law's recipe, makes mouths water in Manhattan. My Texas chili thrills tongues in old Gaul.

John Wayne himself might have been flabbergasted to learn (as I did from my wife, an expert in nineteenth century French fiction) that John Ford's classic Western, *Stagecoach*, in which young Wayne made his starring debut, was inspired by *"Boule de Suif,"* a short story by the French writer Guy de Maupassant. Don't tell me the Duke of Monument Valley actually earned his spurs on the Champs Elysées! I can just see his ornery ghost squirm, purse his dry lips and spit out a dubbed *"Ç'est pas pour demain!* That'll be the day!"

~≈ ~≈ ~≈

New York-born nomad Peter Wortsman has peddled his impressions of elsewhere to the Boston Globe, Los Angeles Times, *and* Washington Post, *among other newspapers, and to the popular web site* World Hum. *His text "Holy Land Blues," first published in the book,* Encounters with the Middle East, *was reissued in Travelers' Tales* The Best Travel Writing 2008. *His column* Rx for Travel *runs in* P&S, *the journal of Columbia University College of Physicians and Surgeons. He is the author of a book of short fiction,* A Modern Way to Die, *and two plays,* The Tattooed Man Tells All *and* Burning Words. *Also a translator from the German, his rendering of the German travel classic* Travel Pictures, *by Heinrich Heine, was published in 2008.*

CHRIS EPTING

❧ ❧ ❧

Let's Spend the Night Together

He goes in search of rock star rooms with a grisly past,
or "places to check out"—permanently.

WHEN BOOKING A HOTEL ROOM, WHAT DRIVES your decision? Price? Location? Size? Amenities? I'm drawn to rooms based less on the usual factors. For me, the most seductive quality in a room is if something notable happened there. Maybe it's a space where an artist worked (the La Quinta bungalow where Frank Capra wrote his classic scripts). Or where an artist simply crashed (Jim Morrison's tiny space at the Alta Cienega Motel). Maybe it's where John and Yoko staged their "Bed In For Peace" in Montreal, or a Palm Springs suite where a frisky Marilyn Monroe lured the occasional lucky gentleman caller. I'm not sure why, but I think it's because I always get the sense that something from the past actions remain in these rooms—a mood, an echo, or just some fleeting phantom sensation.

Sometimes an establishment will promote a room's notoriety, other times they'll deny a room's history altogether (going as far to even change room numbers as a means of discouraging the curious). Either way, if weaving some offbeat history into a trip is in your blood, there are some rooms waiting for you. In most cases, they're tucked away in odd little corners, away from tourists and traffic. What they might lack in glamour they make up for with something else—an event, some random, bizarre brush with history that forever hangs in the air.

If you're a rock and roll fan, most times these compartments take on a darker edge. Death, after all, is forever intertwined with music and hotels. When I listen to the music of some of rock's fallen angels I get lost in trying to decipher what brought them to the last stop—and then I want to go stay in there. It's one part tribute, but another part adventure. What's it like where these young, talented, tortured souls expired? Is there anything to learn after spending the night where they bid farewell? Or is it just a way to feel closer to the legend, and supercharge the music I still wake up listening to? I don't know. All I'm sure of is that you will never forget the nights you spend in these rooms.

Today, it's the Highland Gardens Hotel. Opened in the mid-1950s as the Landmark Hotel, it was designed as a place primarily for entertainers. It's a modest, low-key, rooms-built-around-the-pool sort of hangout where you can still find the occasional celebrity.

In October 1970, Janis Joplin was in Los Angeles laying down tracks for what would be her final album,

Pearl. She left the studio on October 3rd (after laying down the vocal for "Me and Bobby McGee," which would become her first number one record) and headed over to Barney's Beanery, a roadhouse-watering hole that hasn't changed much since then. With band member Ken Pearson, Janis knocked back a few screwdrivers before driving to the Landmark, where she was staying.

Once she got back inside room 105, she shot up her last batch of heroin before wandering into the hotel lobby to get some cigarette change. Janis chatted for a few moments with the clerk who was on duty that night (he didn't know who she was) and then returned to the room. Soon after, she collapsed near the bed from a heroin overdose, ending up wedged against a table with a smoke in her hand. When she failed to show up at the next day's recording session, a band member (John Cook) broke down her door and found the twenty-seven-year-old Joplin dead.

Room 105 has had some work done since 1970, but the layout in the modest room is essentially the same. I settled in one night with my wife, we sipped some good port, and laid back to listen to copy of *Pearl*. The pain and ecstasy of Joplin's cries in the night are still stunning. It's raw, intense music, recorded hours before she died here in this very room. As it fills the room, you wonder what Joplin's last thoughts might have been. Did she have any awareness that this was the end? Was it fast? Did she suffer? I've brought with me some old interviews with Joplin. Reading them in bed, she almost comes to life in the room. Do I hear a distant drawl?

"Being an intellectual creates a lot of questions and no answers. You can fill your life up with ideas and still go home lonely. All you really have that really matters are feelings. That's what music is to me."

"On stage, I make love to 25,000 different people, then I go home alone."

On the stereo she sings "Busted flat in Baton Rouge, waiting for a train…feeling nearly as faded as my jeans…" Some say Janis still wanders around but for us it was quiet—even peaceful. We left with deeper appreciation for the whiskey-throated gal from Port Arthur, Texas. Though a chill did run through me as I cleaned our glasses out in the same sink that Janis used. Hey, what was that?

On a dark desert highway is perhaps my favorite little Hotel California. It's the Joshua Tree Inn located just a few miles from the haunting, beautiful Joshua Tree National Park, where twisting, knotty Joshua Trees dramatically reach up toward the heavens in a permanent, natural pose. U2 found something special out here, but years before, so did Gram Parsons. The influential Byrd, Flying Burrito Brother, and "Grievous Angel" used to escape here with his musical soul mate Keith Richards in the late 1960s. They'd stay in this circa 1950 inn, which features a horseshoe of twelve rooms facing a desert courtyard and huge swimming pool. They'd also climb the nearby craggy rocks at Joshua Tree, getting hypnotized by the black, star-splashed skies while dropping acid and keeping their eyes peeled for UFOs.

In 1973, Gram Parsons died in room 8 at the Joshua Tree Inn after consuming a lethal mix of tequila and morphine. It was a chaotic scene that ended with a pair of groupies trying to save him, but failing. The room is small, and only the mirror on the wall was there the night the deal went down, facing the bed as it did that night. Just before we stayed here, a film crew had become so freaked out, they up and left. Why? Because they say Parsons never really left the room. Reading the bedside journal where travelers record their thoughts, it's clear the soft-spoken musician touched many. As I leafed through the pages, the bedside light started to flicker. I checked the wires and bulb. Nothing was loose. Then it went off. And on. And off again. All by itself.

I settled into bed to read a book called *Road Mangler Deluxe* by Phil Kaufman, Parsons' manager back then. Have you ever read a detailed account of an event while sitting at the exact site where the event took place? It is so appealing to me, even when the event is this horrific. The room just comes to life. On the stereo, the haunting strains of Parsons' tunes including "Hearts on Fire," "Brass Buttons," "Return of the Grievous Angel" and "Love Hurts" filled the room. Parsons' songs feature mournful, ethereal melodies, and they completely fit the mood within room 8. And then the reading lamp went off again, though this time, it wouldn't come back on.

I rigged a different light so that I could finish reading the account of Parsons' death. Days after the death, Kaufman hijacked Gram's body and drove it to the nearby park where he set it afire, completing a pact the two men had (whoever died first, the other was to sacrifice, by fire, the other's body at a sacred site called Cap Rock). Reading this insane (though entertaining) account of Gram Parsons in Joshua Tree, I was distracted by something. A shadow slowly passed over the wall to my left. My wife was asleep, and there was no other movement in the room. I looked outside. Nothing. I am a bit of a cynic on these things, but the shadow is something I

will never forget. It traveled the wall into the bathroom
and disappeared near the shower. That's where the film
crew say a shadow was as well, the one that made them
leave. I didn't sleep much that night, and the next day
we hiked up to where Gram's body was cremated, by
Cap Rock. Nearby is a shrine, maintained by the faith-
ful. The marker reads "Gram, Safe at Home."

The St. Peter's Guest House is in New Orleans.
Though over the years there were always many rumors
that the man had died, this was actually the last stand
for the heroin-addled guitar slinger, Johnny Thunders.
He died here on April 23, 1991. The former New York
Doll legend had thought about moving to New Orleans,
finding some new musicians, and maybe starting a new
band, but he never got the chance to complete his plan.

Thunders checked into room 37 in the late hours of the
23rd of April, and the following morning he was dead.
Apparently, he had scored heroin upon arriving and
dealt himself a lethal shot and died overnight. I remain
a huge New York Dolls fan, I liked the Heartbreakers
as well, and had the chance to see Thunders play many
times (he actually fell over my shoulder one night in
Boston back in the early 1980s and I carried him to a
waiting taxi in front of the old club called Storyville).

Walking through the French Quarter on a muggy
spring afternoon, sixteen years to the day Thunders
checked out, I felt sad. Johnny Thunders was a New
York City wise guy who coulda been a contender. Jimmy
Page knew it. Keith Richards knew it. Thousand of
wannabe guitar heroes knew it. Instead, Thunders remained an underground legend for most of his life and
one of rock and roll's most influential guitar players.

When I checked into the tiny room, I felt sick to my stomach. The thought of how they found Johnny, fetal-positioned on the floor next to the bed, was depressing. But I had to be here. Listening to "You Can't Put Your Arms Around a Memory," I read Nina Antonia's excellent book, *Johnny Thunders...In Cold Blood*. When I got to the part about his death, the window actually rattled a bit. It was 3 A.M. and I was thoroughly absorbed in the book. I actually said aloud, "That you, man?" And it rattled back.

Who knows? Maybe musical spirits are waiting for you to visit, to include them on your vacation itineraries. Maybe they still need an audience. Either way, there are rooms that act as shrines to some tragic, talented figures that left the stage too soon. They feel different than other rooms, because they are different. They hold history. And they hold magic.

～ ～ ～

Chris Epting is the writer/photographer of fifteen books, the most recent being Led Zeppelin Crashed Here: The Rock and Roll Landmarks of North America. *Others include* James Dean Died Here; Elvis Presley Passed Here; Roadside Baseball; *and* The Ruby Slippers, Madonna's Bra, and Einstein's Brain. *He has contributed articles for such publications as the* Los Angeles Times, Westways, Travel + Leisure, *and* Preservation *magazine and is the national spokesman for the Hampton hotel Save-A-Landmark program. Chris lives in Huntington Beach, California with his wife and their two children. His author's web site is www.chrisepting.com*

BRUCE BERGER

~ ~ ~

Discalced

Some things never change, and that is a good thing.

EVER SINCE I STARTED CAMPING IN TENTS, I HAVE enacted a nightly farce. On the advice of desert dwellers who warn that I will step on scorpions or even rattlers if I walk barefoot in the dark, I arrange my shoes by the tent flap so that I may step into them if my bladder wakes me in the night. And when my bladder breaks into a dream, my mind is far too blurry, too resistant to shaking its sleep state, to steer my feet into shoes. Recklessly I advance barefoot to my chosen spot, and over treacherous decades I have stepped on nothing livelier than a stray thorn. The only advantage to this charade is that my shoes are waiting neatly for me at dawn. I was startled, therefore, to crawl out of the tent on New Year's morning, 2006, and discover only one shoe.

As usual, I was hiding out from the holidays at a
ranch along the Gulf of California, arriving before
Christmas and leaving after New Year's hangovers had
cleared from the highway, and this time I had pitched
my tent at the edge of a small dry lakebed that a hill
cut off from the coast. Shoes don't wander off by themselves but nonetheless I initiated a search, scanning the
lakebed, then prowling the more secretive scrub on
the hill, though I could think of no agency that could
get them there from my tent. The rancher was a close
friend, I knew his family well, and I ruled out anyone's
practical joke. Switching to hiking boots that were the
uncomfortable alternative, I held my tongue until mid-
day, hoping the shoe would wander back. Then I mentioned the disappearance to the rancher.

"You didn't leave your shoes out at night?" he asked.
It was a pseudo question.

"Yes," I replied.

"A fox took it."

"A *fox*?"

"Obviously."

"I have been leaving shoes unprotected in the desert
all my life," I protested, "and never even heard of the
problem, let alone losing a shoe."

"You're lucky," replied Lico. "Foxes steal shoes whenever they can. No one knows why, but they love them.
They're regular Imeldas."

I returned to the tent site, looked in vain for paw
prints in the lakebed and scoured the thorn bushes
farther afield, the enormity of this turn taking hold.
There is probably no shoe I have owned in my life,
except for the lost shoe's mate, whose vanishing could
produce such a disproportionate pang. This pair of

shoes, as it happened, represented a conscious turn in my self-presentation to the world, and this theft was the latest plot twist in a most unlikely saga.

The shoe's defection could even be the revenge of its breed on a lifetime of being ignored, for I had always and deliberately worn the plainest of lace-up black or brown oxfords, void of the least splash. Shoes, I held, should be comfortable and anonymous. I hated shopping for them. I wore a pair until it disintegrated, then grudgingly bought another. Once, in Cologne, a shoe literally came apart in the street and I had to hobble in one shoe and one sock to the nearest *Schuhgeshäft* before I could go back to being a tourist.

My scorn of footwear was part of a more general bad attitude toward clothing. Being praised for what concealed you was, by implication, being told that the self underneath was unworthy of comment. People preoccupied by fashion were by definition superficial, and no number of snappy dressers worth knowing had tempered my stance. I didn't need a shrink to tell me how this prejudice had come about. To be sent into public as a small child, undersized among peers, in a little suit jacket, neck-clutching shirt, tie and short pants because one's mother thought it was "cute" was to permanently despise dressing for display. To be maternally nagged about appearance when one became old enough to drape oneself was to dress with scorn for any flourish and, as a statement on formal occasions, to deliberately underdress. By the time a fox made off with an attitude-changing shoe, the mother whose obsession with finery had backfired was fifteen years in the grave and a son's rebellion had become mere unconsidered habit.

But I began to reconsider shoes, at least, when I met
Fernando. Owner of two women's shoe stores in La Paz,
Fernando was obsessed with all footwear. Several times
a year he flew to shoe conventions—in Guadalajara, in
Monterrey, in Los Angeles—where the world's leading
manufacturers of shoes strutted their wares, and I knew
that for Fernando this was more than the acquisition
of inventory. The shoe, forever confined to the shape of
the human foot, mediating between its tenderness and
the world's hard surface, like the pantoum or the sonnet,
expressed the infinity of the human imagination. After
thousands of years its incarnations were still changing, its
forms still emerging and adapting. To be present where
breaking trends, motifs, and profiles converged from the
globe's extremities was to partake of the mind's own far
reaches in one of its myriad specialized pursuits. During
each of his three visits to Aspen, Fernando bought multiple pairs of shoes, and I was fascinated by the secrets
he showed me in my own town. The leather insoles of
American shoes made a fine show from the heel to the
arch and were replaced by synthetics in the unseen part
that stretched to the toe, whereas Brazilian leather insoles
maintained their integrity all the way. Italy once made
the world's finest shoes, but due to labor costs, the Italian
shoes he bought in Aspen might have been commissioned
from China, which turned out a gamut of footgear from
the highest quality to the plastic slippers that flooded the
world's markets. Because of globalization, breakthroughs
in style were less associated with countries than with
individual designers who might not be working in their
homelands—say, a Chinese man working in Italy.

In Fernando's company, I was interested in the phenomenon of shoes without being interested in shoes. He

offered a glimpse into one of the world's unsuspected corners, revealing secrets that literally sustain us, meanwhile
confirming the idiosyncrasy of each person's reality. We
meet in an agreed-upon world, a commons where we in-
teract, while remaining lone citizens of a willfully chosen,
wacky universe of our own. Fernando and I shared visits
to the realm of classical music, a mutual obsession, but I
inhabited a world of deserts and he walked in a world of
shoes. Within our separate kingdoms we were both connoisseurs, even fanatics. Fernando's presence made me
shoe-conscious, and though I didn't upgrade my clunkers,
whenever we were to meet I inspected them for present-
ability. Since I had switched to the kind of convenience
material that didn't take polish, I held them under the
faucet and dried them with paper towels. I knew that
Fernando looked at a person first from the ankle down,
forming a judgment, and I was sure that he suspected me
of soul-rot. I also knew that he was as fascinated by men's
shoes as by women's. How much better shod I would be
if he sold them—why didn't he?

"Men hate to buy shoes. They wear them until they
give out. Manufacturers know this and don't bother to
change the styles. Men's inventory sits in the stockroom
taking space that could be filled by women's shoes,
which turn over once a season. I don't sell men's shoes
because there's no money in it."

I was in a poor position to object, but suddenly an
opportunity opened up: Fernando and I planned a
month-long trip to Spain, Morocco, and Portugal in the
fall of 2005. We would inevitably be hitting shoe stores
on a daily basis, and if Fernando didn't select the perfect
shoes for me himself, his very aura would infuse me
with the juju to buy my breakthrough pair.

I watched Fernando deploy his keen eyes and prob-
ing fingers in Madrid and Marrakech, and when we hit
Sevilla I got serious. I even had a certain street in mind.
A self I could now hardly imagine had spent three years
of his youth in the nearby province of Cádiz, playing
nightclub piano with an Andalucian band, and we made
numerous expeditions to Calle Sierpes in Sevilla to visit
a musical agent who got us gigs and kept our papers in
order. As the name suggests, Sierpes is one of the terms
for snakes and the street was indeed serpentine: narrow,
twisting, and dark, lined with small shops and dense
with vendors, many of them gypsies, selling their wares
in the street. Sierpes had an unsavory reputation and a
Salesian monk once told me he was afraid to enter it.
Without God on my side, I was drawn to Sierpes rather
than frightened, for Franco's police always kept order
and the only Spaniards who frightened me were the
police themselves.

One of my first acts when we reached Sevilla was to
take a nostalgic walk down Sierpes, and I discovered
that it had been widened, straightened and turned into
a pedestrian street for upscale shopping. Clothing stores
abounded and every third showcase was full of shoes.
This was hardly the Sierpes I had known, but neither
was I the person Sierpes had known. I liked that alloy
of continuity and disruption: a passing tourist instead of
a young musician, a street that represented indulgence
and consumerism instead of tyranny and want, yet the
same person in the same place. We entered a store and
inspected. I realized Fernando couldn't actually select
for me, but he approved when I picked up an ankle-
high arc of mahogany leather, somewhere between a
shoe and a boot, and paraded the pair around the store.

I liked the way they looked, felt, and—though I knew it wouldn't last—smelled. I kept them on my feet and had the store box the bituminous oxfords I hoped I would never wear again.

Mission accomplished, or so I thought, but when we had crossed into Portugal and I was exploring downtown Porto with Fernando, pausing as usual at every shoe store window, my gaze was caught by a pair of oxfords of the shape I always wore, except that they were cobbled from leather of three tones—chestnut, tan, and cream—in an aerodynamic configuration. They were simultaneously the old and the new me. "In a style that doesn't lend itself to style, they have style," I said to Fernando, a phrase that comes off crisper in Spanish and which he liked well enough to repeat later. They fit perfectly and were immediately my lifetime favorites. I refused to take them off and had the store box my fresh Sevillian booties. The latter joined the battered oxfords in the small traveling bag I had deliberately kept light to spare my lumbar, and when we reached Lisbon and I lifted the bag from our rental car, my spine tweaked, then my back went into spasm. It was bitter to be laid up in a pension the following day while Fernando was out climbing the five historic hills, but advances in style have their cost.

I saw Fernando to his plane in Madrid, then returned south for a solo visit with old friends in the province of Cádiz, staying with my namesake Bruno, now a lively young man of twenty-three. Wanting to fly home with a single light carry-on, I asked Bruno to box everything I didn't need—reading matter, purchases in Morocco, all shoes but the Portuguese favorites—and ship it to my address in Aspen. That would give the package six

weeks to reach me before I left home for my annual
half-year in La Paz. I gave Bruno more euros than I
thought the postage would cost, and when he remarked
that I had surely overestimated, I told him to spend the
balance on beer.

I became increasingly anxious as the box from Puerto
Real failed to reach Aspen. Friends in La Paz wouldn't
receive the Christmas presents I'd bought them in
Morocco. Where, above all, was my link with Calle
Sierpes? Had Bruno spent every euro on beer? I headed
south in my Portuguese oxfords, not having received the
package from Puerto Real. The ranch where I spend
the holidays is unreachable by road and I tried not to
touch seawater with my precious shoes when Lico's skiff
reached the shore. I was newly protective of my feet
as I commuted gingerly through the dust. And it was
because of that charged, convoluted, trans-Atlantic preliminary that I was so traumatized the morning that I
pictured some vixen barking, "*Portuguese leather*. Happy
New Year!"

On leaving the ranch, I commented to Lico that I was
keeping the other shoe. "There's nothing like throwing
one away to turn up the other."

"Good idea, because we're all over these hills looking
for cows. We could stumble into it."

Not the least of ironies was that after my life's single
binge of shoe-buying, my first obligatory act on reaching La Paz was to buy a pair of shoes. To avoid accusing
Bruno of not sending the package, I waited a few more
weeks, then sent a note mentioning that the items I had
left never arrived. My friends in Puerto Real had not
entered the age of e-mail and it took more weeks for my
handwritten note to cross the ocean and for the reply to

come back. In the meantime, a relevant e-mail arrived from another source: the friend in Aspen who forwarded my mail. A mysterious package had arrived. It was too beat up for him to make out the return address but it looked somehow foreign. Should he forward it?

I e-mailed back, "It's from Spain. Open it and tell me what's in it."

The following day I received the inventory: assorted books and maps, a couple of colorful wool caps, a small box wrapped in Arabic newspaper and three shoes.

I hit Reply. "Three shoes? Not four shoes? *Three* shoes?"

"Three shoes," he confirmed.

"What color?" I added to the e-mail chain.

"One brown and two black."

My new sensibility reeled. I was down to one Portuguese shoe, one Sevillian shoe and the two black clodhoppers that had already spent years on my feet before I flew the Atlantic. I wrote again to Spain. Had only three shoes been put into the box or did one somehow slip out of the battered package en route? Bruno had found only three shoes, had wondered at it, but had mailed everything I had left, following instructions "to the foot of the letter," the Spanish equivalent of English's equally inscrutable "to a *t*" and, in this instance, unwittingly appropriate. The only suspect I could think of was a small street dog that Bruno had adopted, which might have had vulpine tastes. But Bruno lived in a second-floor apartment, the dog only went out in his presence, and surely Bruno would have noticed if the cur had trotted beside him with ankle-length shoe leather in its mouth.

Lico, meanwhile, found no three-toned oxfords in the cactus. "After months in the weather, probably chewed by a fox, by now it won't match the other even if it does turn up," he said. "At this point you're safe in throwing the other shoe away, unless you plan to have it bronzed."

Fernando's hilarity hit new heights. I should ask whether the Sevillian bootie that reached Aspen was a left or a right: perhaps I could assemble an Iberian pair to wear to a harlequinade. It was, furthermore, my fate never to have stylish shoes, even as it was Fernando's destiny ever to be natty from head to toe. I was a follower of St. Teresa of Ávila, founder of the Discalced Carmelites and frequent visitor to Sevilla, who flaunted the worst peasant sandals of her day. I was a permanent member of the Secular Order of the Discalced, an ordained lowlife in footgear. Or so I record Fernando's verdict, shod still in my bituminous oxfords.

~≈ ~≈ ~≈

Bruce Berger's books about the intersections of nature and culture in desert environments include The Telling Distance, *winner of the Western States Book Award, and* Almost an Island, *an account of thirty years' experience in Baja California Sur. For three years a contributing editor with* American Way, *his essays have appeared in* The New York Times, The Yale Review, *and* Orion, *and have won the Ralph Kreiser Nonfiction Award and the Sierra Nature Writing Award. Also a pianist, he currently plays benefit classical recitals in Mexico.*

MARC-EDOUARD LEON

~ ~ ~

Hair to the Throne

Combing the World Beard and Moustache Championships.

ICTT IS MORNING AS SEAGULLS SOAR OVER BRIGHTON'S gold-pebble beach and England's most popular coastal destination prepares for the biennial World Beard and Moustache Championships. In just a few hours, the greatest hirsute creations of man will be judged by a collection of facial-hair connoisseurs with the coveted first-place beer jug at stake. Already, a few elaborately mustachioed gentlemen are huddling in the show grounds of the Brighton Centre, a 1970s-era concrete monstrosity that breaks the otherwise elegant, if decrepit, chain of white Victorian buildings lining the seaside promenade. The participants will compete within the category of their choice or specialization, and a jury of seven will cast their votes in secret. For many, this will be the culmination of two years of intense training in disciplines arcane and formidable: the Dali, the Chinese, and the Garibaldi, as well as the most anticipated and cutthroat of all, the Full Beard Freestyle.

Excitement about these hair Olympics spreads like wildfire through the beach town, as locals report sightings of gravity-defying fluff everywhere, from the rickety roller coasters of the pier to the infamous nude beach. At the crappy youth hostel where I have been sleeping, things are not as peachy. Alexander Antebi, first-time WBMC contestant and occupant of the bunk below me, is freaking out. He scrutinizes his upper lip in the mirror for the zillionth time this morning and rages, "My fucking moustache is all over the place!" The thick, bushy mouth mane that is hanging several inches past the corners of his lips looks majestic to me, but Antebi is frustrated by the lack of composure to his curl. He tries combing it and twirling it. He even tries whispering sweet nothings to it. Nothing will do. Brighton's humid sea air has evidently caused his 'stache to frizz like the bush of a seventies porn star. With only an hour before the WBMC town parade, Antebi has one choice. "I have to go to the headquarters of Beard Team USA," he says.

Antebi takes off for the hotel where his American teammates are staying, hopeful that, with their experience and know-how, they will be able to invigorate his weather-beaten moustache. Until a few days ago, Antebi had a beautiful Musketeer that would've made D'Artagnan jealous. But Phil Olsen, the self-appointed captain of Beard Team USA, and one of the most prominent "stacheletes" on the moustache circuit, advised him to better study his opponents and to strategically shave

his goatee. To a stachelete such as Antebi, this small
change would be akin to a Miss America contestant
undergoing reconstructive surgery the day before a pageant. Still, he followed his mentor's advice and dutifully
undertook this pileous amputation.

When Antebi returns from his teammates' hotel, his
moustache is waxed into the beautiful upward curl that
gives the Imperial Moustache its unmistakable aura of
power and authority. He also has a grin on his face that
a moustache the size of a dead animal couldn't hide. On
the way, Antebi made a necessary stop at the Brighton
Centre for "pre-judging," to get officially assigned to
his proper category, and he was informed that he will
not be competing against Günter Rosin, the Roger
Federer of the moustache universe. Rosin, a cab driver
from Schorndorf, Germany, has placed first in fifty of
fifty-one competitions, thanks to what many consider
to be the most perfect moustache on earth. He also has
a 'stache that is worryingly similar to Antebi's. Yet it
flows out to the sides in a manner that categorizes it as
Hungarian. Because of this, Antebi is so ecstatic that
he accidentally rips his shirt, a minor catastrophe con-
sidering that, like most contestants, he has designed his
costume specifically for the event. But he is already late
for the WBMC town parade, so he must depart without
fixing it.

I tell Antebi to "break a hair" but he is already out the
door, so I wolf down a breakfast of eggs and greasy sau-
sages and head after him. However, as I make my way
to the town hall, I become helplessly lost in Brighton's
meandering streets. As I'm asking for directions from
the sales girl in a local bakery that makes cakes in the
shape of an erect penis, I notice that the jaws of her

customers have dropped in amazement—and not because of the pornographic pastries. I follow their gaze and am frozen by one of the most magnificent sights I have ever seen: an ocean of moustaches, stretching as far as the eye can see. Leading the parade is a stately gentleman ringing a bell and holding a stop sign with the inscription "Hair Crossing," while panting septuagenarian Morris Men perform English folk dances in unison. They are followed by an absolute visual feast of bearded characters: pirates, cowboys, kings, aristocrats, circus ringleaders, musclemen, hippies, dandies, Mandarins, hermits, metal heads, fencers, seamen, surrealists, pioneers, peasants, policemen, Napoleonic generals, Civil War infantry, Scottish Highlanders, Jesuses, and even a Dr. Livingstone (I presume), all marching down the street in a pageant of hirsute heaven on Earth.

By the time the procession of 250 stacheletes, give or take a few, comes to an end at the Brighton Centre, the entire city is muzzy crazy. The organizers have sold a thousand more tickets than expected; countless disappointed fans are being turned away at the door. The contestants are mobbed by reporters and crowds of admirers fight to touch their beards in disbelief, and groupies burst into shrieks of sexual desire. A participant dressed as a priest suggestively tells one of his fans that she can use his beard as a joystick. He demonstrates by imitating a woman grabbing his beard during intercourse and moaning, "Left a bit! Right a bit! Ahh...that's the spot!" She is about to get a live reenactment when a short maharajah bellows, "Ladies! Free moustache rides!!!" and all hell breaks loose.

A husky biker with a two-foot-long beard, who calls himself "Bear," laughs at the commotion. I ask if he's accustomed to people approaching him this way and he nods in the affirmative. "They even pay me for sex," he answers. "Some people came up to me in San Francisco because I had long hair and a beard. They said, 'Do you fancy to do a porn film for us?' I thought it was a joke, so I answered, 'O.K., are you gonna pay me?'" He ended up making $1,500 to star in *Not Pirates of the Caribbean* and *Bear's Bootie Call*. When I ask him about the girls, Bear lets out a big growl. "Girls? What girls? I was sucking dick before you were born."

The competition is about to start inside the Brighton Centre when Nick Cave suddenly makes a surprise entrance as one of the judges, along with the mayor of Brighton and numerous TV celebrities. They are introduced by Michael "Atters" Attree, emcee of the WBMC and honorable chairman of the oldest and most prestigious moustache club in the world, England's Handlebar Club. Atters ceremoniously declares the WBMC games open, and all the greatest international beard and moustache clubs—from the Svenska Mustaschklubben to the Schwäbischen Bart-und Schnauzerclub to the Whisker Club—rise respectfully. The Centre is brimming with the contestants' proud family and friends, as well as a gallery of facial-hair enthusiasts, bemused hipsters, and local drunks. Supporters carry banners for their favorite participants ("Go Michael!"; "Size does not matter!") and hordes of women wear fake moustaches, some of them carrying their sleeping babies who have handlebars Sharpied onto their upper lips. The audience, in unison, chants along to "Bushy Mush," a song written by one of the founders of the Handlebar Club. It plays on a loop through the speakers like an anthem to the competition:

Some women have such funny tastes of what they
    like in chaps
Some like them fat, some like them thin, some
    medium-sized perhaps
Some like a big proboscis with hair that's nearly
    gone
But there's one thing that a chap must have to turn
    the women on
(—now it's got to be a big one!)
Chorus:
Every girl loves a fellah with a big moustache
Every girl loves a geezer with a bush upon his mush
(Repeat)

The Handlebar Club, formed in 1947 as a convivial nest for Royal Air Force veterans, is hosting this year's WBMC in honor of its sixtieth anniversary. Atters, with his slick handlebar moustache, Edwardian attire, and old-fashioned civility, is the embodiment of his club's celebration of English decorum. "Club etiquette demands the wearing of a Club tie and gentlemanly conduct," he explains, "as well as an ability to bore all outsiders with tales of the Empire."

For six decades now, the Handlebar Club has led a courageous battle against the dwindling popularity of moustaches. "The members of the Handlebar Club consider themselves to be at war," observes *Guardian* writer Sam Delaney, in his review of the official guide to the WBMC. "Their war is with a society that tells us to choose the bland, the boring, and the generic. A society that tells us to choose Bacardi Breezers, comfortable leisure wear, and unisex hair salons. A society that tells us to remain cleanshaven. Most of us haven't had the guts to resist this society's oppressive demands. But since 1947, the fine fellows of the Handlebar Club have stood up to such sinister, homogenizing forces in the only way they know how. By growing enormous moustaches."

"I, for one, appreciate this bygone 'Britishness,'" says Atters, "and why not? The future smells of over-egged political correctness, burgers, and warm Fanta." This is why the Handlebar Club upholds the fabric of tradition by allowing membership only to men who, according to its charter, have "a hirsute appendage of the upper lip with graspable extremities." And the HC specifically does not allow beards. This is the cause of a long-lasting feud with the Beard Liberation Front, a British interest group that is lobbying, as you whiskerfaces go about your daily comfortable routine, to end the widespread discrimination against beards.

Keith Flett, the leader of the Beard Liberation Front, believes that the Handlebar Club perpetuates prejudice against beard wearers and has made a call to boycott the WBMC. "Beards are politically progressive," says Flett. "All the great revolutionary socialists had a beard. Stalin had a moustache." For Atters, Flett's logic equals total nonsense. "I'd rather be shot by a mustachioed fascist than bored by the Beard Liberation Front. The Handlebar Club is a *moustache* club. A cycle club bans yachts, kite clubs ban space shuttles, and moustache clubs ban beards. The WBMC is often hosted by beard clubs, but we just showed the beardies how to do the event properly. There is so much glorious facial hair inside that hall, it looks like a woolly mammoth's bollocks."

But the Beard Liberation Front has just about had it with terms like "beardie," and it considers the comparison to an extinct, hairy elephant's balls insulting. "Most of those attending the Brighton Centre spend far more time fiddling, pruning, and, in other ways, fussing about with their facial hair than they would do if they shaved," claims Flett. "These people, whatever their intention, give the hirsute a bad name."

"To be perfectly honest, a huge part of this competition you could call a hairdressing show," concedes Rod Littlewood, vice president of the Handlebar Club. "Most of these guys don't wear their beards as extravagantly all the time. They have bushy beards, and sometimes they even wear ribbons around it and tuck it down. But when the time of the competition comes, you see these fantastic shapes." Littlewood isn't just talking out of his handlebar. The podiatrist once sported the longest beard in England (5.25 feet, according to the Guinness Book of Records) and is more than happy to see participants pimp their 'staches, as long as they don't try to cheat by using false facial hair. In all but the Natural category, aides such as wax, hair spray, and other hair cosmetics are not only accepted but encouraged.

"Victorian etiquette dictated that the moustache should not be too large and that such foppery as twisting the ends upward, too high, was proof of vanity," notes Atters. "Billingsgate! If you've got it, flaunt it, I say!"

"Besides," adds Littlewood, "we go along because it's just friendship and a bit of fun. I like to say we *enter* competitions, we don't compete." Testing his precept, I interview different contestants to find out just how seriously they take the event.

Neil, from Nottingham, a competitor in the Natural Beard class, says, "It's a lazy man's competition. I don't have to take steroids, I don't have to wake up at six o'clock in the morning and run along the canal. I can

drink beers, smoke cigarettes, and drink coffee. All I
have to do is *not* shave. How easy is that?"

Robert Starnes, an IT consultant from New Orleans
who founded the Joseph Palmer League, a brotherhood
devoted to facial foliage, strongly disagrees. "A lot of
people tell me it's not a sport. I say a) it's a competition,
and b) there's defects. Anybody who's tried to keep his
moustache while dating a girl, or applying for a job,
knows how hard it is. That's why the competitive part
of the Joseph Palmer League and I refer to it as 'sport
bearding.'" Starnes, who has an elegant Dali moustache,
reveals that most contestants do a little bit of thinking
about the specific categories in the two years between
each competition, but the real training only starts in
the last months before the event. Then begins the phase
when they pick a category and start to hone their style.

"You don't want to be left at the last minute trying
to figure out how to correctly shave your moustache,"
Starnes explains. "That's actually what happened to me
when I went to the last WBMC in Berlin. I shaved a
little too much off and it brutalized me in terms of thick-
ness and length."

Phil Olsen of Beard Team USA is also full of insight.
"I try to give everybody on the team an idea of what
to expect," he says. "I told them that the outfits were
very important. I told them that last time we were in
Berlin, there was some negative feedback about the
costumes and that some people in our group had costumes that were outlandish." Olsen, who is dressed as a
Revolutionary patriot carrying an American flag, looks
around surreptitiously before whispering, "One man
wore a mask and pretended he was Elvis Presley. It came
to me from...certain sources that there were people who

were involved in this for a long time, who feared that it
was becoming a circus and that people were making fun
of those who were involved in this." He is about to tell
me more when the confidentiality of our conversation is
interrupted by the arrival of a five-foot-tall Italian general with a two-foot-wide moustache. "Rocco!!! Great to
see you!" Olsen exclaims, before turning to me. "We can
continue talking about this later," he says discreetly.

The risk of ridicule is a real one. That's why
Atters cautions against letting inexperienced barbers
trim a 'stache. "One wrong snip and you're Hitler,"
he warns. Yet the dangers of sport bearding can be
even more serious. For Willi Chevalier, an insurance
salesman and dance instructor from Germany, the
situation came close to being far more grave. He narrowly escaped serious injury several years ago, when
his beard got caught in a spinning drill, and follicle
and face were separated in a most rapid and painful
action. But his is a wonderful story of triumph over
adversity—Chevalier later became a world champion. Others have not been so lucky. Starnes's teammate, called by the perfectly Dickensian name Jeffrey
Damnit, accidentally set his goatee on fire in the weeks
leading up to the championships. He was using a very
flammable product to style his beard and it ignited
during a fire-breathing gig he had taken on to pay for
his travel to the WBMC. Damnit burned off half his
beard, along with the insides of his nostrils and had
to go to the hospital, suffering second-degree burns.
The Joseph Palmer League members present at the
WBMC held their flags at half-mast during the town
parade, in honor of their missing teammate. (In the
months following the WBMC, I randomly encounter

Jeffrey Damnit in a Los Angeles coffee shop. He has completely recovered from his wounds. He now allows his beard to grow only on the left side of his face, leaving the right side completely clean-shaven, in mourning for his lost foliage.)

Yet, as a member of the Joseph Palmer League, Damnit was prepared to live dangerously for the sake of his facial hair. After all, his club is named after Joseph Palmer, who, in the early nineteenth century, was beaten and imprisoned for having a beard. A compatriot of Ralph Waldo Emerson and one of America's great un-sung heroes, Palmer fought the rest of his life for the right to affirm his individualism, and demanded that his tomb be inscribed with the following words: "Persecuted for Wearing the Beard."

When it comes to commitment to the beard, though, no man is as true as Elmar Weisser. A demigod of the moustache world, he stunned the competition at the Berlin WBMC, in 2005, when he styled his beard into a convincing representation of the German capital's famous Brandenburg Gate, accessorized with tiny German flags. It remains, without a doubt, one of the greatest creations in the history of bearddom. For this year's event, he flew in his hairstylist from Germany and woke up at 4 A.M. to work on a surprise creation. After a staggering five hours of top-secret preparations, he walked into the Brighton Centre with his beard sculpted into the London Bridge as homage to England for host-ing this year's event. Only one word could define his entrance. Magic.

Jürgen Burkhardt, a German photographer from Leinfelden, also makes quite a sensation thanks to a moustache with a wingspan of more than five feet, from tip to tip. His muzzy is so long that he has to enter the Brighton Centre's gate sideways and hold his arms out to prevent it from gouging someone in the eye. These are the vagaries of life as a world moustache champion. Burkhardt, like most contestants, spends at least half an hour a day grooming his moustache before leaving the house. Atters even sleeps with a whisker hammock, or *snood*, to preserve the shape of his 'stache. For him, though, these moustache-preservation practices are actually part of the fun. "Jauntily worn, the snood makes one look rather dashing," he tells me. "We chaps love a filthy tart in fishnets. Well, I'm no chauvinist. Let's give them a thrill, too! I'd wager there isn't a dolly on this planet who wouldn't get a swollen puffy over my saucy lip-sprouts coquettishly peeping through a gauze."

While the sexual attraction of the sub-nasally well-endowed is a matter of personal taste, Atters's attitude reflects an important feature of the WBMC. "It's a celebration of manhood," says Antebi. "If you look at personal adornment and dress as a mode of communication, women are a lot more articulate than us. Just look at their clothes and shoes. Men are way more inhibited in our modern culture. In European and American society, there are not a lot of opportunities for men to express themselves in a creative way. This is an opportunity for men to be masculine and dandy at the same time."

As the Imperial Moustache category is ushered on stage, it is clear to the audience and judges alike that Antebi has fully embraced this opportunity. If he was nervous this morning, all signs of anxiety are now gone—he even taunts his opponents with a bold rump shaker, to the delight of two fifteen-year-old girls cheering in the audience. The Antebi who walks off the stage is bursting with confidence, and he shares with me some very big news. "Before I got on stage," he confides, "Günter Rosin whistled for my attention and shook his tush, signaling me to do it on stage. I was not going to do anything theatrical, but when the Hungarian World Moustache Champion gives you the O.K., then you go for it."

The competition soon comes to an end and the judges ceremoniously walk on stage, the first-place beer jugs in their hands. Günter Rosin, Elmar Weisser, Willi Chevalier, and Jürgen Burkhardt are deservedly declared the new world champions in their respective categories of Hungarian Moustache, Full Beard Freestyle, Partial Beard Freestyle, and Sideburns Freestyle.

Every competition has its losers, however, and sadly the Joseph Palmer League's president is one of them. Having not made it into the top three in the Dali Moustache category, Robert Starnes cannot hide his bitterness. "I don't think half the judges have ever even seen a picture of Dalí," he says. "They probably don't even know who he is." Yet he won't let his disappointment get the best of him. "At least this WBMC challenges the Hollywood view that moustaches are worn exclusively by the three F's: Fiends, Foreigners, and Fops," he claims.

Antebi anxiously awaits the results for the Imperial Moustache competition and explodes with joy when he is declared the new world champion. He proudly accepts the beer jug, in what is surely one of the greatest moments of his life. After the awards ceremony, he tells me, "The tradition of growing moustaches and beards plugs us into the past, and I think it's important for us to connect with the ideals that the older generations try to impart on us.

"There's a misconception about the WBMC that participants just want to wear costumes and role-play. I think this is more about celebrating individuality and maintaining cultural identity, and less about Halloween. There's a real desire from the participants to hold onto local identity in this global age." Antebi stood upon the moustaches of giants, and now he has joined their ranks.

⤝ ⤝ ⤝

In preparation for his article on the World Beard and Moustache Competition, Marc-Edouard Leon left his job and took four months off to grow a moustache that he could proudly sport during the tournament. Thick. Long. Dark. Illustrious. Words that had never before been mentioned in connection with any part of his body could finally be heard with gusto. Although his moustache has spelled the end of his sex life, it is no surprise that he continues to flaunt it to this very day.

≈ ≈ ≈

My Special Education

The flavor of words leads to a lesson.

THE WOMAN WHO PULLED UP ASIDE ME ON THE rural road in central Italy had me pegged as crazy, retarded, or both. She was screaming at me, but I understood nothing, so she resorted to bad English. "Money. For eating," she said, putting a cupped hand to her mouth. Driving around wasting gasoline seemed like a counterintuitive way to beg for money. So much so I could only stare back at her, saying nothing like some kind of useless imp. She drove away in frustration, but only got about five hundred feet before I saw her turn around. As she got closer, she swung her car over to me again. "You crazy walking this hour," she said, lowering her window. And then she tried handing me a ten-euro bill.

I suppose that walking on a three-mile stretch of barren road between two isolated villages during 100-degree heat while wearing blue jeans probably did make me look like a crazy person in need of money. But it was a small price to pay for a can opener, which I'd gone looking for in a neighboring village so I could open up a can of my favorite soup—chickpea. But because I couldn't understand the directions to the can opener store, I was walking back to Calcata empty handed (and hungry). Maybe I should have taken that ten euros after all.

I've tried learning a handful of languages in my lifetime and, at least at the beginning, I always have the same problem: I can speak adequately well, posing questions like an intermediate speaker, but I can't comprehend anything after that. Which means I can ask a lot of nice sounding questions, and then it's like I'm deaf.

I'd just moved to Calcata, a bewitching medieval hill town about thirty miles north of Rome, which boasts an absurd amount of art galleries and restaurants, but lacks shops that sell household appliances (or anything else, really). I'd come here to write a book about the disappearance of the town relic, the Holy Foreskin (yes, that would be Jesus' foreskin), which vanished under mysterious circumstances about twenty years earlier. And after the woman sped away for the second time, I verbally beat myself up the rest of the way to Calcata: how was I going to find a missing Holy Foreskin if I couldn't even understand directions to a store that sells can openers?

There were several other things I still needed: a lamp to illuminate the loft at night so my soon-to-arrive wife, Jessie, could read in bed, a tea kettle, and a rug for our dog, Abraham Lincoln (besides baths and going to the vet, he hates nothing more than bare floors). Given that there were so few shops around, I wasn't sure where or how I'd get them. More importantly, I wasn't sure how to say that I wanted them.

I had to learn how to speak Italian. Or rather, how to understand Italian. Desperately.

I have a long not-so-storied history of this type of learning (or, more appropriately, not learning). One day in the fourth grade I was yanked out of my class and given a series of tests. I was told I'd have to come to a "special" class for three hours every day. I had, the teacher of this "special" class explained very slowly to me and my parents, a learning disability. Phrases like "slow learner" and "bad comprehension" were mentioned. My parents then relayed the information to my siblings, saying that from now on they'd have to talk to me slowly and give me just...one...command...at...a...time.

When my brother would see me traipsing up to the front door after baseball practice, he'd tell me to go inside and get him a garbage bag. When I'd come out and extend the bag in his direction, he'd point to various piles of leaves he'd just raked, and say, "Now. Put. Leaves. In. Bag." I had suddenly become the village idiot in my house.

I went every day to the "retarded people's class," as everyone in the "normal" class called it, until the day I graduated high school. The teachers in the special education class didn't really teach as much as feed us the information we needed. In junior high, for example, I had the benefit of being able to take all my tests in the special education class. So, when there was a big exam in my history class, my teacher would hand me the test, and I'd leave for the special ed class. Once there, the teacher would hand me the "teacher's edition" of the history book, which had all the answers in the back of the book, wish me "good luck," and walk away. I'd copy down the answers, sometimes verbatim, and head back to my class. A week later, I'd get the test back with an excellent grade, the teachers in my history and science and health-ed classes never questioning how I'd written the exact same answer that was in the teacher's edition of their books. What was the point of studying, I thought, if I was being spoon-fed the answers to the quizzes?

It didn't take a "special person" to figure out that the teachers and school administrators didn't really care if I or my "special" peers overcame whatever learning disabilities we supposedly had; they wanted to get us through the system, so we could go out in the world and become productive underachievers. Even my best friend in high school told his girlfriend (who then told her best friend who happened to be my girlfriend, who then told me) that I'd "never amount to anything in life." If my best friend didn't even believe in me, then why should I?

But somehow, after graduating from high school, I mustered up enough ambition to give college a try. I enrolled in the local community college, which admits everyone. And somehow, I actually excelled, earning great grades and graduating with honors. Then, after two years, I transferred to the University of California, Santa Cruz, a four-year university with a fairly good reputation. Two years later, I graduated with honors again. Eventually, I went on to earn a master's degree in history. And I took the tests without looking at the teacher's edition of the book. Really. I promise.

It gave me a confidence in my intellectual abilities I thought I never had. People could tell me two or more commands at the same time and I'd actually understand. But then here I was in Calcata, trying to learn Italian and still, just like being back in the fourth grade, not comprehending a thing. This time there was no *Classe dei Retardati* in which to flee. There's not even a school in Calcata, of course.

Then, one day, a pile of celebrity weeklies appeared on my doorstep. An American guy named Scot who'd lived in Calcata for the last two years, brought them over, thinking it would be a good way for me to learn. And he was right. It took me about two full days to get through the first issue of *Diva e Donna* (*Diva & Woman*)—which I found amusing that Scot reads so loyally. By the next issue, however, I could see progress: I had to look up fewer and fewer words. I wasn't sure how many times I'd actually say or hear the words and phrases "red carpet," "seduction," "scandal," and "love affair," but at least I was understanding something. And the articles I read about the Pope's cats were actually entertaining.

I tried talking to people again. And I set a goal that I'd have to have at least one conversation a day. So when I was walking to one of the surrounding villages to find a reading lamp, another car slowed down beside me. It was Costantino Morosin, a long-time resident of Calcata and one of the most famous artists living there today. From what I understood, he was asking me if I wanted to accompany him to nearby Lake Bracciano. I jumped in. Costantino speaks no English whatsoever, which made having to spend an entire evening with him a challenge.

I watched, as we sat on the shores of the massive lake that was formed by a volcanic crater as he screamed at a Romanian mason who was doing some reconstruction work on his house. I jotted down words I hadn't heard before and looked them up or asked someone to define them later.

Fare cagare (literally "to make one poop"),
meaning something is very bad.

Non fare un cazzo (literally "to not do a penis"):
a slang term which could be translated as "to do absolutely fucking nothing."

Finisci il lavoro domani: finish the job tomorrow.

I think I had a pretty good idea what the *disaccordo* (disagreement) was about. Later Costantino and I had dinner at a nearby restaurant in the town of Trevignano. We snacked on seafood and talked about...well, I'm not sure what we talked about. He showed me photos of his artwork on his Palm Pilot, which were computer-generated images of maps that, if you looked close enough, were stick figures that seemed to be in a constant state of motion. The only work I'd previously seen of his were the bulbous stone Etruscan thrones that grace one of the squares of Calcata. I'd always admired them, but people here say the thrones are not even close to his best work.

But, as usual, when it came to talking about his art (or, really, anything), I understood little. I'd ask him questions and he'd give me long-winded answers. He'd occasionally ask if I understood and, occasionally, I'd admit that I didn't. He'd stop and, in Italian, try to explain to me what individual words meant. Costantino didn't seem to mind listening to himself talk, even when the person he was talking to couldn't understand a word, but I appreciated that he was giving me the chance. It takes a lot of energy to spend an entire evening with someone who can't understand anything you're saying.

The next day, while sitting on the doorstep at the top of the steps that lead up to my apartment, I saw Gemma, the Belgian woman who runs the tea house. She was standing around looking somewhat bored.

"*Non fai un cazzo?*" I asked. I thought I'd try out my new phrase, the one I heard Costantino use with the Romanian mason.

"What?" she answered back in Italian. Gemma speaks English well and, naturally, that's usually the language we speak in. "Do you mean, 'Am I doing nothing?'"

"*Si,*" I answered, somewhat cheerily because I understood what she had said in Italian.

She walked away. No, scratch that. She stormed away. Maybe, I thought, she heard her phone ringing and had to go answer it. But I saw her a few more times that afternoon around the village and she ignored me.

Oh, no, I thought. What did I say? Well, I knew exactly what I'd said. I just wasn't expecting her to react the way she did—which was as if I'd said something like, "Yo, wassup bitch?"

At the bar in the neighboring village where a group of old men regulars had sort of taken me in, I mentioned the phrase I'd said to Gemma.

"Should I say this to a woman?" I asked.

The seven or eight men, who were sitting in a circle, wagged their fingers at me and erupted into a chorus of "no, no, no, no!"

"Never say this to a woman," one of the men said. Or at least I think he said. "This is talk for the bar—not for ladies."

The next afternoon I went to the tearoom to see Gemma.

"I'd like to apologize for what I said to you yesterday," I said, this time in English.

"For me," she said, "this phrase is worse than cursing."

I explained to her that in trying to learn this language, I was still getting a feel for what is O.K. to say and what's not O.K. to say.

"I understand," she said. "It's just that this is not a phrase an educated person would say. It's for stupid and retarded people."

Retarded people. After that, I swore to myself I'd never use the word "*cazzo*" again. Not even at the bar. Instead, I'd rely on my celebrity gossip to make conversation. And I'd limit my penis-talk to a safer topic: Jesus Christ's penis—or at least the tip of it. The Holy Foreskin.

✿ ✿ ✿

David Farley is the co-editor of Travelers' Tales Prague and the Czech Republic. *His writing appears in* The New York Times, The Washington Post, National Geographic Adventure, New York *magazine, and on Slate.com and WorldHum.com. This essay is a partial excerpt from his travel memoir,* An Irreverent Curiosity: In Search of the Church's Strangest Relic in Italy's Oddest Town. *Farley teaches travel writing at New York University and is the founder of the Restless Legs reading series. Find him online at www.dfarley.com.*

⚞ ⚞ ⚞

A Life in the World

An ever-widening path began with simple choices.

I WAS TWENTY-FOUR, LIGHT ON MY FEET, AND—THANKS to my eight years of studying nothing but litera-ture—going absolutely nowhere. One late-spring day, as music thumped out of the second-floor dorm rooms and the whole of Cambridge, Massachusetts, seemed suddenly to unpeel its winter clothes and flood out into the sun, I saw a flyer—one of a thousand—asking for volunteers for a summer job involving traveling around Europe, writing for a series of student-run guidebooks. "Traveling" and "around Europe" were about all my itinerant life had trained me for, so I descended the few stone steps that led to an icy basement and found a group of students even younger than I was who, as memory imperfectly recalls, asked me to answer a few questions in as many languages as I could.

I scribbled off a sample entry for them—describing my hometown of Santa Barbara, not very graciously, as the weekend mistress of Los Angeles—and the next thing I knew, I was being handed a small (very small) amount of cash and told that I must make it last until the fall. Once a back-of-the-Airbus plane ticket had been bought for the trip across the Atlantic, I worked out that I had roughly $1,400 left for seventy days of hard travel: a guarantee that I would live as cheaply as the low-budget readers I was writing for. After train tickets, postal costs, and pens and paper had been factored in, I calculated that I had enough left over to dine once a week on French fries and stay in a gutter with a streetlight nearby.

I had traveled before, of course; in fact, I had been traveling ever since I was born (to Indian parents in England). Even as a child, I thought of the airport as my second home, and when my parents moved to California while I continued going to school in England, I got into the habit of flying three times a year back and forth between drafty, semi-medieval England and California during the Summer of Love. So much had the fact of movement entered my bloodstream that at seventeen I spent my summer holiday traveling around India, trying to see the country that was supposed to mark my ancestry, and at eighteen I worked as a busboy in a Mexican restaurant in California to save up enough money to travel by bus for three months from Tijuana to Bolivia and back again.

But now I was traveling for a living, and the experience was akin to throwing open the doors of my cobwebbed grad-school life and letting in the world. In Boston, I had just finished learning Old English for the

second time, was teaching Shakespearean tragedy, and
had in front of me Ph.D. oral exams that involved close
acquaintance with the Venerable Bede (the one who told
us that life is like the swift passage of a sparrow through
a banquet hall); now, for ten weeks, I had trains and
sunlight and adventure ahead of me, with no libraries
in sight. Counting the number of bird images that flit
through the second half of *Beowulf* began to pale next
to a study of the broken bed-and-breakfasts that ring
Paddington Station in London.

Not many hours later, as memory regilds it, I was
stumbling around Sussex Gardens, in London, the latest ill-qualified employee to write large sections of *Let's
Go: Britain*; *Let's Go: France*; and *Let's Go: Europe* (the
Harvard-produced guidebooks that were leading impe-
cunious travelers around Europe before Lonely Planet
or Rough Guides were a gleam in their creators' eyes).
I was trying to work out why Sussex Gardens did not
begin to adjoin Sussex Terrace and what archaic num-
bering system meant that 16 Sussex Gardens should
be across from number 61 (maybe my studies in Old
English hadn't been so useless after all).

It seemed, at the time, just a way to travel across
the country I was born in and the France I had always
longed to escape to; to someone who knew nothing but
the lyrics of Caedmon, it seemed, really, a vacation—in
secondhand mufti. Later, I would see that it was the best
vocational training I ever had, a crash course in all kinds
of lessons learned on the fly, and a perfect illustration of
the ancient Calvinist truth that life and a free lunch are
rarely well acquainted. I wandered the inexpensive hos-
telries of central London trying to determine whether

one hole in a carpet was smaller than another, and in the evenings, hunched over my notes in the cheapest gutter I could find, committed page after page of sweeping sentences on Sir John Soane's House, Wimpy Bars, and the gardens of Kew.

At the time, I thought that a summer working for *Let's Go* would allow me to do what came naturally—being alone, far from anywhere, and taking notes—and call it work. In fact, it was difficult work that I only now, at a distance of more than twenty years, can call natural training. But it taught me, the hard way, that what a reader of any guidebook wants is not a wise guy's twenty-page treatise on Art versus Nature in the Cotswolds but the dirt on whether that grimy curry house is less poisonous than the grease-stained burger stand down the street. It taught me to arrive in a town close to dawn, spend the daylight hours walking and walking around every eatery and sight and place of ostensible habitation, and then, when I wanted nothing more than to collapse, to spend the evening writing the whole place up, by hand, on carbon paper that smudged with every word.

It taught me, in fact, just about everything I have used for business and pleasure ever since.

A PC, in those days, was a public constable, and faxing was the kind of thing you heard French boys talk about when you were in the Space Invaders arcade late at night, trying to find a comfortable place in which to write. Every one of the ten or more pages I wrote on lined paper each night—on alternate lines—had to be duplicated on carbon paper and then taken every three weeks, in a breath-held ritual, to the local post office to be mailed to the icy basement. There was no internet on which to check the spelling of *Aix*, and the only responses

I received, once every three weeks in turn, were kept in the *poste restante* section of a building that was generally closed. *Let's Go* taught me that the *Go* was the important thing—the moving on every day and not fussing over colons—and that the *Let's* meant something more than just an individual meander into obscurity.

And what did I do after I finished England and went off to cover twenty-seven French towns in twenty-eight days (as I roughly remember it)? I treated myself to one celebratory sorbet a month when I felt I had the money to splurge. I walked through the streets of Grenoble at 2 A.M., miming Neil Young, as I went back to my Olympic Village hostel, fulfilling a dream I'd had since growing up. I met a vagabond Englishman who was ready to race through the crooked streets of Carcasonne from dawn to dark discussing D. H. Lawrence. I found my way into crowded dorms in the south of France where every traveler was deep, perhaps angrily, into a copy of *Let's Go* (and I was the only one who had to pretend to have no acquaintance with the books).

I fell in love, in short. With the movement, the stimulation, the kind girls at the *syndicats d'initiatives* who were vaguely moved by the shady letter of introduction I had been given by my student bosses; with the thrill of living so simply that my sense of pleasure opened up. The kind of meal I would never have noticed in Cambridge, Massachusetts, became a treat to be savored like a once-in-a-lifetime feast at La Tour d'Argent. Sitting down in a café one day in mid-August to write out a tale for a faraway girl-friend struck me as a grand prize in the lottery. On my one free day of the summer—so indoctrinated had

I become in the glory of movement—I didn't stop my daily routine of getting on a train but intensified it, going out of my no-star hotel at 5 a.m. to take a train all the way from Arles to Monaco and back in time to get up at dawn again the next day. I was learning, on the page and in my life, the luxury of living in very small spaces.

I thought then that I was enjoying an intriguing challenge that kept me on the streets. Better to be working by seeing the world than by going indoors to a place I knew. I felt then that I was just freeing myself from a summer of parsing verse forms. But the more time passed, the more I found, to my great bewilderment, that writing for this student guidebook, as Melville wrote of his whaling ship, was my Harvard College and my Yale. It taught me how to write quickly but with an eye for accuracy. It taught me how to move quickly but with an eye for detail. It taught me to value the reader's needs before my own (as those *Let's Go* readers in southern France never once, I noticed, mused on the delightful *aperçus* of the previous year's edition but had plenty to say about the recommended *pensione* that turned out to be a hellhole). It taught me that the best kind of job could come out of doing what you loved.

I returned for my next year of graduate school—more questions on Dryden's rhyme scheme—and slowly went about trying to make my way as a writer (occasional 200-word reviews in a New York magazine or plaintive letters sent to a literary journal I'd spotted once in a library). I realized that my only reason for being in school was that I couldn't think of anywhere else to be. And as the months rolled on and summer approached, I began to see flyers appearing around campus and I made my slow way down into the icy basement once again.

As a second-time *Let's Go*er, I got some of the prize locations on the itinerary (in those days, the farthest the seven books went was Morocco, and everywhere else we considered was within the tiny bailiwick of Europe). Two weeks after marking my final essay on *The Tempest*, I was in St-Tropez and Cannes, watching visitors with no copy to write get a hands-on taste, so to speak, of cross-cultural relations. I was walking through towns in Italy where citizens had spilled out into the streets, their stores and houses all shuttered, to cheer their beloved team's progression through the World Cup in Spain. And then I was in the middle of a vast crush of blue-clad revelers surging through the piazzas of Rome, all night until dawn, as Paolo Rossi netted goal after goal and the team won the World Cup.

It is dangerous to say that those were among the best times of my life. But memory is a ruthless editor, as tough on redundancies as any of the kids who were butchering my carboned pages back in the icy basement, and what it tells me all these years later is that I can still taste almost every one of my days in France, Greece, and Italy. The bus rides along the haunted Peloponnese, where, for weeks on end, I relished something of the vagabond's freedom of being unknown and off the grid. Island terraces where I sit now, in the photographs, sporting a beard I have not worn since. Silent villages where I read Somerset Maugham after dark, then raced out in the early light, with Philip and Mildred (from *Of Human Bondage*) beside me. Zakynthos and Kythira and Ithaki and places that now sound like the settings of my fairy tale.

Early on in that second summer, I got a message from my parents that someone in New York was trying to make contact with me. I went to the local phone center, but this was Sardinia: It was closed for the weekend. I returned two days later, but this was World Cup season and Italy: The center was not open on Mondays. Finally, what seemed like lifetimes after the message came through—pealing bells and flights of birds in the otherwise silent streets—I was shouting down a telephone receiver to a man in Rockefeller Center who was, I realize now more than then, interviewing me for a job of sorts.

Was I ready to write quickly, about any country that the magazine might throw at me? Could I guarantee making deadlines and being able to write clearly and concisely enough to satisfy any reader? Was I sufficiently confident to forswear the library and write bright sentences about the real world and its urgencies? I looked around me in the clamorous phone hall, the pages of carbon paper heavy against my chest, and was somehow able to tell the truth.

I proofread my entries for that second *Let's Go* season while sitting at a desk in midtown Manhattan writing international affairs articles for *Time* magazine (a job for which I was only marginally less qualified than I was to write for *Let's Go*). And only three months after the fruits of my labors finally came out (or didn't; *Let's Go* also taught me the important writer's lesson that only a few of your immortal lines ever strike the rest of the world as indelible), I took a long vacation from my desk in New York and couldn't stop myself from taking notes as I moved rapidly around the back roads of Southeast Asia.

When I returned to New York, I realized that while only on holiday, as I thought of it, I was again performing an act that looked dangerously like travel writing. I had written hundreds of pages of notes in Thailand and Burma—though this time, sadder but wiser, I had not put them in the mail and had single-spaced them so as to leave no room for editorial intervention. To travel for a living and for life: What, I wondered, could be better? Now, doing the same thing twenty-five years later, I see that the jobs we stumble into often teach us more than all the ideal gigs we so patiently stalk. And getting lost or going on a detour is how we find the places we'd otherwise miss. A summer job, for me, became a way into a life that sometimes seems to have made summer feel eternal.

❦ ❦ ❦

Pico Iyer is the author of two novels and seven works of nonfiction, among them Video Night in Kathmandu, The Lady and the Monk, The Global Soul *and, most recently,* The Open Road, *a record of thirty-three years of talks and travels with the XIVth Dalai Lama. In spite—or because—of his years writing guidebooks when young, he lives in a two-room apartment in rural Japan that looks suspiciously similar to a no-star B&B. This story was originally published in* Condé Nast Traveler.

Acknowledgments

"Escape from Darien" by Cameron McPherson Smith first appeared in *They Lived to Tell the Tale* in 2007. Published with permission from The Lyons Press and the author. Copyright © 2007 by Cameron McPherson Smith.

"Officially a Woman" by Stephanie Elizondo Griest reprinted with permission of Washington Square Press, a Division of Simon & Schuster, Inc., from *MEXICAN ENOUGH: My Life Between the Borderlines*. Copyright © 2008 by Stephanie Elizondo Griest. All rights reserved.

"No Sin in Ecuador" by Justin Peters published with permission from the author. Copyright © 2009 by Justin Peters.

"The Bamenda Syndrome" by David Torrey Peters published with permission from the author. Copyright © 2009 by David Torrey Peters.

"Mother, India" by Jeff Greenwald first appeared in a different form in the *Los Angeles Times* on May 11, 2008. Copyright © 2008 by Jeff Greenwald. Reprinted with permission from the author.

"Crazy Diamond" by Adrian Cole published with permission from the author. Copyright © 2009 by Adrian Cole.

"Raw Meat, Barry White, and the Brothers" by Matthew Gavin Frank published with permission from the author. Copyright © 2009 by Matthew Gavin Frank.

"A Chance Life" by Millicent Susens published with permission from the author. Copyright © 2009 by Millicent Susens.

"Choices Rejected" by Carol Beddo published with permission from the author. Copyright © 2009 by Carol Beddo.

"The Floating Coffin of Tonle Sap Lake" by Michael McCarthy published with permission from the author. Copyright © 2009 by Michael McCarthy.

with permission from the author. Copyright © 2009 by Peter Wortsman.

"Let's Spend the Night Together" by Chris Epting first appeared online in the September/October 2007 issue of *Perceptive Travel*. Copyright 2007 by Chris Epting. Reprinted with permission from the author.

"Discalced" by Bruce Berger published with permission from the author. Copyright © 2009 by Bruce Berger.

"Hair to the Throne" by Marc-Edouard Leon first appeared in *FLAUNT* magazine in February 2008. Published with permission from the author. Copyright © 2008 by Marc-Edouard Leon.

"My Special Education" by David Farley published with permission from the author. Copyright © 2009 by David Farley.

"A Life in the World" by Pico Iyer was originally published in *Condé Nast Traveler* in September 2007. Published with permission from the author. Copyright © 2007 by Pico Iyer.

Photo Credits

Photograph on p. 32 ©iStockphoto.com/Lise Gagne.

Photograph on p. 103 ©iStockphoto.com/Dajas Design.

Photograph on p. 161 ©iStockphoto.com/Jamie Evans.

Photograph on p. 184 ©iStockphoto.com/Tiago Estima.

Photograph on p. 218 ©iStockphoto.com/Peter Jobst.

Photograph on p. 283 ©iStockphoto.com/Hien Nguyen.

Photograph on p. 301 ©iStockphoto.com/Sawayasu Tsuji.

Photograph on p. 332 ©iStockphoto.com/constantgardener.

Images on pp. 1, 11, 21, 67, 81, 121, 136, 146, 153, 167, 188, 203, 223, 235, 256, 261, 272, 294, 308, 318, and 340 © 2009 Jupiterimages Corporation.

About the Editors

James O'Reilly, publisher of Travelers' Tales, was born in Oxford, England and raised in San Francisco. He graduated from Dartmouth College and wrote mystery serials before turning to travel writing and publishing. He's visited nearly fifty countries and lived in four, along the way meditating with monks in Tibet, participating in West African voodoo rituals, living in the French Alps, and hanging out the laundry with nuns in Florence and penguins in Antarctica. He travels extensively with his wife, Wenda, and their three daughters. They live in Palo Alto, California, where they also publish art games and books for children at Birdcage Press (www.birdcagepress.com).

Larry Habegger, executive editor of Travelers' Tales, has been writing about travel since the late '70s. He has visited almost fifty countries and six of the seven continents, traveling from the Arctic to equatorial rainforests, the Himalayas to the Dead Sea. In the early 1980s he co-authored mystery serials for the *San Francisco Examiner* with James O'Reilly, and since 1985 their syndicated column, "World Travel Watch," has appeared in newspapers in five countries and on WorldTravelWatch.com. As series editors of Travelers' Tales, they have worked on more than 100 books, winning many awards for excellence. Habegger regularly teaches the craft of travel writing at workshops and writers' conferences (www.larryhabegger.com). He is editor-in-chief of Triporati.com, a destination discovery site, and is a principal of the Prose Doctors, a consortium of top editors for top writers (prosedoctors.com). He lives with his family on Telegraph Hill in San Francisco.

Sean O'Reilly is director of special sales and editor-at-large for Travelers' Tales. He is a former seminarian, stockbroker, and prison instructor who lives in Virginia with his wife Brenda and their six children. He's had a lifelong interest in philosophy, theology, and travel, and is the author of *How to Manage Your DICK: Redirect Sexual Energy and Discover Your More Spiritually Enlightened, Evolved Self* (www.dickmanagement.com). His travels of late have taken him through China, Thailand, Indonesia, and the South Pacific, and his most recent non-travel project is redbrazil.com, a bookselling site.